COLLATERALIZED MORTGAGE OBLIGATIONS:

STRUCTURES AND ANALYSIS

Second Edition

COLLATERALIZED MORTGAGE OBLIGATIONS:

STRUCTURES AND ANALYSIS

Second Edition

FRANK J. FABOZZI
CHUCK RAMSEY
FRANK R. RAMIREZ

WITH THE ASSISTANCE OF
M. SONG JO AND DAVID T. YUEN

Published by Frank J. Fabozzi Associates

ISBN 1-883249-03-1

Printed in the United States of America
1 2 3 4 5 6 7 8 9 0

FJF
To my wife
Dessa

CR
To the memory of my father
Russell Curtis Ramsey

FRR
To my wife Karen and my children
Rick, Ryan, and Kimberly Ana

ABOUT THE AUTHORS

Frank J. Fabozzi is an Adjunct Professor of Finance at Yale University's School of Organization and Management and the editor of the *Journal of Portfolio Management*. From 1986 to 1992, he was a full-time professor of finance at MIT's Sloan School of Management. He is on the board of directors of the BlackRock complex of closed-end funds, the board of supervisory directors of the Blackstone Fund for Fannie Mae Mortgage Securities and the Blackstone Freddie Mac Mortgage Securities Fund, the board of directors of the family of open-end funds sponsored by The Guardian Life, and an educational consultant to Alex. Brown & Sons. Dr. Fabozzi is a Chartered Financial Analyst and Certified Public Accountant who has authored and edited many books on investment management.

Chuck Ramsey is a principal of Alex. Brown & Sons and a partner and chief executive officer of Mortgage Risk Assessment Co. He was previously a general partner and senior managing director of Bear Stearns where he was responsible for mortgage-backed securities sales. Mr. Ramsey is known as the architect of specified pool analysis and is responsible for the development of computer systems designed to more accurately value these securities.

Frank R. Ramirez is a principal of Alex. Brown & Sons. Mr. Ramirez earned a J.D. from the University of California at Berkeley and an MBA and BA from Stanford University. His prior positions were as a managing director of Bear Stearns and as a staff attorney for the Securities and Exchange Commission. Mr. Ramirez specializes in the use of derivative mortgage-backed securities to enhance total returns and match liabilities.

TABLE OF CONTENTS

PREFACE

The market for collateralized mortgage obligations is the most dynamic and innovative securities market in the world. CMO bond classes have been customized to satisfy the most particular needs of institutional investors, resulting in remarkable growth and a myriad of bonds with appealing risk/return characteristics. CMO structures range from simple products to extremely complex ones.

The traditional tools for evaluating Treasury and corporate bonds prove inadequate for the valuation of CMO products. Few practitioners have had the benefit of formal training in the analysis of CMOs. Even recent MBA graduates specializing in finance have had little exposure to the CMO market in their curriculum because most business schools tend to focus on the equity markets.

Many of the reported problems with certain types of CMO products can be attributed to a lack of understanding of their risk/return characteristics, as well as the total dependence of the portfolio manager on the salesperson who sold him or her the bond. In fact, in the preface to its policy statement covering CMOs, the Federal Financial Institutions Examination Council expresses this concern when it states: "In a number of cases where depository institutions have engaged in speculative or other non-investment activities in their investment portfolios, the portfolio managers appeared to have placed undue reliance on the advice of a securities sales representative."

Money management entails various types of risks. The key to successful money management lies in understanding these risks and knowing how to control them. No one knows what will happen in the future, but a portfolio manager should have an understanding of how particular economic factors will affect the performance of a portfolio. What is unacceptable in money management is not a lack of clairvoyance but ignorance of the effect of potential outcomes on a portfolio — "ignorance risk," if you will.

The goal of *Collateralized Mortgage Obligations: Structures and Analysis: Second Edition* is to reduce ignorance risk. The book is intended not only for money managers, but also for board members of financial institutions who are concerned with their CMO holdings or are contemplating investing in CMOs. Beyond describing the CMO structures, the book discusses critical analytical techniques, the financial accounting treatment of CMOs, and regulatory considerations for depository institutions and insurance companies.

ACKNOWLEDGMENTS

We are grateful to Ron Unz of Wall Street Analytics for allowing us to use his system in some of our analysis. We thank David Canuel of Aeltus Investment Management for permitting publication of the real-world simulations in Chapter 11 and providing helpful comments on the chapters in Section III of the book. We also thank Scott Richard of Miller, Anderson & Sherrerd for allowing us to use the OAS illustrations in Chapter 10.

We have benefited from helpful discussions with: Scott Amero and Keith Anderson (BlackRock Financial Management), Cliff Asness (Goldman Sachs Asset Management), Daniel Dektar (Smith Breeden Associates), Jeff Detwiler (Residential Funding Corporation), Robert Gerber (Sanford Bernstein), Deepak Gulrajani (BARRA), David Jacob (Nomura Securities), Frank Jamison (Alex. Brown & Sons), Frank Jones (The Guardian Life), William Leach (The Boston Company), Brent Lockwood (Alex. Brown & Sons), Edward Murphy (Merchants Mutual Insurance Company), Michael Schumacher (Smith Breeden Associates), William Stewart (Alex. Brown & Sons), and Nicholas Wentworth (Investment Advisors, Inc.).

A very special thanks to M. Song Jo, who structured the hypothetical CMO structures for the illustrations in Section II, and David T. Yuen, who assisted with several chapters, particularly Chapter 8. Their contributions are so important that we have identified them on the title page of the book.

The production team for this book greatly facilitated its completion. The team includes Patricia Peat, who edited the manuscript, and F. Brett Weigl, Chris Palaia, and Toni Zuccarini of Drew University, who provided copyediting and proofreading assistance. Stephen Arbour was responsible for all phases of the production of this book.

Finally, we wish to thank our families for their support.

Frank J. Fabozzi
Chuck Ramsey
Frank R. Ramirez

INDEX OF ADVERTISERS

SECTION I: BACKGROUND

Chapter 1

INTRODUCTION

The largest sector of the debt market in the world is the mortgage market, with an estimated size of $4 trillion as of 1994. Mortgage loans have been used since 1969 as collateral for the creation of securities, popularly referred to as *mortgage-backed securities*. These securities include passthrough securities, collateralized mortgage obligations (CMOs), and stripped mortgage-backed securities. In the world of fixed-income securities, the growth of the U.S. mortgage-backed securities market holds all records, with the CMO sector now dominant. Exhibit 1 shows the number of deals and the dollar volume of CMOs issued between the inception of the market in 1982 and 1993. The CMO's major financial innovation, which is responsible for the rapid growth of this market, is that it provides for redirecting underlying cash flows in order to create securities that much more closely satisfy the asset/liability needs of institutional investors. As Wall Street likes to quickly point out, these securities are truly "custom designed." It is the ever-changing CMO innovation that is the focus of this book.

Exhibit 1: Issuance Volume of Collateralized Mortgage Obligations: 1982 to 1993[*]

Year	Number of Deals	Dollar Volume (in millions)	Number of Tranches	Average Number of Tranches per deal
1982	1	50	2	2.0
1983	8	4,748	53	6.6
1984	18	9,903	143	7.9
1985	59	16,515	434	7.4
1986	89	49,838	951	10.7
1987	94	58,875	1,020	10.9
1988	156	77,066	1,796	11.5
1989	236	95,209	2,608	11.1
1990	280	112,993	3,802	13.6
1991	440	200,810	7,077	16.1
1992	504	260,410	9,688	19.2
1993	441	271,180	10,597	24.0

* Includes agency and private-label CMO/REMICs.
Source: Wall Street Analytics, Inc.

THE CREATION OF A COLLATERALIZED MORTGAGE OBLIGATION

There are a variety of collateralized mortgage obligation structures, arising out of various investment motivations. Here we provide an overview of how these securities are created, using Exhibits 2 through 4 as illustration. Exhibit 2 shows ten mortgage loans and the cash flows from these loans. For the sake of simplicity, we assume that the amount of each loan is $100,000 so that the aggregate value of all ten loans is $1 million.

The cash flows are monthly and consist of three components: (1) interest, (2) scheduled principal repayment, and (3) any payment in excess of the scheduled principal repayment. The third component, payment in excess of the scheduled principal repayment, is referred to as a *prepayment*. It is the amount and timing of this element of the cash flow from a mortgage that makes the analysis of mortgages and mortgage-backed securities complicated. Uncertainty about the amount and timing results in *prepayment risk*. As we show how CMOs are created, it should be clear that the total amount of prepayment risk does not change. The distribution of that risk among investors, however, can be altered.

Exhibit 2: Ten Mortgage Loans

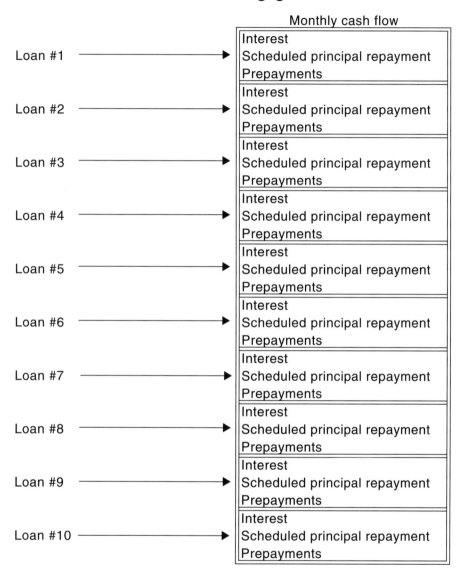

Monthly cash flow

Loan #1	→	Interest Scheduled principal repayment Prepayments
Loan #2	→	Interest Scheduled principal repayment Prepayments
Loan #3	→	Interest Scheduled principal repayment Prepayments
Loan #4	→	Interest Scheduled principal repayment Prepayments
Loan #5	→	Interest Scheduled principal repayment Prepayments
Loan #6	→	Interest Scheduled principal repayment Prepayments
Loan #7	→	Interest Scheduled principal repayment Prepayments
Loan #8	→	Interest Scheduled principal repayment Prepayments
Loan #9	→	Interest Scheduled principal repayment Prepayments
Loan #10	→	Interest Scheduled principal repayment Prepayments

An investor who owns any one of the individual mortgage loans shown in Exhibit 2 faces prepayment risk. In the case of an individual loan, it is particularly difficult to predict prepayments. If an individual investor were to purchase all ten loans, however, prepayments might become more predictable. In fact, if there were 1,000 mortgage loans in Exhibit 2 rather than ten, historical prepayment experience would be one way to improve predictions about the prepayment behavior of homeowners whose loans are in the pool. But that would call for investment of $1 million to buy ten loans and $100 million to buy 1000 loans, assuming each loan is for $100,000.

Suppose, instead, that some entity purchases all ten loans in Exhibit 2 and pools them. The ten loans can be used as collateral for the issuance of a security whose cash flow is based on the cash flow from the ten loans, as depicted in Exhibit 3. Suppose that 40 units of this security are issued. Thus, each unit is initially worth $25,000 ($1 million divided by 40). Each unit will be entitled to 2.5% (1/40) of the cash flow. The security created is called a *mortgage passthrough security*, or, simply, a *passthrough*.

Let's see what has been accomplished by creating the passthrough. The total amount of prepayment risk has not changed. Yet, the investor is now exposed to the prepayment risk spread over ten loans rather than one individual mortgage loan, and for an investment of less than $1 million. So far, this financial engineering has not resulted in the creation of a totally new instrument, as an individual investor could have accomplished the same outcome by purchasing all ten loans.

Mortgage loans that are included in a pool to create a passthrough are said to be *securitized*. The process of creating a passthrough is referred to as the securitization of loans.

The investor in our description of a passthrough remains exposed to the total prepayment risk associated with the underlying pool of mortgage loans, however many there are. Securities can be created, however, where investors do not share prepayment risk equally. Suppose that instead of distributing the monthly cash flow on a pro rata basis, as in the case of a passthrough, the distribution of the principal (both scheduled and prepayments) is carried out on some prioritized basis. How this is done is illustrated in Exhibit 4.

The exhibit shows the cash flow of our original ten mortgage loans and the passthrough. Also shown are three classes of bonds, the par value of each class, and a set of payment rules indicating how the principal from the passthrough is to be distributed to each. Note the following: The sum of the par value of the three classes is equal to $1 million. Although it is not shown in the exhibit, for each of the three classes there will be units representing a proportionate interest in a class. For example, suppose that for Class A, which has a par value of $400,000, there are 50 units of Class A issued. Each unit would receive a proportionate share (2%) of payments received by Class A.

Exhibit 3: Creation of a Passthrough Security

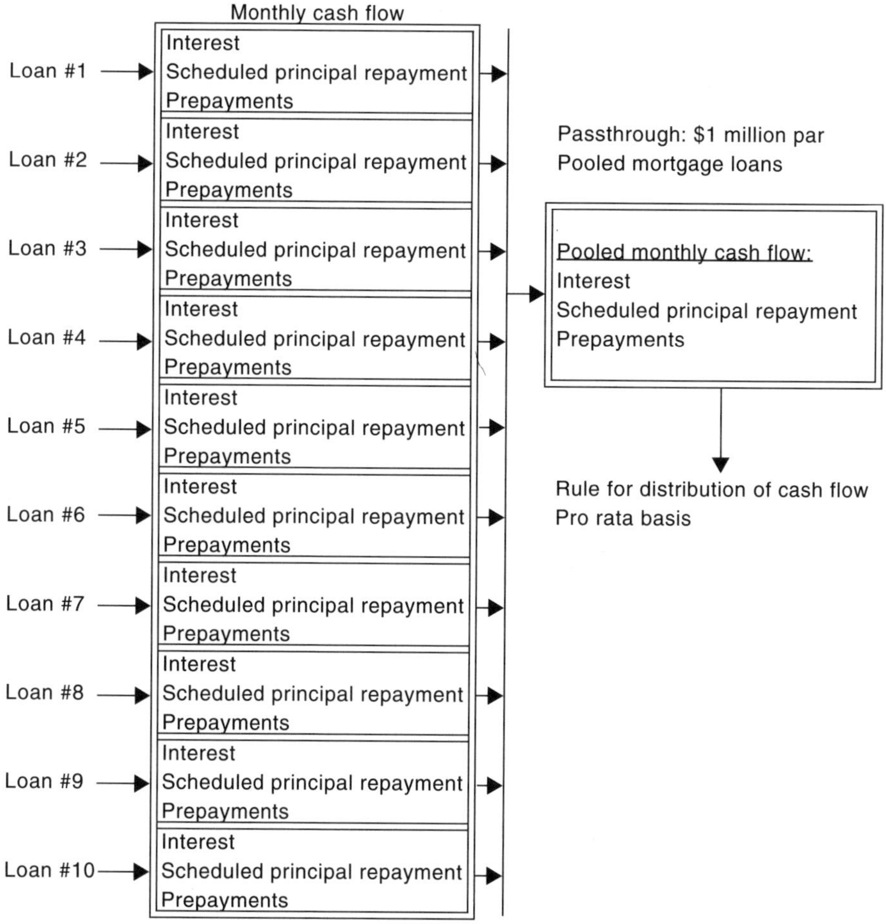

Each loan is for $100,000.
Total loans: $1 million.

The rule for the distribution of principal shown in Exhibit 4 is that Class A will receive all principal (both scheduled and prepayments) until that class receives its entire par value of $400,000. Then, Class B receives all principal payments until it receives its par value of $350,000. After Class B is completely paid off, Class C receives principal payments. The rule for the distribution of cash flow in Exhibit 4 indicates that each of the three classes receives interest on the basis of the amount of par value outstanding.

Exhibit 4: Creation of a Collateralized Mortgage Obligation

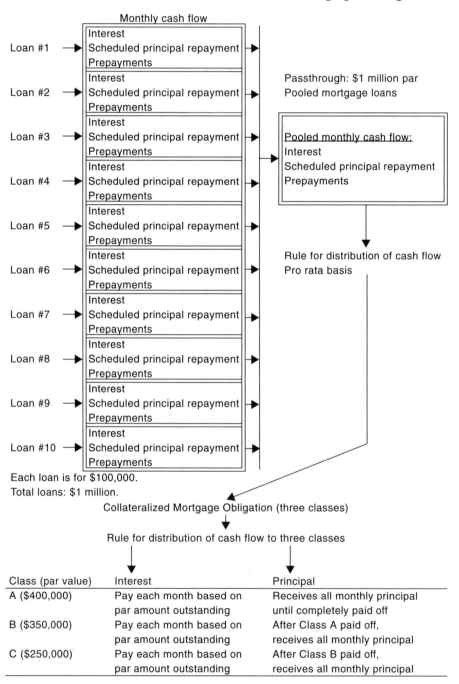

Each loan is for $100,000.
Total loans: $1 million.

Collateralized Mortgage Obligation (three classes)

Rule for distribution of cash flow to three classes

Class (par value)	Interest	Principal
A ($400,000)	Pay each month based on par amount outstanding	Receives all monthly principal until completely paid off
B ($350,000)	Pay each month based on par amount outstanding	After Class A paid off, receives all monthly principal
C ($250,000)	Pay each month based on par amount outstanding	After Class B paid off, receives all monthly principal

The mortgage-backed security that has been created is called a *collateralized mortgage obligation*. The collateral for a CMO may be either one or more passthroughs or a pool of mortgage loans that have not been securitized. Each bond class is commonly referred to as a *tranche*. The ultimate source for the CMO's cash flow is the pool of mortgage loans.

Let's look now at what has been accomplished. Once again, the total prepayment risk for the CMO is the same as the total prepayment risk for the ten mortgage loans. However, the prepayment risk has been distributed differently across the three classes of the CMO. Class A absorbs prepayments first, then Class B, and then Class C. The result of this is that Class A effectively is a shorter-term security than the other two classes; Class C will have the longest maturity. Different institutional investors will be attracted to the different classes, depending on the nature of their liabilities and the effective maturity of the CMO class. Moreover, there is less uncertainty about the maturity of each class of the CMO than there is about the maturity of the passthrough from which it is created. Thus, redirection of the cash flow from the underlying mortgage pool creates classes of bonds that satisfy the asset/liability objectives of certain institutional investors better than a passthrough.

The CMO we describe in Exhibit 4 has a simple set of rules for prioritizing the distribution of the cash flow. Today, much more complicated CMO structures exist. The basic objective is to provide certain CMO classes with less uncertainty about prepayment risk. Note, of course, that this can occur only if the reduction in prepayment risk for some classes is absorbed by other classes in the CMO structure.

CREDIT RISK

A CMO can be viewed as a business entity. The assets of this business are the collateral; that is, the passthrough securities or mortgage loans backing the deal. The collateral for a CMO is held in trust for the exclusive benefit of all the bondholders. The liabilities are the CMO bond classes. The liability obligation consists of the par value and periodic interest payment that is owed to each class of bond. The CMO or, equivalently, the business, is structured so that, even under the worst possible consequences concerning prepayments, all the liabilities will be satisfied.

Since the collateral for a CMO is held in trust for the exclusive benefit of all the bondholders, the credit risk does not depend on who the issuer of the CMO is. It depends on the credit quality of the collateral, although the issuer typically uses its own collateral.

An issuer is either (1) a government-sponsored enterprise (such as the Federal Home Loan Mortgage Corporation, popularly referred to as "Freddie Mac," or the Federal National Mortgage Association, popularly referred to as "Fannie Mae"), (2) the Government National Mortgage Association (popularly referred to as "Ginnie Mae"), a federal-related agency,[1] or (2) a private entity. CMOs issued by government-sponsored enterprises or Ginnie Mae are referred to as *agency CMOs*. Freddie Mac and Fannie Mae can issue CMOs backed by their own passthroughs or backed by passthroughs guaranteed by Ginnie Mae. The latter CMOs are referred to as *cross-agency CMOs*. CMOs issued by a private entity can be divided into two types. A private entity that issues a CMO but whose underlying collateral is a pool of passthroughs guaranteed by an agency is called a *private-label CMOs*. If the collateral for a CMO is a pool of whole loans the structure is referred to as a *whole-loan CMO*.

The guarantee of a government-sponsored entity depends on the financial capacity of the agency to satisfy its obligation and the willingness of the U.S. government to bail out an agency should the entity not be capable of satisfying its obligation. That is, the government guarantee for a government-sponsored entity is an implicit one. CMOs issued by Ginnie Mae are guaranteed by the full faith and credit of the U.S. government. CMOs issued by private entities are rated by commercial rating agencies. There are various ways that such issues can be credit enhanced. We shall describe the methods for credit enhancement in Chapter 8.

REMICs

An entity that issues a mortgage-backed security simply acts as a conduit in passing interest payments received from homeowners through to the security holders, and thus it wants to make sure that any legal structure created to distribute those payments is not taxed. Tax laws provide that the issuer is not treated as a taxable entity if the passthrough is issued through a legal structure known as a *grantor trust*, which is the arrangement used by issuers of passthroughs. There is one major disadvantage of

---

[1] Ginnie Mae began issuing CMOs in 1994.

the grantor trust arrangement: If there is more than one class of bonds (i.e., a multiclass passthrough such as a CMO), the trust does not qualify as a nontaxable entity.

While it is possible to design structures to avoid adverse tax treatment, such structures are inefficient, considering that in the absence of the tax rule restricting more than one class of bonds, the same collateral could be used to create securities with a higher price. Issuers needed a new type of trust device so that mortgage-backed security structures with more than one class of bonds could be issued more efficiently.

The Tax Reform Act of 1986 created a new trust vehicle called the *Real Estate Mortgage Investment Conduit* (REMIC) allowing the issuance of mortgage-backed securities with multiple bondholder classes without adverse tax consequences. While it is common to hear market participants refer to a CMO as a REMIC, not all CMOs are REMICs. In this book, when we refer to a CMO we mean both REMIC and non-REMIC structures.

NUMBER OF BOND CLASSES IN A CMO STRUCTURE

Our basic illustration of a CMO structure assumes three bond classes or tranches. It is not surprising today, however, to see CMO structures with as many as 70 tranches. The last column of Exhibit 1 shows the average number of tranches per deal by year. Between 1983 and 1985, the average number of tranches in a CMO deal was around seven. With the introduction in 1986 of one key innovative bond class, the planned amortization class (PAC), the average number of tranches per deal increased to more than ten. The deals since 1986 when PACs were introduced typically included only one or two PAC tranches. By 1992, there was an average of 19 tranches per deal, and in 1993 there were about 24 tranches per deal.

OVERVIEW OF BOOK

Chapters 2 and 3 complete Section I of this book, which provides background material. In Chapter 2, we review the various types of mortgage loans and agency passthrough securities that have been used as collateral for a CMO. There are also a small number of CMOs in which the collateral is a principal-only security, so we also describe this security in Chapter 2.

To estimate the cash flow of a passthrough or a pool of mortgage loans, prepayments must be projected. Chapter 3 reviews the factors that effect prepayments and the current market convention for estimating prepayments, the Public Securities Association standard prepayment benchmark. The limitations of this market convention are also discussed.

In Section II, Chapters 4 through 8, the various types of CMO structures are explained. Our focus in Chapters 4 through 7 is on CMOs where credit risk is not a concern. We show how the cash flow and the average life (a concept explained in Chapter 2) vary. The plain vanilla sequential-pay CMO bonds are the subject of Chapter 4. In this chapter we also introduce accrual bonds and the residual or equity class of a CMO. In Chapter 5, we show how the redistribution of coupon payments from the underlying collateral can be made so as to create floating-rate and inverse floating-rate CMO bond classes, and interest-only and principal-only bond classes. The most important innovation in the CMO market, the planned amortization class or PAC bond, is explained in Chapter 6. Chapter 7 explains several types of CMO bond classes: targeted amortization class (TAC) bonds, very accurately determined maturity (VADM) bonds, and support bonds. In Chapter 8 we discuss whole-loan CMOs, focusing on the credit enhancement devices.

The analytical techniques for valuing CMO bond classes and for assessing their potential return performance are covered in the four chapters in Section III. There are two analytical techniques used to value CMOs, the static cash flow yield technology and the option-adjusted spread (OAS) technology. The former is covered in Chapter 9 and the latter in Chapter 10. Chapter 11 explains the total return framework and how to incorporate the static cash flow yield and OAS technologies into this framework. We also illustrate how simulation can be used to assess the total return performance characteristics of a CMO bond class. In Chapter 12, we explain how to analyze inverse floaters.

In the final part of this book, Section IV, we discuss the accounting treatment for CMOs and regulations regarding the acquisition of CMOs. Chapter 13 begins with an explanation of the three ways in which a CMO bond class may be classified for financial reporting purposes (held for trading, held for sale, or held for investment) and the accounting treatment for each. Then, the current accounting rules for determining income and balance sheet values for CMOs are illustrated. In Chapter 14, we discuss the regulation of depository institutions with respect to the acquisition of CMOs as specified by the Federal Financial Institutions Examination Council and the regulation for insurance companies as set forth by the National Association of Insurance Commissioners.

Chapter 2

COLLATERAL FOR CMOs

The assets backing a CMO are referred to as its collateral. The collateral may be comprised of as few as one or as many as 1,000 or more pools of passthrough securities, or a single pool of individual mortgage loans (called *whole loans*) that have not been securitized. (Of course, whole loans themselves comprise the collateral for passthrough securities.) There are also some CMOs that are backed by principal-only securities, interest-only securities, and other CMO tranches. When a combination of securities is used as collateral for a CMO deal, the deal is nicknamed a "kitchen sink" deal. Since 1987, passthrough securities have been the collateral for about 95% of the total value of CMOs issued.

The purpose of this chapter is to survey the collateral for CMOs. We begin with a discussion of mortgage loans, follow with a discussion of passthroughs, and then examine principal-only securities.

MORTGAGE (WHOLE) LOANS

A mortgage loan is a loan secured by some specified real estate property, which obliges the borrower to make a predetermined series of payments. The mortgage gives the lender (mortgagee) the right, if the borrower (the mort-

13

gagor) defaults (i.e., fails to make the contracted payments), to "foreclose" on the loan and seize the property in order to ensure that the debt is paid off.

The types of real estate properties that can be mortgaged are divided into two broad categories: residential and nonresidential properties. The former category includes houses, condominiums, cooperatives, and apartments. Residential real estate can be subdivided into single-family (one- to four-family) residences and multifamily residences (apartment buildings in which more than four families reside). Nonresidential property includes commercial and farm properties. Exhibit 1 shows the amount of debt outstanding as of the first quarter of 1993. About 75%, $3 trillion, of the mortgage debt outstanding is for one-to-four family residences. Our focus in this book is on CMOs backed by these mortgages.

Mortgage Originators

The original lender is called the *mortgage originator*. Mortgage originators include commercial banks, thrifts, mortgage bankers, life insurance companies, and pension funds. The three largest originators for all types of residential mortgages are commercial banks, thrifts, and mortgage bankers, originating more than 95% of annual mortgage originations. Mortgage bankers, or more appropriately, mortgage brokers, typically do not invest in the mortgages they originate but rather sell the mortgages to other entities that will invest in them.

Prior to 1990, thrifts were the largest originators, followed by commercial banks. In 1990, thrift origination declined; with an increase in commercial bank origination, the share of thrift origination dropped below that of commercial banks. In 1990 mortgage bankers' share of origination was the largest.

Mortgage originators can either (1) hold the mortgage in their portfolio, (2) sell the mortgage to an investor who (a) holds the mortgage in its portfolio, or (b) places the mortgage in a pool of mortgages that will be used as collateral for the issuance of a security, or (3) use the mortgage themselves as collateral for the issuance of a passthrough security or a CMO. When a mortgage is used as collateral for the issuance of a security or creation of a CMO, the mortgage is said to be securitized.

When a mortgage originator intends to sell the mortgage, it will obtain a commitment from the potential investor (buyer). Two federally sponsored credit agencies and several private companies buy mortgages. Since these agencies and private companies pool these mortgages and sell them to investors, they are called *conduits*.

Exhibit 1: Mortgage Debt Outstanding By Type of Property as of the First Quarter of 1993

Type of property	Millions of dollars
One-to-four family residences	$2,976,287
Multifamily residences	293,382
Commercial	707,041
Farm	80,040
Total	$4,056,750

Source: *Federal Reserve Bulletin*, December 1993, Table A38.

Two agencies, Fannie Mae (Federal National Mortgage Association) and Freddie Mac (Federal Home Loan Mortgage Corporation), purchase only conforming mortgages. A *conforming mortgage* is one meeting the underwriting standards established by these agencies for inclusion in a pool of mortgages underlying a security that they guarantee. The mortgage of an applicant not satisfying the underwriting standards is called a *nonconforming mortgage*. Loans that do not qualify as conforming mortgages because they exceed the maximum loan amount are called *jumbo loans*.[1]

Examples of private conduits are Citimae, Inc. (a subsidiary of Citicorp), Bear Stearns Mortgage Capital Corporation, Residential Funding Corporation (a subsidiary of GMAC), and Sears Mortgage Securities Corporation. They purchase conforming and nonconforming mortgages. Another important conduit is the Resolution Trust Corporation (RTC), a government agency created to liquidate the assets of failed savings and loan associations. The RTC pools mortgages inherited from these savings and loan associations to create passthroughs.

Primary Factors in Evaluating a Borrower's Credit

A potential homeowner who wants to borrow funds to purchase a home will apply for a loan from a mortgage originator. The individual who seeks funds completes an application form, which provides financial information about the applicant, and pays an application fee; then the mortgage originator performs a credit evaluation of the applicant. The two primary factors in determining whether the funds will be lent are the (1) *payment-to-income* (PTI) ratio, and (2) the *loan-to-value* (LTV) ratio. The former ratio is the ratio of monthly payments to monthly income and is a measure of the ability of the applicant to

---

[1] As of 1994, the maximum loan amount is $203,150. This amount is revised annually based on housing prices. In 1993, for example, it was higher than in 1994 ($212,500).

make monthly payments (both mortgage and real estate tax payments). The lower this ratio, the greater the likelihood that the applicant will be able to meet the required payments.

The difference between the purchase price of the property and the amount borrowed is the borrower's down payment. The LTV is the ratio of the amount of the loan to the market (or appraised) value of the property. The lower this ratio, the greater the protection the lender has if the applicant defaults on the payments and the lender must repossess and sell the property. For example, if an applicant wants to borrow $150,000 on property with an appraised value of $200,000, the LTV is 75%. Suppose the applicant subsequently defaults on the mortgage. The lender can then repossess the property and sell it to recover the amount owed. But the amount that will be received by the lender depends on the market value of the property. In our example, even if conditions in the housing market are weak, the lender will still be able to recover the proceeds lent if the value of the property declines by $50,000. Suppose instead that the applicant wanted to borrow $180,000 for the same property. The LTV would then be 90%. If the lender had to sell the property because the applicant defaults, there is less protection for the lender.

Mortgage Insurance

When a lender makes a loan based solely on the credit of the borrower and on the collateral for the mortgage, the mortgage is said to be a *conventional* mortgage.

There are two types of mortgage-related insurance. The first type is originated by the lender to insure against default by the borrower and is called *mortgage insurance*. It is usually required by lenders on loans with loan-to-value (LTV) ratios greater than 80%. The amount insured will be some percentage of the loan and may decline as the LTV ratio declines. While the insurance is required by the lender, the cost of the insurance is borne by the borrower, usually through a higher contract rate.

There are two forms of mortgage insurance: insurance provided by a government agency and private mortgage insurance. The federal agencies that provide this insurance to qualified borrowers are the Federal Housing Administration (FHA), the Veterans Administration (VA), and the Federal Farmers Administration (FMHA). Private mortgage insurance can be obtained from a mortgage insurance company such as Mortgage Guaranty Insurance Company (owned by Northwestern Mutual) and PMI Mortgage Insurance Company (owned by Sears, Roebuck).

The second type of mortgage-related insurance is acquired by the borrower, usually with a life insurance company, and is typically called *credit life*. Unlike mortgage insurance, this type is not required by the lender. The policy provides for a continuation of mortgage payments after the death of the insured person, which allows the survivors to continue living in the house. Since the insurance coverage decreases as the mortgage balance declines, this type of mortgage insurance is simply a term policy.

While both types of insurance have a beneficial effect on the credit-worthiness of the borrower, the first type is more important from the lender's perspective. Mortgage insurance is sought by the lender when the borrower is viewed as being capable of meeting the monthly mortgage payments, but does not have enough funds for a large down payment. For example, suppose a borrower seeks financing of $100,000 to purchase a single-family residence for $110,000, thus making a down payment of $10,000. The LTV ratio is 91%, exceeding the uninsured maximum LTV of 80%. Even if the lender's credit analysis indicates that the borrower's payment-to-income ratio (PTI) is acceptable, the mortgage loan cannot be extended. However, if a private mortgage insurance company insures a portion of the loan, then the lender is afforded protection. Mortgage insurance companies will write policies to insure a maximum of 20% of loans with a LTV ranging from 80% to 90%, and a maximum of 25% of loans with an LTV ranging from 90% to 95%. The lender is still exposed to default by the borrower on the noninsured portion of the mortgage loan, and in the case of private mortgage insurers, exposed to the risk that the insurer will default.

To illustrate what will happen if a borrower covered by private mortgage insurance defaults, suppose that in our previous example mortgage insurance is obtained for $15,000, and a default occurs when the market value of the property is $94,000, and the outstanding mortgage balance is $98,000. The mortgage insurer has two choices. It can simply pay the claim by giving the lender $15,000, thereby fulfilling its insurance obligation. The lender then has $15,000 plus the mortgaged property with a value of $94,000, producing a total value of $104,000 and a profit of $6,000. A more economical alternative for the mortgage insurer would be to pay off the mortgage balance of $98,000 and take title to the property. It can then sell the property for $94,000, realizing a loss of $4,000. This loss, however, is less than the $15,000 loss that would result by paying the claim.

Mortgage insurance can also be obtained for pools of mortgage loans that collateralize mortgage-backed securities issued by private conduits.

Alternative Mortgage Instruments

There are many types of mortgage loans. Here we review several of the popular mortgage designs, restricting our brief survey to those designs that have been used as collateral for CMOs or those that have been securitized with the resulting securities used as collateral for CMOs. Since CMOs are backed by fixed-rate mortgages, we restrict our survey to these types of loans.

Level-Payment, Fixed-Rate Mortgage: The basic idea behind the design of the level-payment, fixed-rate mortgage, or simply level-payment mortgage, is that the borrower pays in equal monthly installments over an agreed-upon period of time, called the maturity or term of the mortgage. Each monthly mortgage payment for a level-payment mortgage is due on the first of each month and consists of:

(1) interest of 1/12th of the fixed annual interest rate times the amount of the outstanding mortgage balance at the beginning of the previous month and
(2) a repayment of a portion of the outstanding mortgage balance (principal).

The difference between the monthly mortgage payment and the portion of the payment that represents interest equals the amount that is applied to reduce the outstanding mortgage balance. The monthly mortgage payment is designed so that after the last scheduled monthly payment of the loan is made, the amount of the outstanding mortgage balance is zero (i.e., the mortgage is fully repaid).

To illustrate a level-payment fixed-rate mortgage, consider a 30-year (360-month), $100,000 mortgage with a 8.125% mortgage rate. The monthly mortgage payment would be $742.50. Exhibit 2 shows for selected months how each monthly mortgage payment is divided between interest and repayment of principal. At the beginning of month 1, the mortgage balance is $100,000, the amount of the original loan. The mortgage payment for month 1 includes interest on the $100,000 borrowed for the month. Since the interest rate is 8.125%, the monthly interest rate is 0.0067708 (0.08125 divided by 12). Interest for month 1 is therefore $677.08 ($100,000 times 0.0067708). The $65.41 difference between the monthly mortgage payment of $742.50 and the interest of $677.08 is the portion of the monthly mortgage payment that represents repayment of principal. This $65.41 in month 1 reduces the mortgage balance.

Exhibit 2: Amortization Schedule
for a Level-Payment, Fixed-Rate Mortgage

Mortgage loan: $100,000
Mortgage rate: 8.125%
Morthly payment: $742.50
Term of loan: 30 years (360 months)

Month	Beginning Mortgage Balance	Scheduled Monthly Payment	Ending Monthly Interest	Principal Repaymeny	Mortgage Balance
1	100,000.00	742.50	677.08	65.41	99,934.59
2	99,934.59	742.50	676.64	65.86	99,868.73
3	99,868.73	742.50	676.19	66.30	99,802.43
4	99,802.43	742.50	675.75	66.75	99,735.68
25	98,301.53	742.50	665.58	76.91	98,224.62
26	98,224.62	742.50	665.06	77.43	98,147.19
27	98,147.19	742.50	664.54	77.96	98,069.23
74	93,849.98	742.50	635.44	107.05	93,742.93
75	93,742.93	742.50	634.72	107.78	93,635.15
76	93,635.15	742.50	633.99	108.51	93,526.64
141	84,811.77	742.50	574.25	168.25	84,643.52
142	84,643.52	742.50	573.11	169.39	84,474.13
143	84,474.13	742.50	571.96	170.54	84,303.59
184	76,446.29	742.50	517.61	224.89	76,221.40
185	76,221.40	742.50	516.08	226.41	75,994.99
186	75,994.99	742.50	514.55	227.95	75,767.04
233	63,430.19	742.50	429.48	313.02	63,117.17
234	63,117.17	742.50	427.36	315.14	62,802.03
235	62,802.03	742.50	425.22	317.28	62,484.75
289	42,200.92	742.50	285.74	456.76	41,744.15
290	41,744.15	742.50	282.64	459.85	41,284.30
291	41,284.30	742.50	279.53	462.97	40,821.33
321	25,941.42	742.50	175.65	566.85	25,374.57
322	25,374.57	742.50	171.81	570.69	24,803.88
323	24,803.88	742.50	167.94	574.55	24,229.32
358	2,197.66	742.50	14.88	727.62	1,470.05
359	1,470.05	742.50	9.95	732.54	737.50
360	737.50	742.50	4.99	737.50	0.00

The mortgage balance at the end of month 1 (beginning of month 2) is then $99,934.59 ($100,000 minus $65.41). The interest for the second monthly mortgage payment is $676.64, the monthly interest rate (0.0066708) times the mortgage balance at the beginning of month 2 ($99,934.59). The difference between the $742.50 monthly mortgage payment and the $676.64 interest is $65.86, representing the amount of the mortgage balance paid off with that monthly mortgage payment. Notice that the last mortgage payment in month 360 is sufficient to pay off the remaining mortgage balance. When a loan repayment schedule is structured in this way, so that the payments made by the borrower will completely pay off the interest and principal, the loan is said to be fully-amortizing. Exhibit 2 is referred to as an amortization schedule.

As Exhibit 2 clearly shows, the portion of the monthly mortgage payment applied to interest declines each month and the portion applied to reducing the mortgage balance increases. The reason for this is that as the mortgage balance is reduced with each monthly mortgage payment, the interest on the mortgage balance declines. Since the monthly mortgage payment is fixed, an increasingly larger portion of the monthly payment is applied to reduce the principal in each subsequent month.

Balloon Mortgages: In a balloon mortgage loan, or simply balloon loan, the borrower is given long-term financing by the lender, but at a specified future date the mortgage rate is renegotiated. Thus, the lender provides long-term funds for what is essentially short-term borrowing; the term depends on the frequency of the renegotiation period. Effectively, a balloon mortgage is a short-term balloon loan in which the lender agrees to provide financing for the remainder of the term of the mortgage. The balloon payment is the original amount borrowed less the amount amortized.

Fannie Mae and Freddie Mac have programs for the purchase of these mortgages. Freddie Mac's 30-year balloon/resets, for example, can have either a renegotiation period of 5 years ("30-due-in-5" FRMs) or 7 years ("30-due-in-7" FRMs). If certain conditions are met, Freddie Mac guarantees the extension of the loan.

"Two-Step" Mortgage Loans: The two-step mortgage loan is similar to a balloon mortgage in that there it is a fixed-rate loan with a single rate reset at some point prior to maturity. Unlike a balloon mortgage, this rate reset occurs without specific action on the part of the borrower.

As an example, a two-step mortgage loan can have a fixed rate seven years, and then resets once. The new rate, or reset rate, on the mortgage can be based on any rate. The two-step mortgage loans available through Fannie Mae's program determines the new rate by adding 250 basis points to a weekly average of the ten-year constant maturity Treasury yield. There are also caps imposed on how much the rate can increase. For example, Fannie Mae limits any increase in the mortgage rate to no more than 600 basis points over the initial mortgage rate.

Unlike in balloon mortgages, the rate reset on the two-step does not consist of a repayment of the initial loan and the origination of a new one. Thus, an investor who holds a 30-year two-step mortgage with a reset after seven years has an investment with a 30-year final maturity. In contrast, the investor who holds a 30-year balloon mortgage with a reset after seven years has an investment with a seven-year final maturity.

Growing Equity Mortgages: A growing equity mortgage (GEM) is a fixed-rate mortgage whose monthly mortgage payments increase over time. The initial monthly mortgage payment is the same as for a level-payment, fixed-rate mortgage. The higher monthly mortgage payments are applied to paying off the principal. As a result, the principal of a GEM is repaid faster. For example, a 30-year $100,000 GEM loan with a mortgage rate of 8.125% might call for an initial monthly payment of $742.50 (the same as a fixed-rate level payment 8.125% 30-year mortgage loan). The GEM payment gradually increases, however, and as a result the loan will be paid off in less than 30 years.

Tiered Payment Mortgages: Another mortgage design with a fixed rate and a monthly payment that graduates over time is the tiered payment mortgage (TPM). The initial monthly mortgage payments are below those of a level-payment fixed-rate mortgage. In the case of a TPM, however, there is no negative amortization because withdrawals are made from a buydown account to supplement the initial monthly payments to cover the shortfall of interest. The buydown account is established at the time the loan is originated by the borrower, the lender, or a third party, such as a real estate developer, home builder, relative, or business associate. In the second half of 1989, 15-year TPMs were used as collateral for a mortgage-backed security.

Prepayment Risk

Our illustration of the cash flow from a level-payment, fixed-rate mortgage assumes that the homeowner does not pay off any portion of the
mortgage balance prior to the scheduled due date. But homeowners do
pay off all or part of their mortgage balance prior to the maturity date.
Payments made in excess of the scheduled principal repayments are
called *prepayments*.

Prepayments occur for many reasons. First, homeowners prepay
the entire mortgage when they sell their home. The sale of a home may
occur because of (1) a change of employment that necessitates moving,
(2) the purchase of a more expensive home ("trading up"), or (3) a death
or divorce in which the will or the settlement requires sale of the marital
residence. Second, the borrower may be moved to pay off part of the
mortgage balance as market rates fall below the mortgage rate on the
loan. Partial prepayments are referred to as *curtailments* and are often
made when a borrower can best utilize excess cash by paying down a
portion of a mortgage. Third, in the case of homeowners who cannot
meet their mortgage obligations, the property is repossessed and sold.
The proceeds of such a sale are used to pay off the mortgage in the case
of a conventional mortgage. For an insured mortgage, the insurer will
pay off the mortgage balance. Finally, if property is destroyed by fire or if
another insured catastrophe occurs, the insurance proceeds are used to
pay off the mortgage.

The effect of prepayments is that the amount and timing of the
cash flow from a mortgage is not known with certainty. For example, all
that the investor in a $100,000, 8.125% 30-year FHA-insured mortgage
knows is that as long as the loan is outstanding, interest will be received
and the principal will be repaid at the scheduled date each month; then
at the end of the 30 years, the investor would have received $100,000 in
principal payments. What the investor does not know — the uncertainty
— is for how long the loan will be outstanding, and therefore what the
timing of the principal payments will be. This is true for all mortgage
loans, not just level-payment, fixed-rate mortgages.

MORTGAGE PASSTHROUGH SECURITIES

A mortgage passthrough security, or simply a passthrough, is created
when one or more mortgage holders form a collection (pool) of mort-

gages and sell shares or participation certificates in the pool. The cash flow of a passthrough depends on the cash flow of the underlying mortgages. It consists of monthly mortgage payments representing interest, the scheduled repayment of principal, and any prepayments.

Payments are made to security holders each month. Neither the amount nor the timing, however, of the cash flow from the pool of mortgages is identical to that of the cash flow passed through to investors. The monthly cash flow for a passthrough is less than the monthly cash flow of the underlying mortgages by an amount equal to servicing and other fees. The other fees are those charged by the issuer or guarantor of the passthrough for guaranteeing the issue. The coupon rate on a passthrough, called the *passthrough coupon rate*, is less than the mortgage rate on the underlying pool of mortgage loans by an amount equal to the servicing and guaranteeing fees.

The timing of the cash flow is also different. The monthly mortgage payment is due from each mortgagor on the first day of each month. There is then a delay in passing through the corresponding monthly cash flow to the security holders, which varies by the type of passthrough. Because of prepayments, the cash flow of a passthrough is not known with certainty.

Types of Passthroughs

There are three major types of passthroughs guaranteed by the following organizations: Government National Mortgage Association ("Ginnie Mae"), Freddie Mac, and Fannie Mae. These are called *agency passthroughs*. Nonagency passthroughs, called conventional or private-label passthroughs, are a small sector of the passthrough market.

An agency can provide one of two types of guarantees. One type guarantees the timely payment of both interest and principal, meaning that the interest and principal will be paid when due, even if any of the mortgagors fail to make their monthly mortgage payments. Passthroughs with this type of guarantee are referred to as *fully modified passthroughs*. The second type guarantees both interest and principal payments, but it guarantees the timeliness of the interest payment only. The scheduled principal is passed through as it is collected, with a guarantee that the scheduled payment will be made no later than a specified time after it is due. Passthroughs with this type of guarantee are called *modified passthroughs*.

Government National Mortgage Association MBS: Ginnie Mae passthroughs are guaranteed by the full faith and credit of the U.S. government. For this reason, Ginnie Mae passthroughs are viewed as risk-free in terms of default risk, just like Treasury securities. The security guaranteed by Ginnie Mae is called a *mortgage-backed security* (MBS). All Ginnie Mae MBSs are fully modified passthroughs.

Only mortgage loans insured or guaranteed by either the Federal Housing Administration, the Veterans Administration, or the Farmers Home Administration can be included in a mortgage pool guaranteed by Ginnie Mae.

Federal Home Loan Mortgage Corporation PC: The second largest type of agency passthroughs is the participation certificate (PC) issued by Freddie Mac. Although a Freddie Mac guarantee is not a guarantee by the U.S. government, most market participants view Freddie Mac PCs as similar, although not identical, in creditworthiness to Ginnie Mae passthroughs.

Freddie Mac has two programs with which it creates PCs: *Cash Program* and *Guarantor/Swap Program*. In the first program, the individual mortgages that back the PC are those purchased from mortgage originators, then pooled by Freddie Mac, and sold in the market or through its dealer network through daily auctions. The PCs created under this program are called *Cash PCs* or *Regular PCs*. Under the Conventional Guarantor/Swap Program, Freddie Mac allows originators to swap pooled mortgages for PCs in those same pools. For example, a thrift may have $50 million of mortgages. It can swap these mortgages for a Freddie Mac PC in which the underlying mortgage pool is the same $50 million in mortgage loans that the thrift swapped for the PC. The PCs created under this program are called *Swap PCs*.

In the fall of 1990, Freddie Mac introduced its *Gold PC*, which has stronger guarantees. Gold PCs are issued now in both programs, and will be the only type of PC issued in the future.

Freddie Mac offers both modified passthroughs and fully modified passthroughs. All non-Gold PCs issued as part of its Cash Program and almost all issued as part of its Guarantor/Swap Program are modified passthroughs. A very small number of non-Gold PCs in the latter program are fully modified passthroughs. All Gold PCs issued are fully modified passthroughs.

For modified PCs issued by Freddie Mac, the scheduled principal is passed through as it is collected, with Freddie Mac guaranteeing only that the scheduled payment will be made no later than one year after it is due.

Federal National Mortgage Association MBS: The passthroughs issued by Fannie Mae are mortgage-backed securities (MBS). Like a Freddie Mac PC, a Fannie Mae MBS is not an obligation of the U.S. government. Fannie Mae also has a swap program similar to that of Freddie Mac, through which it issues most of its MBSs. All Fannie Mae MBSs are fully modified passthroughs.

Private-Label Passthroughs: Private label passthrough securities are issued by thrifts, commercial banks, and private conduits. Private conduits purchase nonconforming mortgages, pool them, and then sell passthroughs in which the collateral is the underlying pool of nonconforming mortgages. Private-label passthroughs are rated by commercial rating agencies such as Moody's, Standard & Poor's, and Fitch. The development of private credit enhancement is the key to the success of this market.

PRINCIPAL-ONLY STRIPPED MORTGAGE-BACKED SECURITIES

A passthrough divides the cash flow from the underlying pool of mortgages on a pro rata basis to the security holders. A stripped MBS is created by changing the distribution of principal and interest from a pro rata distribution to an unequal distribution. In early 1987, stripped MBSs were issued allocating all the interest to one class (called the interest-only or IO class) and all the principal to the other class (called the principal-only or PO class). The IO class receives no principal payments.

The PO security is purchased at a substantial discount from par value. The yield an investor will realize depends on the speed at which prepayments are made. The faster the prepayments, the higher the yield that will be realized. For example, suppose there is a mortgage pool consisting of only 30-year mortgages with $100 million in principal, and that investors can purchase POs backed by this mortgage pool for $43.75 million. The dollar return on this investment will be $56.25 million. How quickly that dollar return is recovered by PO investors determines the yield that will be realized. In the extreme case, if all homeowners in the underlying mortgage pool decide to prepay their mortgages immediately, PO investors will realize the $56.25 million immediately. At the other extreme, if all homeowners decide to keep their home and the same mortgage for 30 years, and make no prepayments, the $56.25 million will be spread out over 30 years, resulting in a reduced yield for PO investors.

As noted earlier, there are CMOs that are backed by POs. Such structures are referred to as *PO-collateralized CMOs*.

PREPAYMENT RISK AND ASSET/LIABILITY MANAGEMENT

The possibility of prepayments means that the cash flow of a passthrough is not known. To understand the risks associated with prepayments, suppose an investor buys a 10% coupon Ginnie Mae MBS when mortgage rates are 10%. Let's consider what will happen to prepayments if mortgage rates in the market decline to, say, 7%. There will be two adverse consequences. First, the price of the MBS will not rise by as much as the price of a Treasury security. This is because homeowners whose mortgages are included in the pool backing the passthrough have a right to prepay their loan, and as market rates for mortgages fall below the rate they are paying, the likelihood that they will refinance increases. When they repay, however, they will do so at par. Any premium above par that the investor has paid will be lost when homeowners prepay. Thus, as rates decline, the passthrough's price appreciation will not move as far above par value as a Treasury security, which has no prepayment risk. This is the same adverse consequence facing the investor in any callable bond; it is referred to as "price compression," or more popularly, "negative convexity." We explain this phenomenon further in Chapter 9.

The second adverse consequence of declining mortgage rates is that the investor must reinvest cash flows received sooner at the lower rate. This is referred to as reinvestment risk. These two consequences that a passthrough investor faces — negative convexity and reinvestment — are referred to together as *contraction risk*.

Now let's look at what happens if mortgage rates rise to, say, 15%. The price of the passthrough, like that of any bond, will decline. But again, it will decline more than the price of a Treasury security because the higher rates will tend to slow down the rate of prepayment, in effect increasing the amount invested at the passthrough coupon rate, which is now lower than the market rate. Prepayments will slow down because homeowners will neither refinance or partially prepay their mortgages when mortgage rates are higher than their mortgage rate of 10%. Yet this is just the time when investors want prepayments to speed up so that they can reinvest the prepayments at the higher market interest rate. This adverse consequence of rising mortgage rates is called *extension risk*.

Therefore, prepayment risk includes contraction risk and extension risk. It comes from the option granted to the borrower/homeowner to prepay a mortgage loan — in whole or in part — at any time.

It should be understood that prepayments are not necessarily an adverse event for an investor. The effect on investment performance will depend upon whether the passthrough is purchased at a discount or at a premium. Prepayments enhance the return from holding a passthrough if it is purchased at a discount for two reasons. First, the investor realizes a capital gain equal to the difference between the par value and the price paid. Second, a passthrough will trade at a discount when the passthrough coupon rate is less than the current coupon rate for newly issued passthroughs. Consequently, prepayments allow the investor to reinvest the proceeds at a higher coupon rate.

For a passthrough purchased at a premium to par, prepayments reduce investment returns for two reasons: (1) the investor realizes a capital loss equal to the difference between the price paid and par value, and (2) the proceeds must be reinvested at a lower coupon rate.

MOTIVATION FOR DEVELOPMENT OF THE CMO STRUCTURE

Until 1983, the most popular vehicle institutional investors used to invest in the mortgage market was passthroughs, despite the effects of prepayment risk. Our discussion is intended to shed light on the motivation for development of the collateralized mortgage obligation.

From an asset/liability perspective, passthroughs are an unattractive investment for many institutional investors because a change in prepayments may result in a mismatch of the funding for their liabilities. The CMO structure broadens the appeal of mortgage-backed products to traditional fixed-income investors. Consider commercial banks and thrifts (S&Ls, savings banks, and credit unions). Such financial institutions want to lock in a spread over their cost of funds, which are raised on a short-term basis either through the issuance of short-term money market obligations or the issuance of certificates of deposit. If they invest the proceeds in fixed-rate passthroughs, they will be mismatched, because a passthrough is a long-term security.

Passthroughs may not be useful for satisfying certain obligations of insurance companies. More specifically, consider a life insurance company that has issued a four-year guaranteed investment contract (GIC). A GIC is an insurance product whose seller agrees to pay a specified interest rate over a predetermined time period in return for a specified sum of money, the premium. If the insurance company purchases a passthrough with the premium received, the security could have a life considerably longer than four years or any other maturity that was anticipated when the passthrough was purchased. That is, the insurance company is exposed to extension risk.

Finally, consider a pension fund or a life insurance company with a predetermined set of liabilities that must be paid over the next 15 years. In the case of a pension fund, this would be the defined benefit payments it must make to beneficiaries; for the life insurance company, it might be obligations resulting from an annuity policy that it has sold. The purchase of a passthrough exposes these institutional investors to the risk that prepayments will speed up, and as a result, the passthrough's maturity will shorten to considerably less than 15 years. Prepayments will speed up if interest rates decline, thereby forcing reinvestment of prepayments at a lower interest rate. In this case, the pension fund and the life insurance company are exposed to contraction risk.

As just demonstrated, some institutional investors are concerned with extension risk and others with contraction risk when they invest in a passthrough. The redirection of cash flows possible in CMOs allows redistribution of prepayment risk, giving investors the opportunity to reduce their exposure to prepayment risk.

Chapter 3

PREPAYMENT CONVENTIONS AND FACTORS AFFECTING PREPAYMENTS

The starting point in the evaluation of any financial asset is estimation of its expected cash flow. As explained in Chapter 2, the cash flow of a mortgage loan consists of (1) monthly mortgage payments representing interest, (2) the scheduled repayment of principal, and (3) any prepayments. The possibility of prepayments means that the cash flow of a passthrough cannot be known with certainty. In this chapter we discuss the current industry convention for projecting the cash flow of a passthrough. Our focus here is simply to illustrate the mechanics involved. In future chapters, we will refer to these conventions whenever we illustrate the cash flow of CMO structures. After discussing the industry convention we will discuss the factors affecting prepayment behavior.

PREPAYMENT BENCHMARK CONVENTIONS

Estimating the cash flow from a passthrough requires making an assumption about future prepayments. Several conventions have been used as a benchmark for prepayment rates: (1) Federal Housing Administration (FHA) experience, (2) the constant prepayment rate, and (3) the Public Securities

Association (PSA) prepayment benchmark. While the first convention is no longer used, we discuss it because of its historical significance.

In the earliest stages of the passthrough market's development, cash flows were calculated assuming no prepayments for the first 12 years at which time all the mortgages in the pool were assumed to prepay. This naive approach was replaced by the "FHA prepayment experience" approach, which also is no longer in use.

The prepayment experience for 30-year mortgages derived from an FHA table on mortgage survival factors was once the most commonly used benchmark for prepayment rates. It calls for the projection of the cash flow for a mortgage pool on the assumption that the prepayment rate will be the same as the FHA experience (referred to as "100% FHA"), or some multiple of FHA experience (faster or slower than FHA experience).

Despite the method's past popularity, prepayments based on FHA experience are not necessarily indicative of the prepayment rate for a particular pool, mainly because FHA prepayments are for mortgages originated over all sorts of interest rate periods. Prepayment rates are tied to interest rate cycles, however, so an average prepayment rate over various cycles is not very useful in estimating prepayments. Moreover, new FHA tables are published periodically, causing confusion about which FHA table prepayments should be based on. Finally, because FHA mortgages are assumable, unlike FNMA, FHLMC, and most nonconforming mortgages which have due-on-sale provisions, FHA statistics underestimate prepayments for non-FHA mortgages. Because estimated prepayments using FHA experience may be misleading, the resulting cash flow is not meaningful for valuing passthroughs.

Constant Prepayment Rate

Another benchmark for projecting prepayments and the cash flow of a passthrough requires assuming that some fraction of the remaining principal in the pool is prepaid each month for the remaining term of the mortgage. The prepayment rate assumed for a pool, called the *constant prepayment rate* (CPR),[1] is based on the characteristics of the pool (including its historical prepayment experience) and the current and expected future economic environment. The advantage of this approach is its simplicity. What's more, changes in economic conditions that impact prepayment rates or changes in the historical prepayment pattern of a pool can be analyzed quickly.

---

[1] It is also called the *conditional prepayment rate*.

The Single-Monthly Mortality Rate: The CPR is an annual prepayment rate. To estimate monthly prepayments, the CPR must be converted into a monthly prepayment rate, commonly referred to as the *single-monthly mortality rate* (SMM). A formula can be used to determine the SMM for a given CPR:

$$SMM = 1 - (1 - CPR)^{1/12} \tag{1}$$

Suppose that the CPR used to estimate prepayments is 6%. The corresponding SMM is:

$$SMM = 1 - (1 - 0.06)^{1/12} = 1 - (0.94)^{0.08333} = 0.005143$$

The SMM Rate and the Monthly Prepayment: An SMM of w% means that approximately w% of the remaining mortgage balance at the beginning of the month, less the scheduled principal payment, will prepay that month. That is,

Prepayment for month t = SMM ×

(Beginning mortgage balance for month t –

Scheduled prinicpal payment for month t)

For example, suppose that an investor owns a passthrough in which the remaining mortgage balance at the beginning of some month is $290 million. Assuming that the SMM is 0.5143% and the scheduled principal payment is $3 million, the estimated prepayment for the month is:

$$0.005143 \times (\$290,000,000 - \$3,000,000) = \$1,476,041$$

PSA Prepayment Benchmark

The Public Securities Association (PSA) prepayment benchmark is expressed as a monthly series of annual prepayment rates.[2] The basic PSA model assumes that prepayment rates are low for newly originated mortgages and then will speed up as the mortgages become seasoned.

---

[2] This benchmark is commonly referred to as a prepayment model, suggesting that it can be used to estimate prepayments. Characterization of this benchmark as a prepayment model is inappropriate. It is simply a market convention.

Exhibit 1: Graphical Depiction of 100 PSA

The PSA standard benchmark assumes the following prepayment rates for 30-year mortgages:

(1) a CPR of 0.2% for the first month, increased by 0.2% per year per month for the next 29 months when it reaches 6% per year, and

(2) a 6% CPR for the remaining years.

This benchmark, referred to as "100% PSA" or simply "100 PSA," is graphically depicted in Exhibit 1. Mathematically, 100 PSA can be expressed as follows:

if $t \le 30$ then CPR = 6% (t/30)
if $t > 30$ then CPR = 6%

where t is the number of months since the mortgage originated.

Slower or faster speeds are then referred to as some percentage of PSA. For example, 50 PSA means one-half the CPR of the PSA benchmark prepayment rate; 150 PSA means 1.5 times the CPR of the PSA benchmark prepayment rate; 300 PSA means three times the CPR of the benchmark prepayment rate. This is illustrated graphically in Exhibit 2 for 50 PSA, 100 PSA, and 150 PSA. A prepayment rate of 0 PSA means that no prepayments are assumed.

The CPR is converted to an SMM using equation (1). For example, the SMMs for month 5, month 20, and months 31 through 360 assuming 100 PSA are calculated as follows:

for month 5:

$$CPR = 6\% \ (5/30) = 1\% = 0.01$$
$$SMM = 1 - (1 - 0.01)^{1/12} = 1 - (0.99)^{0.083333} = 0.000837$$

for month 20:

$$CPR = 6\% \ (20/30) = 4\% = 0.04$$
$$SMM = 1 - (1 - 0.04)^{1/12} = 1 - (0.96)^{0.083333} = 0.003396$$

for month 31-360:

$$CPR = 6\%$$
$$SMM = 1 - (1 - 0.06)^{1/12} = 1 - (0.94)^{0.083333} = 0.005143$$

The SMMs for month 5, month 20, and months 31 through 360 assuming 165 PSA are computed as follows:

for month 5:

$$CPR = 6\% \ (5/30) = 1\% = 0.01$$
$$165 \ PSA = 1.65 \ (0.01) = 0.0165$$
$$SMM = 1 - (1 - 0.0165)^{1/12} = 1 - (0.9835)^{0.08333} = 0.001386$$

for month 20:

$$CPR = 6\% \ (20/30) = 4\% = 0.04$$
$$165 \ PSA = 1.65 \ (.04) = 0.066$$
$$SMM = 1 - (1 - 0.066)^{1/12} = 1 - (0.934)^{0.08333} = 0.005674$$

for month 31-360:

$$CPR = 6\%$$
$$165 \ PSA = 1.65 \ (0.06) = 0.099$$
$$SMM = 1 - (1 - 0.099)^{1/12} = 1 - (0.901)^{0.08333} = 0.007828$$

Notice that the SMM assuming 165 PSA is not just 1.65 times the SMM assuming 100 PSA. It is the CPR that is a multiple of the CPR assuming 100 PSA.

Exhibit 2: Graphical Depiction of 50 PSA, 100 PSA, and 300 PSA

The SMMs for month 5, month 20, and months 31 through 360 assuming 50 PSA are as follows:

for month 5:

$$CPR = 6\% \ (5/30) = 1\% = 0.01$$
$$50 \ PSA = 0.5 \ (0.01) = 0.005$$
$$SMM = 1 - (1 - 0.005)^{1/12} = 1 - (0.995)^{0.08333} = 0.000418$$

for month 20:

$$CPR = 6\% \ (20/30) = 4\% = 0.04$$
$$50 \ PSA = 0.5 \ (0.04) = 0.02$$
$$SMM = 1 - (1 - 0.02)^{1/12} = 1 - (0.98)^{0.08333} = 0.001682$$

for month 31-360:

$$CPR = 6\%$$
$$50 \ PSA = 0.5 \ (0.06) = 0.03$$
$$SMM = 1 - (1 - 0.03)^{1/12} = 1 - (0.97)^{0.08333} = 0.002535$$

Once again, notice that the SMM assuming 50 PSA is not just one-half the SMM assuming 100 PSA. It is the CPR that is a multiple of the CPR assuming 100 PSA.

Illustration of Monthly Cash Flow Construction: We now show how to construct a monthly cash flow for a hypothetical passthrough given a PSA assumption. For the purpose of this illustration, the underlying mortgages for this hypothetical passthrough are assumed to be fixed-rate level-payment mortgages with a weighted average coupon (WAC) rate of 8.125%. It will be assumed that the passthrough rate is 7.5% with a weighted average maturity (WAM) of 357 months.

Exhibit 3 shows the cash flow for selected months assuming 100 PSA. The cash flow is broken down into three components: (1) interest (based on the passthrough rate), (2) the regularly scheduled principal repayment, and (3) prepayments based on 100 PSA.

Let's walk through Exhibit 3 column by column.

Column 1: This is the month.

Column 2: This column gives the outstanding mortgage balance at the beginning of the month. It is equal to the outstanding balance at the beginning of the previous month reduced by the total principal payment in the previous month.

Column 3: This column shows the SMM for 100 PSA. Two things should be noted in this column. First, for month 1, the SMM is for a passthrough that has been seasoned three months. That is, the CPR is .8%. This is because the WAM is 357. Second, from month 27 on, the SMM is 0.00514 which corresponds to a CPR of 6%.

Column 4: The total monthly mortgage payment is shown in this column. Notice that the total monthly mortgage payment declines over time as prepayments reduce the mortgage balance outstanding. There is a formula to determine what the monthly mortgage balance will be for each month given prepayments.[3]

Column 5: The monthly interest paid to the passthrough investor is found in this column. This value is determined by multiplying the outstanding mortgage balance at the beginning of the month by the passthrough rate of 7.5% and dividing by 12.

Column 6: This column gives the regularly scheduled principal repayment. This is the difference between the total monthly mortgage payment [the amount shown in column (4)] and the gross

---

[3] The formula is presented in Chapter 20 of Frank J. Fabozzi, *Fixed Income Mathematics: Analytical and Statistical Techniques* (Chicago: Probus Publishing, 1993).

coupon interest for the month. The gross coupon interest is 8.125% multiplied by the outstanding mortgage balance at the beginning of the month, then divided by 12.

Column 7: The prepayment for the month is reported in this column. The prepayment is found by using equation (2):

SMM × (Beginning mortgage balance for month t –
  Scheduled prinicpal payment for month t)

So, for example, in month 100, the beginning mortgage balance is $231,249,776, the scheduled principal payment is $332,298, and the SMM at 100 PSA is 0.00514301 (only 0.00514 is shown in the exhibit to save space), so the prepayment is:

0.00514301 × ($231,249,776 – $332,928) = $1,187,608.

Column 8: The total principal payment, which is the sum of columns (6) and (7), is shown in this column.

Column 9: The projected monthly cash flow for this passthrough is shown in this last column. The monthly cash flow is the sum of the interest paid to the passthrough investor [column (5)] and the total principal payments for the month [column (8)].

Exhibits 4 and 5 show selected monthly cash flows for the same passthrough assuming 165 PSA and 300 PSA, respectively.

Average Life and Macaulay Duration

Market participants want some measure of the "life" of a mortgage-backed security. As we explain in Chapter 9, the typical practice is to compare the yield on an MBS to that of a comparable Treasury security, meaning a Treasury security with the same average life or Macaulay duration.

Average Life: The average life of an MBS is the weighted average time to receipt of principal payments (scheduled payments and projected prepayments). The formula for the average life is:

$$\frac{1\,(\text{Principal at time 1}) + 2\,(\text{Principal at time 2}) + \ldots + T\,(\text{Principal at time T})}{12\,(\text{Total principal received})}$$

where T is the number of months.

Exhibit 3: Monthly Cash Flow for a $400 Million Passthrough with a 7.5% Passthrough Rate, a WAC of 8.125%, and a WAM of 357 Months Assuming 100 PSA

Month	Outstanding Balance	SMM	Mortgage Payment	Net Interest	Scheduled Principal	Prepayment	Total Principal	Cash Flow
1	400,000,000	0.00067	2,975,868	2,500,000	267,535	267,470	535,005	3,035,005
2	399,464,995	0.00084	2,973,877	2,496,656	269,166	334,198	603,364	3,100,020
3	398,861,631	0.00101	2,971,387	2,492,885	270,762	400,800	671,562	3,164,447
4	398,190,069	0.00117	2,968,399	2,488,688	272,321	467,243	739,564	3,228,252
5	397,450,505	0.00134	2,964,914	2,484,066	273,843	533,493	807,335	3,291,401
6	396,643,170	0.00151	2,960,931	2,479,020	275,327	599,514	874,841	3,353,860
7	395,768,329	0.00168	2,956,453	2,473,552	276,772	665,273	942,045	3,415,597
8	394,826,284	0.00185	2,951,480	2,467,664	278,177	730,736	1,008,913	3,476,577
9	393,817,371	0.00202	2,946,013	2,461,359	279,542	795,869	1,075,410	3,536,769
10	392,741,961	0.00219	2,940,056	2,454,637	280,865	860,637	1,141,502	3,596,140
11	391,600,459	0.00236	2,933,608	2,447,503	282,147	925,008	1,207,155	3,654,658
12	390,393,304	0.00254	2,926,674	2,439,958	283,386	988,948	1,272,333	3,712,291
13	389,120,971	0.00271	2,919,254	2,432,006	284,581	1,052,423	1,337,004	3,769,010
14	387,783,966	0.00288	2,911,353	2,423,650	285,733	1,115,402	1,401,134	3,824,784
15	386,382,832	0.00305	2,902,973	2,414,893	286,839	1,177,851	1,464,690	3,879,583
16	384,918,142	0.00322	2,894,117	2,405,738	287,900	1,239,739	1,527,639	3,933,378
17	383,390,502	0.00340	2,884,789	2,396,191	288,915	1,301,033	1,589,949	3,986,139
18	381,800,553	0.00357	2,874,992	2,386,253	289,884	1,361,703	1,651,587	4,037,840
19	380,148,966	0.00374	2,864,730	2,375,931	290,805	1,421,717	1,712,522	4,088,453
20	378,436,444	0.00392	2,854,008	2,365,228	291,678	1,481,046	1,772,724	4,137,952
21	376,663,720	0.00409	2,842,830	2,354,148	292,503	1,539,658	1,832,161	4,186,309
22	374,831,559	0.00427	2,831,201	2,342,697	293,279	1,597,525	1,890,804	4,233,501

Exhibit 3: Monthly Cash Flow for a $400 Million Passthrough with a 7.5% Passthrough Rate, a WAC of 8.125%, and a WAM of 357 Months Assuming 100 PSA (Continued)

Month	Outstanding Balance	SMM	Mortgage Payment	Net Interest	Scheduled Principal	Prepayment	Total Principal	Cash Flow
23	372,940,755	0.00444	2,819,125	2,330,880	294,005	1,654,618	1,948,623	4,279,503
24	370,992,132	0.00462	2,806,607	2,318,701	294,681	1,710,908	2,005,589	4,324,290
25	368,986,543	0.00479	2,793,654	2,306,166	295,307	1,766,368	2,061,675	4,367,841
26	366,924,868	0.00497	2,780,270	2,293,280	295,883	1,820,970	2,116,852	4,410,133
27	364,808,016	0.00514[a]	2,766,461	2,280,050	296,406	1,874,688	2,171,094	4,451,144
28	362,636,921	0.00514	2,752,233	2,266,481	296,879	1,863,519	2,160,398	4,426,879
29	360,476,523	0.00514	2,738,078	2,252,978	297,351	1,852,406	2,149,758	4,402,736
30	358,326,766	0.00514	2,723,996	2,239,542	297,825	1,841,347	2,139,173	4,378,715
100	231,249,776	0.00514	1,898,682	1,445,311	332,928	1,187,608	1,520,537	2,965,848
101	229,729,239	0.00514	1,888,917	1,435,808	333,459	1,179,785	1,513,244	2,949,052
102	228,215,995	0.00514	1,879,202	1,426,350	333,990	1,172,000	1,505,990	2,932,340
103	226,710,004	0.00514	1,869,538	1,416,938	334,522	1,164,252	1,498,774	2,915,712
104	225,211,230	0.00514	1,859,923	1,407,570	335,055	1,156,541	1,491,596	2,899,166
105	223,719,634	0.00514	1,850,357	1,398,248	335,589	1,148,867	1,484,456	2,882,703
200	109,791,339	0.00514	1,133,751	686,196	390,372	562,651	953,023	1,639,219
201	108,838,316	0.00514	1,127,920	680,239	390,994	557,746	948,740	1,628,980
202	107,889,576	0.00514	1,122,119	674,310	391,617	552,863	944,480	1,618,790
203	106,945,096	0.00514	1,116,348	668,407	392,241	548,003	940,243	1,608,650
204	106,004,852	0.00514	1,110,607	662,530	392,866	543,164	936,029	1,598,560
205	105,068,823	0.00514	1,104,895	656,680	393,491	538,347	931,838	1,588,518

Exhibit 3: Monthly Cash Flow for a $400 Million Passthrough with a 7.5% Passthrough Rate, a WAC of 8.125%, and a WAM of 357 Months Assuming 100 PSA (Concluded)

Month	Outstanding Balance	SMM	Mortgage Payment	Net Interest	Scheduled Principal	Prepayment	Total Principal	Cash Flow
300	32,383,611	0.00514	676,991	202,398	457,727	164,195	621,923	824,320
301	31,761,689	0.00514	673,510	198,511	458,457	160,993	619,449	817,960
302	31,142,239	0.00514	670,046	194,639	459,187	157,803	616,990	811,629
303	30,525,249	0.00514	666,600	190,783	459,918	154,626	614,545	805,328
304	29,910,704	0.00514	663,171	186,942	460,651	151,462	612,113	799,055
305	29,298,591	0.00514	659,761	183,116	461,385	148,310	609,695	792,811
350	4,060,411	0.00514	523,138	25,378	495,645	18,334	513,979	539,356
351	3,546,432	0.00514	520,447	22,165	496,435	15,686	512,121	534,286
352	3,034,311	0.00514	517,770	18,964	497,226	13,048	510,274	529,238
353	2,524,037	0.00514	515,107	15,775	498,018	10,420	508,437	524,213
354	2,015,600	0.00514	512,458	12,597	498,811	7,801	506,612	519,209
355	1,508,988	0.00514	509,823	9,431	499,606	5,191	504,797	514,228
356	1,004,191	0.00514	507,201	6,276	500,401	2,591	502,992	509,269
357	501,199	0.00514	504,592	3,132	501,199	0	501,199	504,331

a. Since the WAM is 357 months, the underlying mortgage pool is seasoned an average of three months. Therefore, the CPR for month 27 is 6%.

Exhibit 4: Monthly Cash Flow for a $400 Million Passthrough with a 7.5% Passthrough Rate, a WAC of 8.125%, and a WAM of 357 Months Assuming 165 PSA

Month	Outstanding Balance	SMM	Mortgage Payment	Net Interest	Scheduled Principal	Prepayment	Total Principal	Cash Flow
1	400,000,000	0.00111	2,975,868	2,500,000	267,535	442,389	709,923	3,209,923
2	399,290,077	0.00139	2,972,575	2,495,563	269,048	552,847	821,896	3,317,459
3	398,468,181	0.00167	2,968,456	2,490,426	270,495	663,065	933,560	3,423,986
4	397,534,621	0.00195	2,963,513	2,484,591	271,873	772,949	1,044,822	3,529,413
5	396,489,799	0.00223	2,957,747	2,478,061	273,181	882,405	1,155,586	3,633,647
6	395,334,213	0.00251	2,951,160	2,470,839	274,418	991,341	1,265,759	3,736,598
7	394,068,454	0.00279	2,943,755	2,462,928	275,583	1,099,664	1,375,246	3,838,174
8	392,693,208	0.00308	2,935,534	2,454,333	276,674	1,207,280	1,483,954	3,938,287
9	391,209,254	0.00336	2,926,503	2,445,058	277,690	1,314,099	1,591,789	4,036,847
10	389,617,464	0.00365	2,916,666	2,435,109	278,631	1,420,029	1,698,659	4,133,769
11	387,918,805	0.00393	2,906,028	2,424,493	279,494	1,524,979	1,804,473	4,228,965
12	386,114,332	0.00422	2,894,595	2,413,215	280,280	1,628,859	1,909,139	4,322,353
13	384,205,194	0.00451	2,882,375	2,401,282	280,986	1,731,581	2,012,567	4,413,850
14	382,192,626	0.00480	2,869,375	2,388,704	281,613	1,833,058	2,114,670	4,503,374
15	380,077,956	0.00509	2,855,603	2,375,487	282,159	1,933,203	2,215,361	4,590,848
16	377,862,595	0.00538	2,841,068	2,361,641	282,623	2,031,931	2,314,554	4,676,195
17	375,548,041	0.00567	2,825,779	2,347,175	283,006	2,129,159	2,412,164	4,759,339
18	373,135,877	0.00597	2,809,746	2,332,099	283,305	2,224,805	2,508,110	4,840,210
19	370,627,766	0.00626	2,792,980	2,316,424	283,521	2,318,790	2,602,312	4,918,735
20	368,025,455	0.00656	2,775,493	2,300,159	283,654	2,411,036	2,694,690	4,994,849
21	365,330,765	0.00685	2,757,296	2,283,317	283,702	2,501,466	2,785,169	5,068,486
22	362,545,596	0.00715	2,738,402	2,265,910	283,666	2,590,008	2,873,674	5,139,584

Exhibit 4: Monthly Cash Flow for a $400 Million Passthrough with a 7.5% Passthrough Rate, a WAC of 8.125%, and a WAM of 357 Months Assuming 165 PSA (Continued)

Month	Outstanding Balance	SMM	Mortgage Payment	Net Interest	Scheduled Principal	Prepayment	Total Principal	Total Cash Flow
23	359,671,922	0.00745	2,718,823	2,247,950	283,545	2,676,588	2,960,133	5,208,083
24	356,711,789	0.00775	2,698,575	2,229,449	283,338	2,761,139	3,044,477	5,273,926
25	353,667,312	0.00805	2,677,670	2,210,421	283,047	2,843,593	3,126,640	5,337,061
26	350,540,672	0.00835	2,656,123	2,190,879	282,671	2,923,885	3,206,556	5,397,435
27	347,334,116	0.00865[a]	2,633,950	2,170,838	282,209	3,001,955	3,284,164	5,455,002
28	344,049,952	0.00865	2,611,167	2,150,312	281,662	2,973,553	3,255,215	5,405,527
29	340,794,737	0.00865	2,588,581	2,129,967	281,116	2,945,400	3,226,516	5,356,483
30	337,568,221	0.00865	2,566,190	2,109,801	280,572	2,917,496	3,198,067	5,307,869
100	170,142,350	0.00865	1,396,958	1,063,390	244,953	1,469,591	1,714,544	2,777,933
101	168,427,806	0.00865	1,384,875	1,052,674	244,478	1,454,765	1,699,243	2,751,916
102	166,728,563	0.00865	1,372,896	1,042,054	244,004	1,440,071	1,684,075	2,726,128
103	165,044,489	0.00865	1,361,020	1,031,528	243,531	1,425,508	1,669,039	2,700,567
104	163,375,450	0.00865	1,349,248	1,021,097	243,060	1,411,075	1,654,134	2,675,231
105	161,721,315	0.00865	1,337,577	1,010,758	242,589	1,396,771	1,639,359	2,650,118
200	56,746,664	0.00865	585,990	354,667	201,767	489,106	690,874	1,045,540
201	56,055,790	0.00865	580,921	350,349	201,377	483,134	684,510	1,034,859
202	55,371,280	0.00865	575,896	346,070	200,986	477,216	678,202	1,024,273
203	54,693,077	0.00865	570,915	341,832	200,597	471,353	671,950	1,013,782
204	54,021,127	0.00865	565,976	337,632	200,208	465,544	665,752	1,003,384
205	53,355,375	0.00865	561,081	333,471	199,820	459,789	659,609	993,080

Exhibit 4: Monthly Cash Flow for a $400 Million Passthrough with a 7.5% Passthrough Rate, a WAC of 8.125%, and a WAM of 357 Months Assuming 165 PSA (Concluded)

Month	Outstanding Balance	SMM	Mortgage Payment	Net Interest	Scheduled Principal	Prepayment	Total Principal	Cash Flow
300	11,758,141	0.00865	245,808	73,488	166,196	100,269	266,465	339,953
301	11,491,677	0.00865	243,682	71,823	165,874	97,967	263,841	335,664
302	11,227,836	0.00865	241,574	70,174	165,552	95,687	261,240	331,414
303	10,966,596	0.00865	239,485	68,541	165,232	93,430	258,662	327,203
304	10,707,934	0.00865	237,413	66,925	164,912	91,196	256,107	323,032
305	10,451,827	0.00865	235,360	65,324	164,592	88,983	253,575	318,899
350	1,235,674	0.00865	159,202	7,723	150,836	9,384	160,220	167,943
351	1,075,454	0.00865	157,825	6,722	150,544	8,000	158,544	165,266
352	916,910	0.00865	156,460	5,731	150,252	6,631	156,883	162,614
353	760,027	0.00865	155,107	4,750	149,961	5,277	155,238	159,988
354	604,789	0.00865	153,765	3,780	149,670	3,937	153,607	157,387
355	451,182	0.00865	152,435	2,820	149,380	2,611	151,991	154,811
356	299,191	0.00865	151,117	1,870	149,091	1,298	150,389	152,259
357	148,802	0.00865	149,809	930	148,802	0	148,802	149,732

a. Since the WAM is 357 months, the underlying mortgage pool is seasoned an average of three months. Therefore, the CPR for month 27 is $1.65 \times 6\%$.

Exhibit 5: Monthly Cash Flow for a $400 Million Passthrough with a 7.5% Rate, a WAC of 8.125%, and a WAM of 357 Months Assuming 300 PSA

Month	Outstanding Balance	SMM	Mortgage Payment	Net Interest	Scheduled Principal	Prepayment	Total Principal	Cash Flow
1	400,000,000	0.00202	2,975,868	2,500,000	267,535	808,396	1,075,931	3,575,931
2	398,924,069	0.00254	2,969,850	2,493,275	268,802	1,010,610	1,279,412	3,772,688
3	397,644,657	0.00305	2,962,321	2,485,279	269,936	1,212,259	1,482,194	3,967,474
4	396,162,462	0.00357	2,953,284	2,476,015	270,934	1,413,032	1,683,966	4,159,982
5	394,478,496	0.00409	2,942,743	2,465,491	271,795	1,612,620	1,884,415	4,349,905
6	392,594,081	0.00462	2,930,705	2,453,713	272,516	1,810,711	2,083,227	4,536,940
7	390,510,854	0.00514	2,917,179	2,440,693	273,095	2,006,998	2,280,093	4,720,786
8	388,230,761	0.00567	2,902,176	2,426,442	273,530	2,201,171	2,474,701	4,901,143
9	385,756,061	0.00621	2,885,709	2,410,975	273,819	2,392,925	2,666,745	5,077,720
10	383,089,316	0.00674	2,867,796	2,394,308	273,962	2,581,958	2,855,920	5,250,229
11	380,233,395	0.00728	2,848,454	2,376,459	273,957	2,767,971	3,041,928	5,418,387
12	377,191,468	0.00783	2,827,703	2,357,447	273,803	2,950,670	3,224,472	5,581,919
13	373,966,995	0.00838	2,805,567	2,337,294	273,498	3,129,767	3,403,265	5,740,559
14	370,563,730	0.00893	2,782,069	2,316,023	273,044	3,304,979	3,578,023	5,894,047
15	366,985,707	0.00948	2,757,238	2,293,661	272,439	3,476,033	3,748,472	6,042,133
16	363,237,234	0.01004	2,731,103	2,270,233	271,684	3,642,660	3,914,344	6,184,577
17	359,322,890	0.01060	2,703,694	2,245,768	270,779	3,804,603	4,075,381	6,321,149
18	355,247,509	0.01116	2,675,045	2,220,297	269,723	3,961,611	4,231,335	6,451,632
19	351,016,174	0.01173	2,645,191	2,193,851	268,519	4,113,447	4,381,966	6,575,817
20	346,634,209	0.01230	2,614,169	2,166,464	267,167	4,259,880	4,527,047	6,693,511
21	342,107,162	0.01287	2,582,018	2,138,170	265,668	4,400,694	4,666,362	6,804,532
22	337,440,800	0.01345	2,548,779	2,109,005	264,023	4,535,684	4,799,707	6,908,712

Exhibit 5: Monthly Cash Flow for a $400 Million Passthrough with a 7.5% Rate, a WAC of 8.125%, and a WAM of 357 Months Assuming 300 PSA (Continued)

Month	Outstanding Balance	SMM	Mortgage Payment	Net Interest	Scheduled Principal	Prepayment	Total Principal	Cash Flow
23	332,641,093	0.01403	2,514,493	2,079,007	262,235	4,664,657	4,926,892	7,005,899
24	327,714,201	0.01462	2,479,204	2,048,214	260,306	4,787,432	5,047,737	7,095,951
25	322,666,464	0.01521	2,442,957	2,016,665	258,237	4,903,843	5,162,080	7,178,745
26	317,504,384	0.01580	2,405,800	1,984,402	256,031	5,013,739	5,269,770	7,254,172
27	312,234,614	0.01640[a]	2,367,779	1,951,466	253,690	5,116,981	5,370,672	7,322,138
28	306,863,943	0.01640	2,328,944	1,917,900	251,219	5,028,934	5,280,153	7,198,053
29	301,583,790	0.01640	2,290,745	1,884,899	248,772	4,942,371	5,191,143	7,076,042
30	296,392,646	0.01640	2,253,173	1,852,454	246,348	4,857,268	5,103,616	6,956,070
100	86,232,535	0.01640	708,014	538,953	124,148	1,412,314	1,536,462	2,075,416
101	84,696,073	0.01640	696,402	529,350	122,939	1,387,133	1,510,072	2,039,423
102	83,186,001	0.01640	684,980	519,913	121,741	1,362,385	1,484,127	2,004,039
103	81,701,874	0.01640	673,745	510,637	120,555	1,338,063	1,458,618	1,969,255
104	80,243,256	0.01640	662,695	501,520	119,381	1,314,158	1,433,539	1,935,060
105	78,809,717	0.01640	651,825	492,561	118,218	1,290,665	1,408,883	1,901,444
200	13,118,210	0.01640	135,464	81,989	46,643	214,394	261,037	343,026
201	12,857,173	0.01640	133,242	80,357	46,188	210,120	256,309	336,666
202	12,600,864	0.01640	131,057	78,755	45,739	205,924	251,662	330,418
203	12,349,201	0.01640	128,907	77,183	45,293	201,804	247,097	324,279
204	12,102,105	0.01640	126,793	75,638	44,852	197,758	242,610	318,248
205	11,859,495	0.01640	124,713	74,122	44,415	193,786	238,201	312,323

Exhibit 5: Monthly Cash Flow for a $400 Million Passthrough with a 7.5% Rate, a WAC of 8.125%, and a WAM of 357 Months Assuming 300 PSA (Concluded)

Month	Outstanding Balance	SMM	Mortgage Payment	Net Interest	Scheduled Principal	Prepayment	Total Principal	Total Cash Flow
300	1,239,791	0.01640	25,918	7,749	17,524	20,047	37,571	45,320
301	1,202,220	0.01640	25,493	7,514	17,353	19,434	36,787	44,301
302	1,165,433	0.01640	25,075	7,284	17,184	18,833	36,017	43,301
303	1,129,416	0.01640	24,664	7,059	17,017	18,245	35,262	42,321
304	1,094,154	0.01640	24,259	6,838	16,851	17,669	34,520	41,359
305	1,059,634	0.01640	23,861	6,623	16,687	17,106	33,793	40,415
350	87,994	0.01640	11,337	550	10,741	1,267	12,008	12,558
351	75,985	0.01640	11,151	475	10,637	1,072	11,708	12,183
352	64,277	0.01640	10,968	402	10,533	881	11,414	11,816
353	52,863	0.01640	10,788	330	10,430	696	11,126	11,457
354	41,736	0.01640	10,611	261	10,329	515	10,844	11,105
355	30,893	0.01640	10,437	193	10,228	339	10,567	10,760
356	20,325	0.01640	10,266	127	10,128	167	10,296	10,423
357	10,030	0.01640	10,098	63	10,030	0	10,030	10,092

a. Since the WAM is 357 months, the underlying mortgage pool is seasoned an average of three months. Therefore, the CPR for month 27 is $3.00 \times 6\%$.

Exhibit 6: Average Life of a $400 Million, 7.5% Coupon Passthrough with a WAM of 357 Under Various Prepayment Scenarios

	PSA Speed								
	50	100	165	200	300	400	500	600	700
Average Life	15.11	11.66	8.76	7.68	5.63	4.44	3.68	3.16	2.78

Exhibit 6 reports the average life for our hypothetical passthrough under various prepayment assumptions. Notice that the average life ranges from 2.78 years assuming 700 PSA to 15.11 years assuming 50 PSA. An investor might purchase this passthrough assuming that the prepayment speed would be 165 PSA and the average life would be 8.76 years, but obviously the average life could extend or contract considerably.

Macaulay Duration. Macaulay duration is a weighted average term to maturity where the weights are the present value of the cash flows. The yield used to discount the cash flow is the cash flow yield, which we discuss in Chapter 9. The formula for Macaulay duration is:

$$\frac{1\,(\text{PV of CF 1}) + 2\,(\text{PV of CF 2}) + \ldots + T\,(\text{PV of CF T})}{\text{Price plus accrued interest}}$$

PV of CF = Present value of cash flow

Beware of Conventions

The PSA prepayment benchmark is simply a market convention, originally introduced to provide a standard measure for pricing CMOs backed by 30-year fixed-rate, fully amortizing mortgages. It is a product of a study by the PSA that evaluated the mortality rates of residential loans insured by the FHA. Data that the PSA committee examined seemed to suggest that mortgages became "seasoned" (i.e., prepayment rates tended to level off) after 29 months at which time the CPR tended to hover at approximately 6%. How did the PSA come up with the CPRs used for months 1 through 29? It was not based on recent empirical evidence of FHA mortgages. Instead, a linear increase from month 1 to month 30 was arbitrarily selected, so that at month 1 the CPR assumption is 0.2% and at month 30 the CPR assumption is 6%.

In adopting this convention, the seasonal nature of prepayment activity was assumed away as were the differences in underlying borrower characteristics. FHA/VA borrowers, conventional borrowers, and jumbo borrowers all evidence different prepayment behavior not to mention the fact that FHA/VA loans are assumable while conventional loans carry due-on-sale provisions. Moreover, the same benchmark or seasoning process is used in quoting passthroughs regardless of the collateral — 30- and 15-year loans, balloon loans, fixed- and adjustable-rate loans.

A strong case can be made against using the PSA standard to price balloon passthroughs since balloon loans mature in 5 to 7 years when more than 90% of the original principal balance becomes payable to the lender. Although balloon mortgages have only been securitized for a little more than 3 years, recent analysis suggests that balloons season much faster than 30-year mortgages and that (all else equal) after 7 months the CPR of a 7-year balloon reaches 50% of the level it will attain when fully seasoned and that after 15 months such a balloon prepays at about 80% of its fully seasoned level. The conclusion is that to avoid misleading comparisons, balloon prepayment speeds should be quoted in terms of CPR rather than PSA.

Astute money managers recognize that the CPR is a convenient convention, useful for quoting yield and/or price, but that it also has many limitations in determining the value of a passthrough. The message is that money managers must take care in using any measure that is based on the PSA prepayment benchmark. It is simply a market convention.

Vector Analysis

One practice market participants use to overcome the drawback of the PSA benchmark is to assume that the PSA speed can change over time. This technique, *variable prepay vector array analysis*, is more commonly referred to as *vector analysis*. A vector is simply a single prepay assumption that is held constant for one or more months. In the case of a CMO backed by 30-year mortgages, a vector analysis could have as many as 360 prepayment vectors. This type of analysis is crucial in evaluating many CMO structures because differing levels of prepayment activity dramatically affect the cash flows of certain classes.

To illustrate vector analysis, Exhibit 7 shows the variation in the average life for the sample passthrough assuming nine different prepayment scenarios. In each scenario, the prepayment speed begins at 165 PSA and changes twice.

Exhibit 7: Average Life of a $400 Million, 7.5% Coupon Passthrough with a WAM of 357 Using Vector Analysis

PSA Vector Scenario

Months	(1)	(2)	(3)	(4)	(5)	(6)	(7)	(8)	(9)
1- 36	165	165	165	165	165	165	165	165	165
37-138	50	50	300	400	400	400	400	500	600
139-357	250	400	400	200	700	500	165	200	1000
Average Life	10.89	10.07	6.29	5.65	5.40	5.45	5.69	5.00	4.48

Source: Calculated using SFW Software Copyright (c) 1989 by WallStreet Analytics, Inc.

Additonal motivation for the use of vector analysis can be seen from the following situation. Suppose that a passthrough that is seasoned 5 months has experienced prepayments at 1000 PSA. The CPR for 5 months is 1% for 100 PSA and therefore 10% CPR for 1000 PSA. However, if a 1000 PSA is assumed for the life of the passthrough, then from month 30 on, the CPR would be 60%. This rather large CPR may be unrealistic. This problem can be overcome by using vector analysis wherein the PSA is assumed to be less than 1000 PSA over time.

FACTORS AFFECTING PREPAYMENT BEHAVIOR

In this section we review the factors that have been observed to affect prepayments. The factors that affect prepayment behavior are (1) the prevailing mortgage rate, (2) characteristics of the underlying mortgage pool, (3) seasonal factors, and (4) general economic activity.

Prevailing Mortgage Rate

The current mortgage rate affects prepayments in three ways. First, the spread between the prevailing mortgage rate and the contract rate affects the incentive to refinance. Second, the path of mortgage rates since the loan was originated affects prepayments through a phenomenon referred to as *refinancing burnout*. Both the spread and path of mortgage rates affect prepayments that are the product of refinancing. The third way in which the prevailing mortgage rate affects prepayments is through its effect on the affordability of housing and housing turnover. We discuss each below.

Spread Between Contract Rate and Prevailing Mortgage Rate: The single most important factor affecting prepayments because of refinancing is the current level of mortgage rates relative to the borrower's contract rate. The greater the difference between the two, the greater the incentive to refinance the mortgage loan. For refinancing to make sense, the interest savings must be greater than the total costs associated with the process. These costs include legal expenses, origination fees, title insurance, and the value of the time associated with obtaining another mortgage loan. Some of these costs — such as title insurance and origination points — will vary proportionately with the amount to be financed. Other costs such as the application fee and legal expenses are typically fixed.

Historically, it has been observed that when mortgage rates fall to more than 200 basis points below the contract rate, prepayment rates increase. However, the creativity of mortgage originators in designing mortgage loans such that the refinancing costs are folded into the amount borrowed and the ability to obtain 100% financing in California has changed the view that mortgage rates must drop dramatically below the contract rate to make refinancing economic. Moreover, mortgage originators now do an effective job of advertising to make homeowners cognizant of the economic benefits of refinancing.

The present value of the benefits from refinancing depends on the initial level of the contract rate. Specifically, the present value of the benefits of a 200 basis point decline from an initial contract rate of 8% is greater than for a 200 basis point decline from an initial contract rate of 17%. Consequently, in modeling prepayment behavior one would expect that prepayments caused by refinancing might be more highly correlated with a percentage change in the rates rather than a spread.

Because of the lack of observations in a wide range of mortgage rate environments, it has not been possible to evaluate empirically whether a spread measured in basis points or in percentage terms better explains prepayment behavior. As a result, refinancing opportunities can be measured in a variety of ways. In the Goldman, Sachs prepayment model, for example, refinancing opportunities are measured by the ratio of the contract rate to the mortgage refinancing rate.[4] For a specific pool, the contract rate is the weighted average of the contract rates for the underlying mortgage loans. To reflect the lags in the refinancing process, the Goldman, Sachs prepayment model uses a weighted average of the past five month ratio of the contract rate to the mortgage refinancing rate.

Path of Mortgage Rates: The historical pattern of prepayments and economic theory suggests that it is not only the level of mortgage rates that affects prepayment behavior but also the path that mortgage rates take to get to the current level.

To illustrate why, suppose the underlying contract rate for a pool of mortgage loans is 11% and that three years after origination, the prevailing mortgage rate declines to 8%. Let's consider two possible paths of the mortgage rate in getting to the 8% level. In the first path, the mortgage rate declines to 8% at the end of the first year, then rises to 13% at the end of the second year, and then falls to 8% at the end of the third year. In the second path, the mortgage rate rises to 12% at the end of the first year, continues its rise to 13% at the end of the second year, and then falls to 8% at the end of the third year.

If the mortgage rate follows the first path, those who can benefit from refinancing will more than likely take advantage of this opportunity when the mortgage rate drops to 8% in the first year. When the mortgage rate drops again to 8% at the end of the third year, the likelihood is that prepayments because of refinancing will not surge; those who can benefit by taking advantage of the refinancing opportunity will have done so already when the mortgage rate declined for the first time. This is the prepayment behavior referred to as the refinancing burnout (or simply, burnout) phenomenon.

In contrast, the expected prepayment behavior when the mortgage rate follows the second path is quite different. Prepayment rates are expected to be low in the first two years. When the mortgage rate declines to 8% in the third year, refinancing activity and therefore prepayments are expected to surge. Consequently, the burnout phenomenon is related to the path of mortgage rates.

The difficulty in modeling prepayments has been to quantify path dependency. Some researchers have used the ratio of the remaining mortgage balance outstanding for the pool to the original mortgage balance. This ratio is called the *pool factor*. The argument is that the lower the pool factor, the greater prepayments have been historically and

---

[4] The Goldman, Sachs prepayment model is described in Scott F. Richard and Richard Roll, "Prepayments on Fixed-Rate Mortgage-Backed Securities," *The Journal of Portfolio Management* (Spring 1989), pp. 73-74, and Scott F. Richard, "Relative Prepayment Rates on Thirty-Year FNMA, FHLMC and GNMA Fixed Rate Mortgage-Backed Securities," in Frank J. Fabozzi (ed.), *Advances and Innovations in the Bond and Mortgage Markets* (Chicago, IL: Probus Publishing, 1989), pp. 351-369.

therefore the more likely it is that burnout will occur. One researcher who has tested various measures of path dependency reports that the pool factor is the best measure.[5] In contrast, the Goldman, Sachs prepayment model adjustment for burnout is a nonlinear function generated from the entire history of the ratio of the contract rate to the mortgage refinancing rate since the mortgage was issued.

Level of Mortgage Rates: As we discussed earlier, prepayments occur because of housing turnover and refinancing. Our focus so far has been on the factors that affect prepayments caused by refinancing. The level of mortgage rates affects housing turnover to the extent that a lower rate increases the affordability of homes. Such rate environments provide an opportune time to purchase a more expensive home (trade up) or to change location for other reasons.

Characteristics of the Underlying Mortgage Loans

The following characteristics of the underlying mortgage loans affect prepayments: (1) the contract rate, (2) whether the loans are FHA/VA-guaranteed or conventional, (3) the amount of seasoning, (4) the type of loan, for example, a 30-year level payment mortgage, 5-year balloon mortgage, etc.,[6] (5) the pool factor, and (6) the geographical location of the underlying properties. We have already discussed how the contract rate affects prepayment behavior and how the pool factor has been used by some researchers as a measure to proxy for path dependency. Below we focus on the other four characteristics.

FHA/VA Mortgages versus Conventional Mortgages: The underlying mortgage loans for GNMA passthroughs are guaranteed by either the FHA or VA. Most FNMA and FHLMC passthroughs are conventional loans. There are four characteristics of FHA- and VA-guaranteed loans that cause their prepayment characteristics to differ from those of conventional loans. First, FHA- and VA-guaranteed loans are assumable. Consequently, prepayments should be lower than for otherwise comparable conventional loans when the contract rate is less than the current

---

[5] Charles N Shorin, "Fixed-Rate MBS Prepayment Models," Chapter 10 in Frank J. Fabozzi (ed.), *Handbook of Mortgage-Backed Securities* (Chicago, IL: Probus Publishing, 1992).

[6] We restrict our discussion to fixed-rate mortgage loans because adjustable rate mortgages have not been used as collateral for a CMO.

mortgage rate. This is because purchasers will assume the seller's mortgage loan in order to acquire the below-market interest rate and, as a result, there will be no prepayment resulting from the sale of the property. Second, the amount of the mortgage loan is typically small, reducing the incentive to refinance as mortgage rates decline and thereby producing a rate of prepayment because of refinancing that is less than for conventional loans. Third, the income level of those who must obtain a mortgage loan guaranteed by the FHA or VA is typically less than that of borrowers with conventional loans. Their ability to take advantage of a refinancing opportunity is limited because they often do not have the funds to pay the costs associated with refinancing. While these three characteristics suggest that prepayments for these loans will be less than for conventional loans, the last characteristic also suggests faster prepayments. Historically, default rates are greater for FHA and VA-guaranteed loans compared to conventional loans. Defaults result in prepayments. However, the factor of faster prepayments because of default is swamped by the other characteristics that cause slower prepayments.

Empirical research suggests that for a given refinancing incentive, the prepayment rate is greater for FNMA/FHLMC passthroughs relative to GNMA passthroughs and that FNMA/FHLMC passthroughs burnout faster than GNMA passthroughs.[7]

Seasoning: Seasoning refers to the aging of the mortgage loans. Empirical evidence suggests that prepayment rates are low after the loan is originated and increase after the loan is somewhat seasoned. Then prepayment rates tend to level off, in which case the loans are referred to as fully seasoned. This is the underlying theory for the PSA prepayment benchmark discussed earlier in this chapter.

Geographical Location of the Underlying Properties: The prepayment behavior described thus far is for generic pools. In some regions of the country the prepayment behavior tends to be faster than the average national prepayment rate, while other regions exhibit slower prepayment rates. This is caused by differences in local economies that affect housing turnover.[8]

---

[7] Richard, "Relative Prepayment Rates on Thirty-Year FNMA, FHLMC and GNMA Fixed Rate Mortgage-Backed Securities," pp. 354 and 358.

Seasonal Factors

There is a well-documented seasonal pattern in prepayments. This pattern is related to activity in the primary housing market, with home buying increasing in the spring, and gradually reaching a peak in the late summer. Home buying declines in the fall and winter. Mirroring this activity are the prepayments that result from the turnover of housing as home buyers sell their existing homes and purchase new ones. Prepayments are low in the winter months and begin to rise in the spring, reaching a peak in the summer months. However, probably because of delays in passing through prepayments, the peak may not be observed until early fall.

General Economic Activity

Economic theory would suggest that general economic activity affects prepayment behavior through its effect on housing turnover. The link is as follows: a growing economy results in a rise in personal income and in opportunities for worker migration; this increases family mobility and as a result increases housing turnover. The opposite holds for a weak economy. Some researchers suggest that prepayments can be projected by identifying and forecasting the turnover rate of the single-family housing stock.[9]

Although some modelers of prepayment behavior may incorporate macroeconomic measures of economic activity such as gross national product, industrial production, or housing starts, the trend has been to ignore them or limit their use to specific applications. There are two reasons why macroeconomic measures have been ignored by some modelers. First, empirical tests suggest that the relationship between residuals of a prepayment forecasting model that does not include macroeconomic measures and various macroeconomic measures is either statistically insignificant or, if it is statistically significant, explanatory power is low.[10] Second, as explained later, prepayment models are based on a projection of a path for future mortgage rates. The inclusion of macroeconomic variables in a prepayment model would require the forecasting of the value of these variables over long time periods.

---

[8] Chuck Ramsey and J. Michael Henderson, "Investing in Specified Pools," Chapter 5 in *The Handbook of Mortgage-Backed Securities*.

[9] See, for example, Joseph C. Hu, "An Alternative Prepayment Projection Based on Housing Activity," in Frank J. Fabozzi (ed.), *The Handbook of Mortgage-Backed Securities* (Chicago: Probus Publishing, 1988), pp. 639-648.

[10] Richard and Roll, "Prepayments on Fixed-Rate Mortgage-Backed Securities," pp. 78-79.

Macroeconomic variables, however, have been used by some researchers in prepayment models in two ways. One way is to capture the effect of housing turnover on prepayments by specifying a relationship between interest rates and housing turnover. This is the approach used in the Prudential Securities Model.[11] A second way is to incorporate macroeconomic variables and their forecasts in projecting short-term rather than long-term prepayments. As will be explained in Chapter 11, in assessing the potential total return from investing in CMOs, short-term prepayment forecasts are required.

PREPAYMENT MODELS AND PROJECTIONS

A prepayment model begins by modeling the statistical relationships among the factors that are expected to affect prepayments. One study suggests that the four factors discussed above explain about 95% of the variation in prepayment rates: refinancing incentives, burnout, seasoning, and seasonality.[12] These factors are then combined into one model. For example, in the Goldman, Sachs prepayment model the effects interact proportionally through the following multiplicative function, which is used to project prepayments:

Monthly prepayment rate = refinancing incentive × seasoning multiplier × month multiplier × burnout multiplier

where the various multipliers are adjustments for the effects we discussed earlier in this chapter.

For two of the effects, the only information that is needed is the amount of seasoning and the month. For the refinancing incentive and burnout, it is necessary to know the contract rate on the underlying pool and the refinancing mortgage rate. While the former is known and is unchanged over the life of the mortgage pool, the latter will change. The practice in prepayment modeling has been to generate a path of monthly

---

[11] Lakbhir S. Hayre, Kenneth Lauterbach, and Cyrus Mohebbi, "Prepayment Models and Methodologies," in Fabozzi (ed.), *Advances and Innovations in the Bond and Mortgage Markets*, p. 338.

[12] Richard, "Relative Prepayment Rates on Thirty-Year FNMA, FHLMC and GNMA Fixed Rate Mortgage-Backed Securities," pp. 359-360.

mortgage rates as follows. First, a path for monthly short-term interest rates that is consistent with the prevailing term structure of interest rates (discussed in Chapter 10) is generated. Based on an assumed relationship between short-term interest rates and long-term interest rates, a path for monthly mortgage rates can be obtained. From these monthly mortgage rates, prepayment rates caused by refinancing incentives and burnout are projected. Consequently, the prepayment projection is contingent on the interest rate path projected.

The product of a prepayment forecast is not one prepayment rate but a set of prepayment rates for each month of the remaining term of a mortgage pool. The set of monthly prepayment rates, however, is not reported by Wall Street firms or vendors. Instead, a single prepayment rate is reported. One way to convert a set of monthly prepayment rates into a single prepayment rate is to calculate a simple average of the prepayment rates. The obvious drawback to this approach is that it does not take into consideration the outstanding balance each month. An alternative approach is to use some type of weighted average, selecting the weights to reflect the amount of the monthly cash flow corresponding to a monthly prepayment rate. This is done by first computing the cash flow yield (discussed in Chapter 9) for a passthrough given its market price and the set of monthly prepayment rates. Then a single prepayment rate (CPR or PSA multiple) that gives the same cash flow yield is found.

SUMMARY

This chapter has described the current market practice for determining the cash flow of a passthrough based on some prepayment convention and the factors affecting prepayment behavior. The convention used is the PSA prepayment benchmark, which is a series of CPRs. The PSA standard benchmark, referred to as 100 PSA, assumes that for the first 30 months the CPR begins at 0.2% per month and increases each month by 0.2%. From month 30 on, the passthrough is assumed to have seasoned and the CPR is assumed to be 6%. The benchmark is based on FHA prepayment data; there is no recent empirical evidence that future prepayment rates will follow the pattern assumed.

Two measures are commonly used to estimate the life of a passthrough: average life and Macaulay duration. Vector analysis is a technique for allowing the PSA to change over the life of the passthrough.

There are four factors that affect prepayment behavior: (1) prevailing mortgage rate, (2) characteristics of the underlying mortgage pool, (3) seasonal factors, and (4) general economic activity. A prepayment model begins by modeling the statistical relationships among the factors that are expected to affect prepayments. The product of a prepayment forecast is a set of prepayment rates for each month of the remaining term of a mortgage pool which are then converted into a PSA speed.

SECTION II:
CMO STRUCTURES

Chapter 4

SEQUENTIAL-PAY CMOS

We earlier noted the prepayment risks associated with investing in passthroughs. Some institutional investors are concerned with extension risk and others with contraction risk when they invest in a passthrough. Structuring a passthrough in different classes makes it possible to redistribute prepayment risk to investors who want to reduce their exposure to it by redirecting cash flows to the various bond classes. As the total prepayment risk of a passthrough is not changed by altering the cash flows, however, it must be that there are other investors willing to accept the unwanted prepayment risk.

Collateralized mortgage obligations (CMOs) are made up of bond classes created by redirecting the cash flows of mortgage-related products (passthroughs and whole loans) so as to mitigate prepayment risk. The creation of a CMO cannot eliminate prepayment risk; it can only distribute the various forms of this risk among different classes of bondholders. Redistribution of the interest from the underlying mortgage-related products to different classes results in CMO classes with different coupon rates from the underlying collateral. The result is instruments that have different price performance characteristics that may be more suitable to the particular needs and expectations of investors, which broadens the appeal of mortgage-backed products to traditional fixed-income investors.

In this chapter, we will introduce the CMO structure and describe the simplest type, the sequential-pay CMO. In the next three chapters, we introduce more complicated CMO structures.

THE SEQUENTIAL-PAY CMO

The first generation of CMOs was structured so that each class of bond would be retired sequentially; such structures are referred to as sequential-pay CMOs. To illustrate a sequential-pay CMO, we discuss FRR-01, a hypothetical deal made up to illustrate the basic features of the structure. The collateral for this hypothetical CMO is a hypothetical passthrough with a total par value of $400 million and the following characteristics: (1) the passthrough coupon rate is 7.5%, (2) the weighted average coupon (WAC) is 8.125%, and (3) the weighted average maturity (WAM) is 357 months. This is the same passthrough that we used in the previous chapter to describe the cash flow characteristics of passthroughs.

From this $400 million of collateral, four bond classes, called tranches, are created. Their characteristics are summarized in Exhibit 1. The total par value of the four tranches is equal to the par value of the collateral (i.e., the passthrough security). In this simple structure, the coupon rate is the same for each tranche and also the same as the coupon rate on the collateral. There is no reason why this must be so, and we shall see structures where the coupon rate differs for each tranche.

The payment rules in Exhibit 1 describe how the cash flow from the collateral is to be distributed to the four tranches. There are separate rules for the payment of the coupon interest and the payment of principal, the principal being the total of the regularly scheduled principal payment and any prepayments. In FRR-01, each tranche receives periodic coupon payments based on the amount of the outstanding balance. The disbursement of the principal, however, is made in a special way. A tranche is not entitled to receive principal until the entire principal of the tranche before it has been paid off. More specifically, tranche A receives all the principal payments until the entire principal amount owed to that bond class, $194,500,000, is paid off; then tranche B begins to receive principal and continues to do so until it is paid the entire $36,000,000. Tranche C then receives principal, and when it is paid off, tranche D starts receiving principal payments.

Exhibit 1: FRR-01 – A Hypothetical Four-Tranche Sequential-Pay Structure

Tranche	Par Amount	Coupon Rate (%)
A	$194,500,000	7.5
B	36,000,000	7.5
C	96,500,000	7.5
D	73,000,000	7.5
Total	$400,000,000	

Payment rules:

1. For payment of periodic coupon interest: Disburse periodic coupon interest to each tranche on the basis of the amount of principal outstanding at the beginning of the period.

2. For disbursement of principal payments: Disburse principal payments to tranche A until it is completely paid off. After tranche A is completely paid off, disburse principal payments to tranche B until it is completely paid off. After tranche B is completely paid off, disburse principal payments to tranche C until it is completely paid off. After tranche C is completely paid off, disburse principal payments to tranche D until it is completely paid off.

Cash Flow

While the priority rules for the disbursement of the principal payments are known, the precise amount of the principal in each period is not. This will depend on the cash flow, and therefore principal payments, of the collateral, which depends on the actual prepayment rate of the collateral. An assumed PSA speed allows the cash flow to be projected. Exhibit 4 in the previous chapter shows the cash flow (interest, regularly scheduled principal repayment, and prepayments) assuming 165 PSA. Assuming that the collateral does prepay at 165 PSA, the cash flow available to all four tranches in FRR-01 will be precisely the cash flow shown in Exhibit 4 of the previous chapter.

To demonstrate how the priority rules for FRR-01 work, Exhibit 2 shows the cash flow for selected months assuming the collateral pays down at 165 PSA. For each tranche, the exhibit shows: (1) the balance at the end of the month, (2) the principal paid down (regularly scheduled principal repayment plus prepayments), and (3) interest. In month 1, the cash flow for the collateral consists of principal payment of $709,923 and interest of $2.5 million (0.075 times $400 million divided by 12). The interest payment is distributed to the four classes based on the amount of the par value outstanding. So, for example, tranche A receives $1,215,625 (0.075 times $194,500,000 divided by 12) of the $2.5 million. The principal, however, is all distributed to tranche A. Therefore, the cash flow for tranche A in month 1 is $1,925,548.

The principal balance at the end of month 1 for tranche A is $193,790,076 (the original principal balance of $194,500,000 less the principal payment of $709,923). No principal payment is distributed to the three other tranches because there is still a principal balance outstanding for tranche A. This will be true for months 2 through 80.

After month 81, the principal balance will be zero for tranche A. For the collateral, the cash flow in month 81 is $3,318,521, consisting of a principal payment of $2,032,196 and interest of $1,286,325. At the beginning of month 81 (end of month 80), the principal balance for tranche A is $311,926. Therefore, $311,926 of the $2,032,196 of the principal payment from the collateral will be disbursed to tranche A. After this payment is made, no additional principal payments are made to this tranche as the principal balance is zero. The remaining principal payment from the collateral, $1,720,271, is disbursed to tranche B. According to the assumed prepayment speed of 165 PSA, tranche B then begins receiving principal payments in month 81.

Exhibit 2 shows that tranche B is fully paid off by month 100, when tranche C now begins to receive principal payments. Tranche C is not fully paid off until month 178, at which time bond class D begins receiving the remaining principal payments. The maturity (i.e., the time until the principal is fully paid off) for these four tranches assuming 165 PSA would be 81 months for tranche A, 100 months for tranche B, 178 months for tranche C, and 357 months for tranche D.

Exhibit 3 graphs the cash flow for FRR-01 assuming a prepayment speed of 165 PSA.

The *principal paydown window* for a tranche is the time period between the beginning and the ending of the principal payments to that tranche. So, for example, for tranche A, the principal pay down window would be month 1 to month 81 assuming 165 PSA. For tranche B it is from month 82 to month 100. The window is also specified in terms of the length of the time from the beginning of the principal pay down window to the end of the principal pay down window. For tranche A, the window would be stated as 80 months, for tranche B 19 months.

Effect on Average Life

Let's look at what has been accomplished by creating the CMO. First, recall that in the previous chapter we show that the average life for the collateral of this passthrough is 8.76 years, assuming a prepayment speed of 165 PSA. Moreover, the average life has considerable variability based on the prepayment speed.

Exhibit 2: Monthly Cash Flow for Selected Months for FRR-01 Assuming 165 PSA

Month	Tranche A			Tranche B		
	Balance	Principal	Interest	Balance	Principal	Interest
1	194,500,000	709,923	1,215,625	36,000,000	0	225,000
2	193,790,077	821,896	1,211,188	36,000,000	0	225,000
3	192,968,181	933,560	1,206,051	36,000,000	0	225,000
4	192,034,621	1,044,822	1,200,216	36,000,000	0	225,000
5	190,989,799	1,155,586	1,193,686	36,000,000	0	225,000
6	189,834,213	1,265,759	1,186,464	36,000,000	0	225,000
7	188,568,454	1,375,246	1,178,553	36,000,000	0	225,000
8	187,193,208	1,483,954	1,169,958	36,000,000	0	225,000
9	185,709,254	1,591,789	1,160,683	36,000,000	0	225,000
10	184,117,464	1,698,659	1,150,734	36,000,000	0	225,000
11	182,418,805	1,804,473	1,140,118	36,000,000	0	225,000
12	180,614,332	1,909,139	1,128,840	36,000,000	0	225,000
75	12,893,479	2,143,974	80,584	36,000,000	0	225,000
76	10,749,504	2,124,935	67,184	36,000,000	0	225,000
77	8,624,569	2,106,062	53,904	36,000,000	0	225,000
78	6,518,507	2,087,353	40,741	36,000,000	0	225,000
79	4,431,154	2,068,807	27,695	36,000,000	0	225,000
80	2,362,347	2,050,422	14,765	36,000,000	0	225,000
81	311,926	311,926	1,950	36,000,000	1,720,271	225,000
82	0	0	0	34,279,729	2,014,130	214,248
83	0	0	0	32,265,599	1,996,221	201,660
84	0	0	0	30,269,378	1,978,468	189,184
85	0	0	0	28,290,911	1,960,869	176,818
95	0	0	0	9,449,331	1,793,089	59,058
96	0	0	0	7,656,242	1,777,104	47,852
97	0	0	0	5,879,138	1,761,258	36,745
98	0	0	0	4,117,880	1,745,550	25,737
99	0	0	0	2,372,329	1,729,979	14,827
100	0	0	0	642,350	642,350	4,015
101	0	0	0	0	0	0
102	0	0	0	0	0	0
103	0	0	0	0	0	0
104	0	0	0	0	0	0
105	0	0	0	0	0	0

Exhibit 2 (Concluded)

Month	Tranche C			Tranche D		
	Balance	Principal	Interest	Balance	Principal	Interest
1	96,500,000	0	603,125	73,000,000	0	456,250
2	96,500,000	0	603,125	73,000,000	0	456,250
3	96,500,000	0	603,125	73,000,000	0	456,250
4	96,500,000	0	603,125	73,000,000	0	456,250
5	96,500,000	0	603,125	73,000,000	0	456,250
6	96,500,000	0	603,125	73,000,000	0	456,250
7	96,500,000	0	603,125	73,000,000	0	456,250
8	96,500,000	0	603,125	73,000,000	0	456,250
9	96,500,000	0	603,125	73,000,000	0	456,250
10	96,500,000	0	603,125	73,000,000	0	456,250
11	96,500,000	0	603,125	73,000,000	0	456,250
12	96,500,000	0	603,125	73,000,000	0	456,250
95	96,500,000	0	603,125	73,000,000	0	456,250
96	96,500,000	0	603,125	73,000,000	0	456,250
97	96,500,000	0	603,125	73,000,000	0	456,250
98	96,500,000	0	603,125	73,000,000	0	456,250
99	96,500,000	0	603,125	73,000,000	0	456,250
100	96,500,000	1,072,194	603,125	73,000,000	0	456,250
101	95,427,806	1,699,243	596,424	73,000,000	0	456,250
102	93,728,563	1,684,075	585,804	73,000,000	0	456,250
103	92,044,489	1,669,039	575,278	73,000,000	0	456,250
104	90,375,450	1,654,134	564,847	73,000,000	0	456,250
105	88,721,315	1,639,359	554,508	73,000,000	0	456,250
175	3,260,287	869,602	20,377	73,000,000	0	456,250
176	2,390,685	861,673	14,942	73,000,000	0	456,250
177	1,529,013	853,813	9,556	73,000,000	0	456,250
178	675,199	675,199	4,220	73,000,000	170,824	456,250
179	0	0	0	72,829,176	838,300	455,182
180	0	0	0	71,990,876	830,646	449,943
181	0	0	0	71,160,230	823,058	444,751
182	0	0	0	70,337,173	815,536	439,607
183	0	0	0	69,521,637	808,081	434,510
184	0	0	0	68,713,556	800,690	429,460
185	0	0	0	67,912,866	793,365	424,455
350	0	0	0	1,235,674	160,220	7,723
351	0	0	0	1,075,454	158,544	6,722
352	0	0	0	916,910	156,883	5,731
353	0	0	0	760,027	155,238	4,750
354	0	0	0	604,789	153,607	3,780
355	0	0	0	451,182	151,991	2,820
356	0	0	0	299,191	150,389	1,870
357	0	0	0	148,802	148,802	930

Exhibit 3: Graphical Presentation of Cash Flow
for FRR-01 Assuming 165 PSA

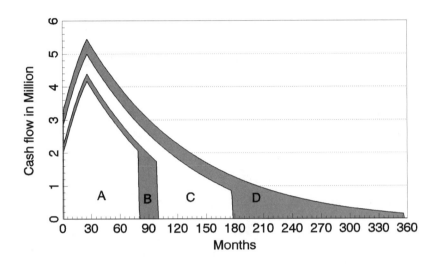

Exhibit 4 reports the average life of the collateral and the four tranches assuming different prepayment speeds. Note that the average life for the collateral ranges from 15.11 years (at 50 PSA) to 2.78 years (at 700 PSA). Different prepayment speeds mean that the average life could extend or contract considerably.The four tranches created have a different average life than the collateral at a given prepayment speed. The tranches have greater protection against prepayment risk than the collateral. For example, consider tranche A. While the average life could extend if the speed is less than 165 PSA, it can only extend to 7.48 years at 50 PSA, not 15.11 as the collateral could. For tranche D, the average life could contract to 5.95 years if the speed is 700 PSA while the collateral could contract to 2.78 years at the same speed.

Prioritizing the distribution of principal (i.e., establishing the payment rules for principal) effectively protects the shorter-term tranche A in this structure against extension risk. This protection must come from somewhere, so it comes from the three other tranches. Similarly, tranches C and D provide protection against extension risk for tranche B. At the same time, tranches C and D benefit because they are provided protection against contraction risk, the protection coming from tranches A and B.

Exhibit 4: Average Life for the Collateral and the Four Tranches of FRR-01

Prepayment Speed (PSA)	Average life for				
	Collateral	A	B	C	D
50	15.11	7.48	15.98	21.02	27.24
100	11.66	4.90	10.86	15.78	24.58
165	8.76	3.48	7.49	11.19	20.27
200	7.68	3.05	6.42	9.60	18.11
300	5.63	2.32	4.64	6.81	13.36
400	4.44	1.94	3.70	5.31	10.34
500	3.68	1.69	3.12	4.38	8.35
600	3.16	1.51	2.74	3.75	6.96
700	2.78	1.38	2.47	3.30	5.95

ACCRUAL BONDS

In FRR-01, the payment rules for interest provide for all tranches to be paid interest each month. In many sequential-pay CMO structures, at least one tranche does not receive current interest. Instead, the interest for that tranche would accrue and be added to the principal balance. Such a bond class is commonly referred to as an accrual bond, or a Z bond (because the bond is similar to a zero-coupon bond). The interest that would have been paid to the accrual bond class is then used to speed up pay down of the principal balance of earlier bond classes.

To see this, consider FRR-02, a hypothetical CMO structure with the same collateral as FRR-01 and with four tranches, each with a coupon rate of 7.5%. The difference is in the last tranche, Z, which is an accrual bond. The structure for FRR-02 is shown in Exhibit 5.

Cash Flow

Exhibit 6 shows cash flows for selected months. Let's look at month 1 and compare it to month 1 in Exhibit 2. Both cash flows are based on 165 PSA. The principal payment from the collateral is $709,923. In FRR-01, this is the principal paydown for tranche A. In FRR-02, the interest for tranche Z, $456,250, is not paid to that tranche but instead is used to pay down the principal of tranche A. So, the principal payment to tranche A in Exhibit 6 is $1,166,173, the collateral's principal payment of $709,923 plus the interest of $456,250 that was diverted from tranche Z.

Exhibit 5: FRR-02 – A Hypothetical Four-Tranche Sequential-Pay Structure with An Accrual Bond Class

Tranche	Par Amount	Coupon Rate (%)
A	$194,500,000	7.5
B	36,000,000	7.5
C	96,500,000	7.5
Z (Accrual)	73,000,000	7.5
Total	$400,000,000	

Payment rules:

1. For payment of periodic coupon interest Disburse periodic coupon interest to tranches A, B, and C on the basis of the amount of principal outstanding at the beginning of the period. For tranche Z, accrue the interest based on the principal plus accrued interest in the previous period. The interest for tranche Z is to be paid to the earlier tranches as a principal paydown.

2. For disbursement of principal payments: Disburse principal payments to tranche A until it is completely paid off. After tranche A is completely paid off, disburse principal payments to tranche B until it is completely paid off. After tranche B is completely paid off, disburse principal payments to tranche C until it is completely paid off. After tranche C is completely paid off, disburse principal payments to tranche Z until the original principal balance plus accrued interest is completely paid off.

The expected final maturity for tranches A, B, and C has shortened as a result of the inclusion of tranche Z. The final payout for tranche A is 64 months rather than 81 months; for tranche B it is 77 months rather than 100 months; and for tranche C it is 112 rather than 178 months.

Exhibit 7 graphs the cash flow for FRR-02 assuming a prepayment speed of 165 PSA.

Effect on Average Life

The average lives for FRR-02 and FRR-01 are compared in Exhibit 8. Notice that the average life for the three non-accrual bond classes is reduced as a a result of the presence of the accrual bond class. Even the accrual bond class has a lower average life than tranche D in FRR-01 under any prepayment speed assumption, which may at first seem odd. The explanation is that the average lives for the accrual bond in Exhibit 8 are calculated according to a certain market convention. Recall that the principal payment is weighted by the month when it will be received. In the earliest years, however, the principal payment is negative because there is negative amortization. Therefore, it is possible to obtain an average life greater than the collateral's WAM. To prevent this, the practice is to ignore the negative amortization in calculating the average life.

Exhibit 6: Monthly Cash Flow for Selected Months
for FRR-02 Assuming 165 PSA

Month	Tranche A Balance	Principal	Interest	Tranche B Balance	Principal	Interest
1	194,500,000	1,166,173	1,215,625	36,000,000	0	225,000
2	193,333,827	1,280,997	1,208,336	36,000,000	0	225,000
3	192,052,829	1,395,531	1,200,330	36,000,000	0	225,000
4	190,657,298	1,509,680	1,191,608	36,000,000	0	225,000
5	189,147,619	1,623,350	1,182,173	36,000,000	0	225,000
6	187,524,269	1,736,446	1,172,027	36,000,000	0	225,000
7	185,787,823	1,848,875	1,161,174	36,000,000	0	225,000
8	183,938,947	1,960,543	1,149,618	36,000,000	0	225,000
9	181,978,404	2,071,357	1,137,365	36,000,000	0	225,000
10	179,907,047	2,181,225	1,124,419	36,000,000	0	225,000
11	177,725,822	2,290,054	1,110,786	36,000,000	0	225,000
12	175,435,768	2,397,755	1,096,474	36,000,000	0	225,000
60	15,023,406	3,109,398	93,896	36,000,000	0	225,000
61	11,914,007	3,091,812	74,463	36,000,000	0	225,000
62	8,822,195	3,074,441	55,139	36,000,000	0	225,000
63	5,747,754	3,057,282	35,923	36,000,000	0	225,000
64	2,690,472	2,690,472	16,815	36,000,000	349,863	225,000
65	0	0	0	35,650,137	3,023,598	222,813
66	0	0	0	32,626,540	3,007,069	203,916
67	0	0	0	29,619,470	2,990,748	185,122
68	0	0	0	26,628,722	2,974,633	166,430
69	0	0	0	23,654,089	2,958,722	147,838
70	0	0	0	20,695,367	2,943,014	129,346
71	0	0	0	17,752,353	2,927,508	110,952
72	0	0	0	14,824,845	2,912,203	92,655
73	0	0	0	11,912,642	2,897,096	74,454
74	0	0	0	9,015,546	2,882,187	56,347
75	0	0	0	6,133,358	2,867,475	38,333
76	0	0	0	3,265,883	2,852,958	20,412
77	0	0	0	412,925	412,925	2,581
78	0	0	0	0	0	0

Exhibit 6 (Concluded)

Month	Tranche C Balance	Principal	Interest	Tranche Z Balance	Principal	Interest
1	96,500,000	0	603,125	73,000,000	-456,250	456,250
2	96,500,000	0	603,125	73,456,250	-459,102	459,102
3	96,500,000	0	603,125	73,915,352	-461,971	461,971
4	96,500,000	0	603,125	74,377,323	-464,858	464,858
5	96,500,000	0	603,125	74,842,181	-467,764	467,764
6	96,500,000	0	603,125	75,309,944	-470,687	470,687
7	96,500,000	0	603,125	75,780,632	-473,629	473,629
8	96,500,000	0	603,125	76,254,261	-476,589	476,589
9	96,500,000	0	603,125	76,730,850	-479,568	479,568
10	96,500,000	0	603,125	77,210,417	-482,565	482,565
11	96,500,000	0	603,125	77,692,983	-485,581	485,581
12	96,500,000	0	603,125	78,178,564	-488,616	488,616
70	96,500,000	0	603,125	112,209,468	-701,309	701,309
71	96,500,000	0	603,125	112,910,777	-705,692	705,692
72	96,500,000	0	603,125	113,616,469	-710,103	710,103
73	96,500,000	0	603,125	114,326,572	-714,541	714,541
74	96,500,000	0	603,125	115,041,113	-719,007	719,007
75	96,500,000	0	603,125	115,760,120	-723,501	723,501
76	96,500,000	0	603,125	116,483,621	-728,023	728,023
77	96,500,000	2,425,710	603,125	117,211,644	-732,573	732,573
78	94,074,290	2,824,504	587,964	117,944,217	-737,151	737,151
79	91,249,786	2,810,565	570,311	118,681,368	-741,759	741,759
80	88,439,221	2,796,816	552,745	119,423,126	-746,395	746,395
110	9,701,953	2,467,192	60,637	143,967,757	-899,798	899,798
111	7,234,762	2,458,796	45,217	144,867,555	-905,422	905,422
112	4,775,966	2,450,558	29,850	145,772,978	-911,081	911,081
113	2,325,408	2,325,408	14,534	146,684,059	-799,707	916,775
114	0	0	0	147,483,765	1,512,045	921,774
115	0	0	0	145,971,721	1,498,508	912,323
116	0	0	0	144,473,213	1,485,089	902,958
117	0	0	0	142,988,123	1,471,787	893,676
118	0	0	0	141,516,336	1,458,601	884,477
119	0	0	0	140,057,735	1,445,530	875,361
120	0	0	0	138,612,205	1,432,573	866,326

Exhibit 7: Graphical Presentation of Cash Flow for FRR-02 Assuming 165 PSA

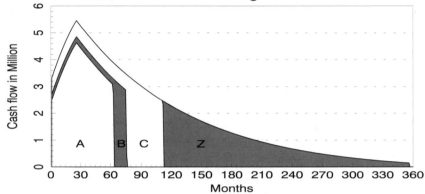

Exhibit 8: Average Life for the Four Tranches of FRR-02 and FRR-01

Prepayment Speed (PSA)	Structure	Average life for tranche			
		A	B	C	Z/D [*]
50	FRR-02	4.98	9.94	12.46	22.15
50	FRR-01	7.48	15.98	21.02	27.24
100	FRR-02	3.74	7.63	9.97	19.35
100	FRR-01	4.90	10.86	15.78	24.58
165	FRR-02	2.90	5.86	7.87	16.03
165	FRR-01	3.48	7.49	11.19	20.27
200	FRR-02	2.61	5.22	7.06	14.52
200	FRR-01	3.05	6.42	9.60	18.11
300	FRR-02	2.09	4.03	5.48	11.18
300	FRR-01	2.32	4.64	6.81	13.36
400	FRR-02	1.78	3.33	4.51	8.95
400	FRR-01	1.94	3.70	5.31	10.34
500	FRR-02	1.58	2.88	3.85	7.41
500	FRR-01	1.69	3.12	4.38	8.35
600	FRR-02	1.43	2.57	3.38	6.30
600	FRR-01	1.51	2.74	3.75	6.96
700	FRR-02	1.31	2.34	3.03	5.47
700	FRR-01	1.38	2.47	3.30	5.95

[*] Tranche Z in FRR-02 and tranche D in FRR-01.

Exhibit 9: FRR-03 – A Hypothetical Sequential-Pay Structure with an Accrual Bond Class and a Residual Class

Tranche	Par amount	Coupon rate (%)
A	$194,500,000	6.00
B	36,000,000	6.50
C	96,500,000	7.00
Z (Accrual)	73,000,000	7.25
R	0	0
Total	$400,000,000	

Payment rules:

1. For payment of periodic coupon interest: Disburse periodic coupon interest to tranches A, B, and C on the basis of the amount of principal outstanding at the beginning of the period. For tranche Z, accrue the interest based on the principal plus accrued interest in the previous period. The interest for tranche Z is to be paid to the earlier tranches as a principal paydown.

2. For disbursement of principal payments: Disburse principal payments to tranche A until it is completely paid off. After tranche A is completely paid off, disburse principal payments to tranche B until it is completely paid off. After tranche B is completely paid off, disburse principal payments to tranche C until it is completely paid off. After tranche C is completely paid off, disburse principal payments to tranche Z until the original principal balance plus accrued interest is completely paid off.

3. Tranche R (the residual class) receives any monthly excess interest payment and reinvestment income.

DIFFERENT COUPON RATES

In FRR-01 and FRR-02, the coupon rate for all the tranches in the CMO structure is the same. Moreover, the coupon rate is the same as the coupon rate on the collateral, 7.5%. There is no reason why this has to be true, and in fact, it is often not. The coupon rate is commonly set equal to a rate that will make the tranche's price close to par. So, in an upward sloping yield curve environment, the longer the average life, the higher the coupon rate.

In FRR-03, we have created a five-tranche CMO structure with an accrual bond class and different coupon rates for each tranche. The highest coupon rate is for tranche Z, 7.25%, 25 basis points less than that for the collateral. FRR-03 is described in Exhibit 9. With the exception of the coupon rate for each tranche and the tranche labeled R, the structure is the same as in FRR-02.

RESIDUAL CLASS

Recall that in Chapter 1 we note that the CMO can be viewed as a business. The assets of the business are the collateral; the liabilities are the bond classes. As in any business, if the cash inflow exceeds the cash outflow, the difference accrues to the owners of the business. In the case of a CMO, the cash inflow includes the interest and principal payments from the collateral as well as any interest income earned before the cash flow must be distributed; the cash outflow is the interest and principal obligations to the bond classes.

When CMO cash inflow exceeds cash outflow for the period, the difference accrues to the owner of the CMO. The bond class that is entitled to receive the excess cash flow is called the *CMO residual class*, or the *CMO equity class*.

Sources of Cash Flow for the CMO Residual
The cash flow for the CMO residual can come from four sources:

1. the difference between the interest payment from the collateral and the interest payment to all the bond classes based on the highest coupon rate of all the tranches. This source is called the *premium income*.

2. the difference between the interest payment to all the bond classes based on the highest coupon rate of all the tranches and the total interest payment to all the other tranches. This source is called the *coupon differential*.

3. the interest arising from reinvestment of the cash flow from the collateral until the payments must be distributed to the tranches. This source is called the *reinvestment income*.

4. any excess principal from the collateral over the amount that must be paid to the bond classes.

The residual class in FRR-03 is class R. In FRR-03, the highest coupon rate is for tranche Z, 7.25%. The coupon rate for the collateral is 7.5%. Therefore, in each month the interest payment to all the tranches based on 7.25% is 25 basis points less than the interest payment from the collateral. Let's look at the first month. The principal outstanding is

$400 million so the interest payment from the collateral is $2,500,000 ($400 million times 7.5% divided by 12). The interest payment to all tranches on the basis of the coupon rate for tranche Z is $2,416,667 ($400 million times 7.25% divided by 12). Therefore, in the first month the excess interest payment resulting from premium income is $83,333.

Let's look at how the coupon differential interest works in the case of FRR-03. While the interest payment of $2,416,667 is based on a coupon rate of 7.25%, the actual interest payment to all the tranches in the first month totals $2,171,459, as shown below:

A	$194,500,000 × 6.00%/12	=	$972,500
B	36,000,000 × 6.50%/12	=	195,000
C	96,000,000 × 7.00%/12	=	562,917
Z	73,000,000 × 7.25%/12	=	441,042
Total		=	$2,171,459

Therefore, the coupon differential for the first month is $245,208 ($2,416,667 minus $2,171,459). Disregarding reinvestment income, the cash flow for the first month is $328,541 ($83,333 plus $245,208). Exhibit 10 gives the cash flow of the residual for selected months for various prepayment speeds assuming no reinvestment income.

Reinvestment income depends on the interest rate at which the cash flow can be reinvested until payments must be made to the tranches. More specifically, the reinvestment income depends on the short-term interest rate at the time and the amount of time between the date the cash flow is received from the collateral and the date the payments are due to the tranches. In a quarterly-pay CMO structure, reinvestment income will be greater than in a monthly-pay CMO structure.

Finally, excess principal payments occur whenever there is overcollateralizing. For example, if the par value of the collateral is $401 million, and the total par value of all the bond classes is $400 million, there will be a total of $1 million excess principal payment over the life of the structure. In the three CMO structures in this chapter there is no overcollateralization.

Cash Flow

Both the amount and the timing of the cash flow are uncertain for the CMO residual. The cash flow will depend on (1) the prepayment rate on the collateral, and (2) the reinvestment rate. This contrasts with the nonresidual bond classes, also referred to as the *regular class interest bond*, where the amount of the principal that will be returned is known but its timing is not.

Exhibit 10: Cash Flow from the Premium Income Plus Coupon Differential for the Residual Class in FRR-03 for Selected Months Assuming Various Prepayment Speeds

Month	PSA Assumption					
	50	100	100	200	300	500
1	328,542	328,542	328,542	328,542	328,542	328,542
2	327,581	327,413	327,195	327,077	326,737	326,051
3	326,574	326,197	325,705	325,439	324,676	323,131
4	325,520	324,893	324,073	323,630	322,358	319,783
5	324,420	323,500	322,300	321,650	319,785	316,010
6	323,274	322,021	320,384	319,500	316,959	311,816
7	322,081	320,454	318,329	317,180	313,882	307,207
8	320,842	318,800	316,133	314,692	310,555	302,188
9	319,558	317,059	313,799	312,038	306,983	296,767
10	318,227	315,233	311,327	309,218	303,167	290,952
11	316,851	313,321	308,719	306,235	299,112	284,753
12	315,429	311,324	305,976	303,090	294,822	278,180
13	313,962	309,243	303,098	299,785	290,300	271,245
14	312,450	307,078	300,089	296,323	285,553	263,960
15	310,893	304,830	296,948	292,705	280,583	256,338
16	309,291	302,499	293,679	288,935	275,398	248,395
17	307,644	300,086	290,283	285,015	270,002	240,145
18	305,953	297,593	286,762	280,948	264,402	231,604
19	304,218	295,020	283,118	276,736	258,604	222,789
20	302,439	292,367	279,353	272,383	252,614	213,718
21	300,617	289,636	275,470	267,893	246,440	204,408
22	298,751	286,828	271,470	263,267	240,089	194,878
23	296,841	283,943	267,357	258,511	233,568	185,148
24	294,889	280,982	263,132	253,627	226,885	175,238
100	129,611	69,671	43,283	32,172	17,965	5,783
101	127,335	67,944	42,402	31,286	17,645	5,606
102	125,056	67,146	41,526	30,408	17,330	5,434
103	122,773	66,349	40,655	29,536	17,021	5,267
104	120,486	65,555	39,790	28,671	16,717	5,105
105	118,195	64,763	38,930	28,134	16,419	4,948
340	4,564	1,938	611	322	47	1
341	4,314	1,827	574	301	44	1
342	4,063	1,717	537	282	41	1
343	3,812	1,607	501	262	38	0
344	3,561	1,497	465	243	35	0
345	3,309	1,387	430	224	32	0
346	3,057	1,278	395	205	29	0
347	2,804	1,170	360	187	26	0
348	2,552	1,061	325	168	24	0
349	2,298	953	291	151	21	0
350	2,044	846	257	133	18	0
351	1,790	739	224	115	16	0
352	1,536	632	191	98	13	0
353	1,281	526	158	81	11	0
354	1,026	420	126	64	9	0
355	770	314	94	48	6	0
356	514	209	62	32	4	0
357	257	104	31	16	2	0

For a CMO residual, it is possible that the investor will not recover the amount invested. This occurs if prepayments become very high because long-term interest rates have dropped.

Variety of Residual Classes

There can be more than one residual class in a structure, although the earlier CMO structures included only one residual class, which received all the premium income, the coupon differential, and reinvestment income. In later deals, there have been two significant changes.

First, the coupon differential has been used to create a bond class called an *IOette*. This is a regular class interest bond, not a residual class, that receives only interest and a nominal amount of principal. Prior to 1992, some principal had to be paid to this class because the tax law governing Real Estate Investment Mortgage Conduits (REMICs) required that all regular class interest bonds receive some principal, i.e., there can be no interest-only classes. Consequently, one can quickly identify the IOette class in a CMO structure by its extremely high coupon rate. In 1992, this provision was changed to allow an interest-only class.

The second change came about after the passage of the REMIC legislation. In the pre-REMIC structures, the sole residual class in the structure not only received the cash flows described above, but it also was responsible for any tax due on the structure. Keep in mind that the residual class represents an equity position, so any excess of income over expenses is taxable. Financial accounting for discounts and premiums, moreover, gives rise to phantom income and expenses, which means that taxable income may differ from the actual cash flow.

Today, it is typical for two residual classes to be included in a structure. One is a residual class that receives part of the coupon differential. This residual class is typically denoted R. The other is a residual class that is responsible for the tax liability, typically denoted as RL, and referred to as a *de minimus residual*. Investors pay to purchase the residual class R; investors in the RL residual class typically either do not pay or are paid to purchase this class. An investor who purchases the RL is typically using it for a tax strategy.

AN ACTUAL DEAL: FN92-G24

Now let's look at an actual sequential-pay deal, FNMA REMIC Trust,

GNMA Series 1992-24, which we refer to simply as FN92-G24. Exhibit 11 provides summary information about the deal and its collateral. The exhibit is divided into three panels. The first panel indicates the tranches in the structure. The second panel shows average life and principal pay-down window based on the prepayment rate assumed when the deal was offered. The third panel describes the collateral.

FN92-G24 is a 10 tranche deal with a total par value of $1.25 billion. As noted in the first panel of Exhibit 11, all the tranches have the same coupon rate, 6.5%. There is an accrual bond class, Z, in this structure.

The collateral for FN92-G24 is two pools of GNMA Is with a passthrough rate of 9%. The mortgage loans have a WAC of 9.5% and a WAM of 343 months.

Payment of interest is made to each tranche, except tranche Z, which accrues interest. The rules for the payment of principal are as follows. Tranches B and A have first priority on the principal payments and pay down simultaneously. Specifically, 2.974% of the principal payment is distributed to tranche B and the balance to tranche A. So, for example, in month 1, the principal payment based on 160 PSA is $6,870,000. Thus, $204,314 (2.974% times $6,870,000) of the principal payment is distributed to tranche B, and $6,665,686 is distributed to tranche A. Once tranche B is completely paid off (which is in month 34 assuming 160 PSA), tranche C pays down simultaneously with tranche A, using the same allocation as for tranche B: 2.974% to tranche C and the balance to tranche A. Once tranches B and C are fully paid off — in month 86 assuming 160 PSA — then tranches D and E are paid down in sequence.

Let's look at the rules for tranches G, H, J, and Z. The accrued interest on tranche Z is the only portion of the cash flow from the collateral that is used to pay down the principal of tranches G, H, and J. These tranches are paid off in sequence, starting with tranche G, then tranche H, and finally tranche J. As we will see, the use of tranche Z in this way results in a stable average life for tranches G, H, and J. The use of an accrual bond in this way produces bond classes that are called *very accurately determined maturity*, or VADM, bonds. In FN92-G24 the VADM bonds are therefore G, H, and J. We discuss VADM bonds further in Chapter 7.

Exhibit 12 shows what happens to the average life for each tranche at slower and faster prepayment speeds. Notice the stability of the average life for the VADM bonds.

Exhibit 11: Description of FNMA REMIC Trust, GNMA Series 1992-24

	Tranche	Balance ($000)	Coupon rate (%)	Type of bond
		Bond Structure:		
1	B	9,000	6.5	sequential-pay
2	C	11,000	6.5	sequential-pay
3	A	652,500	6.5	pays down with B and C
4	D	89,500	6.5	sequential-pay
5	E	300,000	6.5	sequential-pay
6	G	25,000	6.5	sequential-pay
7	H	40,000	6.5	sequential-pay
8	J	56,625	6.5	sequential-pay
9	Z	66,375	6.5	sequential-pay, Z
10	R	100	6.5	residual
	Total	$1,250,100,000		

	Tranche	Average life	Principal pay window	
		Average Life and Principal Paydown at 160 PSA:		
1	B	1.43	5/92	- 2/95
2	C	4.82	2/95	- 6/99
3	A	3.30	5/92	- 6/99
4	D	7.90	6/99	- 12/00
5	E	11.89	12/00	- 5/08
6	G	2.62	5/92	- 4/97
7	H	7.93	4/97	- 11/02
8	J	13.49	11/02	- 5/08
9	Z	21.04	5/08	- 11/20
10	R	8.36	5/92	- 11/20

Type	Balance	WAM	WAC (%)	P/T Rate (%)
		Collateral:		
GNMA-I	$347,250,000	343	9.5	9.0
GNMA-I	902,850,000	343	9.5	9.0

Average life for collateral at 160 PSA: 8.36 years

Exhibit 12: Average Life for All Tranches of FN92-G24 for Various Prepayment Assumptions

	Tranche	Average life assuming a PSA speed of					
		80	120	165	250	400	600
1	B	2.52	1.82	1.43	0.99	0.67	0.47
2	C	8.53	6.19	4.82	3.20	2.05	1.39
3	A	5.82	4.22	3.30	2.21	1.43	0.98
4	D	13.46	10.06	7.90	5.23	3.28	2.16
5	E	18.52	14.76	11.89	7.99	5.00	3.23
6	G	2.62	2.62	2.62	2.62	2.62	2.60
7	H	7.93	7.93	7.93	7.93	6.79	4.71
8	J	13.49	13.49	13.49	11.61	7.97	5.40
9	Z	25.66	21.04	23.54	16.95	11.92	8.05
10	R	12.40	8.36	10.08	5.86	3.75	2.45
	Collateral	12.40	8.36	10.08	5.86	3.75	2.45

Chapter 5

FLOATER, INVERSE FLOATER, PO, IO, AND HIGH-COUPON BOND CLASSES

In this chapter we describe the creation of bond classes offering a floating coupon rate, an inverse floating coupon rate, principal only (no coupon rate), interest only (no principal), and high coupon rate.

FLOATING-RATE AND INVERSE FLOATING-RATE BOND CLASSES

The CMO structures discussed in the previous chapter offered a fixed coupon rate on all tranches. If CMO classes could be created only with fixed-rate coupons, the market for CMOs would be limited. Many financial institutions prefer floating-rate assets, which provide a better match for their liabilities. For example, because the liabilities of depository institutions (commercial banks, savings and loan associations, and credit unions) float with market interest rates, such institutions would prefer a floating-rate asset whose coupon rate changes according to changes in a reference rate that is highly correlated with the rate it must pay on its deposits.

Creating a Floater From Fixed-Rate Collateral

Can a floating-rate CMO bond class be created from fixed-rate collateral? At first this does not seem possible, given that the underlying collateral pays a fixed interest rate. For example, in our hypothetical CMO structures in the previous chapter, the coupon rate for the $400 million collateral is 7.5%. So, if a floating-rate bond class is created that pays, say, one-month LIBOR (London Interbank Offered Rate) plus 65 basis points, and one-month LIBOR at some reset date is 8%, this means that the coupon rate for the floating-rate bond class would be 8.65%. But the coupon rate on the collateral is only 7.5%, 115 basis points less than the rate that must be paid to the floating-rate bond class. Where is this interest shortfall going to be made up?

At the end of the last chapter, we described the excess interest income built into a CMO structure, which means that more than 7.5% could be paid to a floating-rate tranche. But there is still a cap or maximum coupon rate that can be paid to the floating-rate tranche. Some earlier CMO structures with a floating-rate tranche handled this problem by imposing a ceiling or cap on the coupon rate so that the collateral could support the maximum. This feature made floating-rate CMO bond classes a less attractive vehicle for financial institutions and foreign investors that use them for asset/liability management.

To overcome this drawback, an inverse floating-rate bond class can be used. The coupon rate on an inverse floating-rate bond class changes in the opposite direction from the reference rate used to set the coupon rate for the floating-rate bond class. Inclusion of an inverse floater with a floating-rate bond class allows a higher maximum coupon rate to be paid to the floating-rate class. The cap on the floating-rate bond class remains, determined by the floor (the minimum coupon rate) on the inverse floating-rate bond class.

The practice of creating a floating-rate tranche and an inverse floating-rate tranche from fixed-rate collateral is not unique to the CMO market. In the municipal bond market, for example, issuers have been reluctant to issue securities with a floating coupon rate in low interest rate environments. At the same time, investor appetite for floating-rate municipal securities increases. Floating-rate municipal securities are created synthetically by taking a fixed-rate municipal security and splitting it into a floating-rate and an inverse floating-rate security. The same practice occurs in the corporate bond market.

Creation of a Floater and Inverse Floater

We illustrate the creation of a floating-rate and inverse floating-rate bond class using the hypothetical CMO structure FRR-02, which is a four-tranche sequential-pay structure with an accrual bond. We can select any of the tranches from which to create a floating-rate and inverse floating-rate tranche. In fact, we can create these two securities for more than one of the four tranches or for only a portion of one tranche.

In this case, we create a floater and an inverse floater from tranche C. The par value for this tranche is $96.5 million, and we create two tranches that have a combined par value of $96.5 million. We refer to this CMO structure with a floater and an inverse floater as FRR-04. It has five tranches, designated A, B, FL, IFL, and Z, where FL is the floating-rate tranche and IFL is the inverse floating-rate tranche. Exhibit 1 describes FFR- 04.

Any reference rate — short-term, intermediate-term, or long-term — can be used to create a floater and the corresponding inverse floater. The reference rate can be a market-determined rate such as LIBOR, a Treasury bill rate, a Constant Maturity Treasury rate, or a computed rate such as the 11th District Cost of Funds. The reference rate for setting the coupon rate for FL and IFL in FRR-04 is taken as one-month LIBOR.

Floating-Rate Bond Class: The amount of the par value of the floating-rate bond class will be some portion of the $96.5 million. There are an infinite number of ways to cut up the $96.5 million between the floater and inverse floater, and final partitioning will be driven by the demands of investors.

In the FRR-04 structure, we made the floater from $72,375,000 or 75% of the $96.5 million. The coupon rate on the floater is set at one-month LIBOR plus 50 basis points. So, for example, if LIBOR is 3.75% at the reset date, the coupon rate on the floater is 3.75% + 0.5%, or 4.25%. There remains a cap on the coupon rate for the floater (discussed below under inverse floater).

Unlike a floating-rate note in the corporate bond market, whose principal is unchanged over the life of the instrument, the floater's principal balance declines over time as principal paydowns are made. The principal payments to the floater are determined by the principal payments from the tranche from which the floater is created. In our CMO structure, this is bond class C.

Exhibit 1: FRR-04 – A Hypothetical Five-Tranche Sequential-Pay Structure with Floater, Inverse Floater, and Accrual Bond Classes

Tranche	Par amount	Coupon rate
A	$194,500,000	7.50%
B	36,000,000	7.50
FL	72,375,000	1-mo. LIBOR + 0.50
IFL	24,125,000	28.50 - 3 x (1-mo. LIBOR)
Z (Accrual)	73,000,000	7.50
Total	$400,000,000	

Payment rules:

1. For payment of periodic coupon interest: Disburse periodic coupon interest to tranches A, B, FL, and IFL on the basis of the amount of principal outstanding at the beginning of the period. For tranche Z, accrue the interest based on the principal plus accrued interest in the previous period. The interest for tranche Z is to be paid to the earlier tranches as a principal paydown. The maximum coupon rate for FL is 10%; the minimum coupon rate for IFL is 0%.

2. For disbursement of principal payments: Disburse principal payments to tranche A until it is completely paid off. After tranche A is completely paid off, disburse principal payments to tranche B until it is completely paid off. After tranche B is completely paid off, disburse principal payments to tranches FL and IFL until they are completely paid off. The principal payments between tranches FL and IFL should be made in the following way: 75% to tranche FL and 25% to tranche IFL. After tranches FL and IFL are completely paid off, disburse principal payments to tranche Z until the original principal balance plus accrued interest is completely paid off.

Inverse Floater: Since the floater's par value is $72,375,000 of the $96.5 million, the balance is the par value of the inverse floater. Assuming that one-month LIBOR is the reference rate, the coupon rate on the inverse floater takes the following form:

$$K - L \times (\text{1-month LIBOR})$$

In FRR-04, K is set at 28.50% and L at 3. Thus, if one-month LIBOR is 3.75%, the coupon rate for the period is:

$$28.50\% - 3 \times (3.75\%) = 17.25\%$$

K is the cap or maximum coupon rate for the inverse floater. In FRR-04, the cap for the inverse floater is 28.50%.

The L or multiple in the formula to determine the coupon rate for the inverse floater is called the *coupon leverage*. The higher the coupon leverage, the more the inverse floater's coupon rate changes for a given change in one-month LIBOR. For example, a coupon leverage of 3.0 means that a 10-basis point change in one-month LIBOR will change the coupon rate on the inverse floater by 300 basis points; a coupon leverage of 0.7 means that the coupon rate will change by 70 basis points for a 100-basis point change in one-month LIBOR. Inverse floaters with a wide variety of coupon leverages are available in the market. Participants refer to low-leverage inverse floaters as those with a coupon leverage between 0.5 and 2.1; medium-leverage as those with a coupon leverage higher than 2.1 but not exceeding 4.5; and high-leverage as those with a coupon leverage higher than 4.5.

The issuer develops the coupon leverage according to investor desire. In FRR-04, the coupon leverage is set at 3.

Let's see how the total interest paid on the floater and inverse floater can be supported by the bond class with a coupon rate of 7.5% from which they are created. The coupon rate for the floating-rate class is:

1-month LIBOR + 0.50

For the inverse floater the coupon rate is:

$28.50 - 3 \times (1\text{-month LIBOR})$

Since the floater is 75% of the $96.5 million and the inverse floater is 25%, the weighted average coupon rate is:

0.75 (Floater coupon rate) + 0.25 (Inverse floater coupon rate)

The weighted average coupon rate is 7.5%, regardless of the level of LIBOR. For example, if one-month LIBOR is 9%, then

Floater coupon rate = 9.0% + 0.5% = 9.5%

Inverse floater coupon rate = 28.5% − 3 (9.0%) = 1.5%

The weighted average coupon rate is:

0.75 (9.5%) + 0.25 (1.5%) = 7.5%

Consequently, the 7.5% coupon rate on the bond class from which these two classes were created can support the aggregate interest payments that must be made to them.

As in the case of the floater, the principal paydown of an inverse floater will be a proportionate amount of the principal paydown of bond class C.

Floater Caps and Inverse Floater Floors and Caps

Because one-month LIBOR is always positive, the coupon rate paid to the floating-rate bond class cannot be negative. If there are no restrictions placed on the coupon rate for the inverse floater, however, it is possible for the coupon rate for that bond class to be negative. To prevent this, a floor, or minimum, can be placed on the coupon rate. In many structures, the floor is set at zero. Once a floor is set for the inverse floater, a cap or ceiling is imposed on the floater.

In FRR-04, a floor of zero is set for the inverse floater. The floor results in a cap or maximum coupon rate for the floater of 10%. This is found by substituting zero for the coupon rate of the inverse floater in the formula for the weighted average coupon rate, and then setting the formula equal to 7.5%.

The cap for the floater and the inverse floater, the floor for the inverse floater, the coupon leverage, and the margin spread are not determined independently. Any cap or floor imposed on the coupon rate for the floater and the inverse floater must be selected so as to maintain the integrity of the combined coupon rate. That is, the combined coupon rate must be less than or equal to the collateral's coupon rate. The relationships among the parameters for the collateral, floater, and inverse floater are shown in Exhibit 2. Combinations for the parameters for the floater and inverse floater for FRR-04 assuming a floor for the inverse of floater of zero are given below:

Floater cap (%)	Coupon leverage	Cap for Inverse floater assuming a spread of:		
		50 bps	75 bps	100 bps
9.0	5.000	42.500	41.250	40.000
9.5	3.750	33.750	32.813	31.875
10.0	3.000	28.500	27.750	27.000
10.5	2.500	25.000	24.375	23.750
11.0	2.143	22.500	21.964	21.429
11.5	1.875	20.625	20.156	19.688
12.0	1.667	19.167	18.750	18.333

Exhibit 2: Relationships for Principal and Coupon for Creation of Floater and Inverse Floater Tranches *

Parameters for collateral:
  Collateral principal
  Collateral coupon rate

Parameters for floater tranche:
  Floater spread
  Floater cap
  Floater floor
  Current value of reference rate

Parameters for inverse floater tranche:
  Coupon leverage
  Inverse floater cap
  Inverse floater floor

* Assumes that all of the collateral principal and interest will be distributed to the floater and inverse floater.

Exhibit 2: Relationships for Principal and Coupon for Creation of Floater and Inverse Floater Tranches (Concluded)

Relationships:

Floater coupon = Current value of reference rate + Floater spread

$$\text{Floater principal} = \frac{\text{Coupon leverage} \times \text{Collateral principal}}{(1 + \text{Coupon leverage})}$$

Inverse principal = Collateral principal − Floater principal

$$\text{Inverse interest} = (\text{Collateral principal} \times \text{Collateral coupon rate}) - (\text{Floater principal} \times \text{Floater coupon rate})$$

$$\text{Floater cap} = \frac{\text{Collateral coupon}}{\text{Floater principal}}$$

$$\text{Inverse floor} = \frac{\text{Inverse interest when floater coupon at cap}}{\text{Inverse principal}}$$

$$\text{Inverse cap} = \frac{\text{Inverse interest when floater coupon at floor}}{\text{Inverse principal}}$$

Exhibit 3: FRR-05 – A Hypothetical Five-Tranche Sequential-Pay Structure with Superfloater, Inverse Superfloater, and Accrual Bond Classes

Tranche	Par amount	Coupon rate
A	$194,500,000	7.50%
B	36,000,000	7.50
SFL	60,312,500	3 x (1-mo. LIBOR) - 16.5
ISFL	36,187,500	47.5 - 5 x (1-mo. LIBOR)
Z (Accrual)	73,000,000	7.50
Total	$400,000,000	

Payment rules:

1. For payment of periodic coupon interest: Disburse periodic coupon interest to tranches A, B, SFL, and ISFL on the basis of the amount of principal outstanding at the beginning of the period. For tranche Z, accrue the interest based on the principal plus accrued interest in the previous period. The interest for tranche Z is to be paid to the earlier tranches as a principal paydown. The minimum (floor) coupon rate for SFL is 6%, and the maximum (cap) is 12%. The minimum (floor) coupon rate for ISFL is 0%, and the maximum (cap) is 10%.

2. For disbursement of principal payments: Disburse principal payments to tranche A until it is completely paid off. After tranche A is completely paid off, disburse principal payments to tranche B until it is completely paid off. After tranche B is completely paid off, disburse principal payments to tranches SFL and ISFL until they are completely paid off. The principal payments between tranches SFL and ISFL should be made in the following way: 62.5% to tranche SFL and 37.5% to tranche ISFL. After tranches SFL and ISFL are completely paid off, disburse principal payments to tranche Z until the original principal balance plus accrued interest is completely paid off.

Superfloaters

A superfloater is a floating-rate CMO whose coupon rate is a multiple of a reference rate. A superfloater takes the same form as an inverse floater, except that the superfloater's coupon rate increases with the reference rate. The form is as follows, assuming that the reference rate is one-month LIBOR:

$$C \times (1\text{-month LIBOR}) - M$$

where C is the coupon leverage, and M is a constant.

For example, if C is 3 and M is 16.5%, then the formula for the coupon rate for the superfloater is: $3 \times (1\text{-month LIBOR}) - 16.5\%$. If one-month LIBOR is 8%, for example, then the superfloater's coupon rate for the month is $3 \times 8\% - 16.5\% = 7.5\%$. There must be a floor on the coupon rate to prevent it from becoming negative. As with the conventional floater, an inverse floater is needed so that the collateral can support the interest payments regardless of the level of one-month LIBOR.

To illustrate a superfloater, let's consider once again FRR-02. From tranche C, we created a floater and an inverse floater, described as FRR-04. In FRR-05 we create a superfloater and inverse superfloater from tranche C. Exhibit 3 summarizes this CMO structure. The super-floater (labeled tranche SFL in the deal) is created from 62.5% of the $96.5 million of bond tranche C, and the inverse superfloater (labeled tranche ISFL) is created from the balance. The coupon rate and restrictions on the superfloater and inverse superfloater are summarized below:

Tranche	Coupon	Floor	Cap
Superfloater	$3 \times$ (1-month LIBOR) $- 16.5\%$	6%	12%
Inverse superfloater	$47.5 - 5 \times$ (1-month LIBOR)	0%	10%

Exhibit 4 gives the coupon rate for the superfloater and inverse superfloater for a range of rates for one-month LIBOR. Notice that there are two critical levels for LIBOR where the restrictions on the super-floater and inverse superfloater will take effect. If LIBOR is 7.5% or less, the superfloater's coupon rate reaches its floor (6%) while the inverse superfloater's coupon rate realizes its cap (10%). Thus, LIBOR of 7.5% is referred to as the *strike rate* for the superfloater, since for any LIBOR level below 7.5%, the coupon rate is 6%. It is referred to as the strike rate as it is nothing more than an interest rate floor agreement. In such agreements, the buyer of the floor is guaranteed a minimum interest rate, and that minimum rate is the strike rate. Thus, the buyer of a superfloater has effectively purchased an interest rate floor agreement. Viewed from the perspective of the buyer of the inverse superfloater, the 7.5% is effectively the strike rate on an interest rate cap sold.

The other critical LIBOR level is 9.5%. At that level, the super-floater reaches its cap (12%) and forgoes any upside potential should LIBOR rise above 9.5%. At 9.5%, the inverse superfloater reaches its floor (0%). Thus, 9.5% is also a strike rate. In this case, the buyer of the superfloater has effectively sold an interest rate cap agreement. Viewed from the perspective of the buyer of the inverse superfloater, the 9.5% is effectively the strike rate on an interest rate floor purchased.

Between these two strike rates, the coupon rates for the super-floater and inverse superfloater change according to the respective formula. Because of the two strike rates that create a lower and upper tier for the coupon rates, this type of superfloater is referred to as a *two-tier index bond*, or *TTIB*.

In earlier CMO structures with superfloaters, there were no strike rates. The usual practice today is to create superfloaters that are two-tier index bonds.

Exhibit 4: Coupon Rate for Superfloater (SFL) and Inverse Superfloater (ISFL) in FRR-05 Structure at Different Levels of LIBOR

1-Month LIBOR (%)	Superfloater (%)	Inverse superfloater (%)
1.00	6.00	10.00
2.00	6.00	10.00
3.00	6.00	10.00
4.00	6.00	10.00
5.00	6.00	10.00
6.00	6.00	10.00
7.00	6.00	10.00
7.25	5.25	11.25
7.50	6.00	10.00
7.75	6.75	8.75
8.00	7.50	7.50
8.25	8.25	6.25
8.50	9.00	5.00
8.75	9.75	3.75
9.00	10.50	2.50
9.25	11.25	1.25
9.50	12.00	0.00
11.00	12.00	0.00
12.00	12.00	0.00
13.00	12.00	0.00

PRINCIPAL-ONLY AND INTEREST-ONLY BOND CLASSES

As we explained in Chapter 2, stripped mortgage-backed securities are created by paying all the principal to one bond class and all the interest to another bond class. These two classes are referred to as the *principal-only* or *PO* bond class, and the *interest-only* or *IO* bond class.

A PO bond class is sold at a substantial discount from par. Therefore, it benefits from a decline in mortgage rates as prepayments accelerate. This results in a return of principal at par value for a security purchased at less than par. Thus, investors who expect prepayments to rise will realize superior performance from PO bond classes. The shortening of the average life occurs because of faster prepayments, enhancing the performance of a PO. A lengthening of the average life will come with slower prepayments, resulting in inferior performance for a PO.

Exhibit 5: FRR-06 – A Hypothetical Six-Tranche Sequential-Pay Structure with a Floater, Inverse Floater, PO, IO, and Accrual Bond Classes

Tranche	Par amount	Coupon rate (%)
A	$194,500,000	7.50
IO	0	Interest equal to 7.5% times the balance outstanding for the PO tranche
PO	36,000,000	0
FL	72,375,000	1-mo. LIBOR + 0.50
IFL	24,125,000	28.50 - 3 x (1-mo. LIBOR)
Z (Accrual)	73,000,000	7.50
Total	$400,000,000	

Payment rules:

1. For payment of periodic coupon interest: Disburse periodic coupon interest to tranches A, B, FL, and IFL on the basis of the amount of principal outstanding at the beginning of the period. Disburse periodic coupon interest to tranche IO based on the amount of principal outstanding at the beginning of the period for tranche PO. For tranche Z, accrue the interest based on the principal plus accrued interest in the previous period. The interest for tranche Z is to be paid to the earlier tranches as a principal paydown. The maximum coupon rate for FL is 10%; the minimum coupon rate for IFL is 0%.

2. For disbursement of principal payments: Disburse principal payments to tranche A until it is completely paid off. After tranche A is completely paid off, disburse principal payments to tranche PO until it is completely paid off. After tranche PO is completely paid off, disburse principal payments to tranches FL and IFL until they are completely paid off. The principal payments between tranches FL and IFL should be made in the following way: 75% to tranche FL and 25% to tranche IFL. After tranches FL and IFL are completely paid off, disburse principal payments to tranche Z until the original principal balance plus accrued interest is completely paid off.

The opposite is true for an IO bond class. Since only interest and no principal is received by the holder of this security, slower prepayments represent more cash flow than faster prepayments. Thus, the performance of an IO is enhanced by slower prepayments but hurt when there are faster prepayments.

Creation of an IO and a PO from One Tranche

CMO structures can be created so that a tranche can receive only the principal or only the interest. For example, consider FRR-04. Suppose that tranche B in this structure is divided into two tranches, a principal-only tranche and an interest-only tranche. We will call this structure FRR-06, described in Exhibit 5.

In the calculation of the average life for a tranche, only the principal received is considered. Since an IO does not return principal, an average life can not be calculated. Instead, a *cash flow average life* can be computed by used cash flow in lieu of principal in the average life formula. Obviously, the cash flow is just the interest.

Exhibit 6: FRR-07 – A Three-Tranche Structure with a Floater, Inverse IO Floater, and PO

Tranche	Par amount	Coupon rate
FL	$300,000,000	1-mo. LIBOR + 0.50
IIO	0	Interest equal to:
		[28.50% - 3 x (1-mo. LIBOR)]
		x PO balance outstanding
PO	100,000,000	0
Total	$400,000,000	

Payment rules:

1. For payment of periodic coupon interest: Disburse periodic coupon interest to tranche FL determined by the specified formula and on the basis of the amount of principal outstanding at the beginning of the period. Disburse periodic coupon interest to tranche IIO using the IIO specified formula and according to the amount of principal outstanding at the beginning of the period for tranche PO. The maximum coupon rate for FL is 10%; the minimum coupon rate for IIO is 0%.

2. For disbursement of principal payments: Disburse principal payments to tranche FL and tranche PO on the following basis: for each principal payment of $1, distribute $.75 to tranche FL and $.25 to tranche PO.

To illustrate other types of CMO structures including a PO or an IO, consider FRR-07 shown in Exhibit 6. This is a three-tranche structure using the $400 million, 7.5% coupon, 357 WAM collateral. Tranche F is a floater with a coupon rate of one-month LIBOR plus 50 basis points; its par value is $300 million. There is a 10% cap on tranche F. The balance of the collateral, $100 million, is used to create the remaining two tranches. There is a PO tranche, and there is a tranche denoted IIO, which is a bond class that receives only interest (i.e., an IO tranche) based on the outstanding balance of the PO tranche. Rather than a fixed coupon rate, the interest is based on a formula where the coupon rate changes inversely with one-month LIBOR (i.e., it is an inverse floater). The formula is the same as for FRR-04, $28.5\% - 3 \times (1\text{-month LIBOR})$. This bond class is referred to as an inverse IO (IIO).

The principal payment from the collateral is distributed to the floater and PO tranches on the basis of their par value relative to the total par value of the collateral, $400 million. Thus, for each $100 of principal payment from the collateral, $75 is distributed to the floater and $25 to the PO. The average life for the floater and the PO is the same as the tranche from which these two bond classes were created.

Creation of an IO From More than One Tranche

In our previous illustration of how an IO tranche is created, we used a simple CMO structure in which all the tranches have the same coupon rate (7.5%) and that coupon rate is the same as the collateral. Let's look at how an IO is more commonly created from a CMO structure where the coupon rate is different for each tranche.

In Chapter 4 we introduced such a structure, FRR-03. That structure is a four-tranche sequential-pay with an acrrual bond and a residual class. All the the excess interest — premium income and coupon differential — from the collateral is paid to the to the residual class. Instead of paying the excess interest to that residual class, the excess interest can be paid to an IO class.This is done in FRR-08 shown in Exhibit 7. Notice that for this structure the par amount for the IO class is shown as $52,566,667 and the coupon rate is 7.5%. Since this is an IO class there is no par amount. The amount shown is the amount upon which the interest payments will be determined, not the amount that will be paid to the holder of this bond. Therefore, it is called a *notional amount.*

Let's look at how the notional amount is determined. Consider first tranche A. The par value is $194.5 million and the coupon rate is 6%. Since the collateral's coupon rate is 7.5%, the excess interest is 150 basis points (1.5%). Therefore, an IO with a 1.5% coupon rate and a notional amount of $194.5 million can be created from tranche A. But this is equivalent to an IO with a notional amount of $38.9 million and a coupon rate of 7.5%. Mathematically, this notional amount is found as follows:

$$\text{Notional amount for 7.5\% IO} = \frac{\text{Tranche's par value} \times \text{Excess interest}}{0.075}$$

where

$$\text{Excess interest} = \text{Collateral coupon rate} - \text{Tranche coupon rate}$$

For example, for tranche A:

$$\text{Excess interest} = 0.075 - 0.060 = 0.015$$

$$\text{Tranche's par value} = \$194,500,000$$

$$\text{Notional amount for 7.5\% IO} = \frac{\$194,500,000 \times 0.015}{0.075} = \$38,900,000$$

Exhibit 7: FRR-08 – A Hypothetical Five Tranche Sequential Pay with an Accrual Tranche, an Interest-Only Tranche, and a Residual Class

Tranche	Par amount	Coupon rate (%)
A	$194,500,000	6.00
B	36,000,000	6.50
C	96,500,000	7.00
Z	73,000,000	7.25
IO	52,566,667 (Notional)	7.50
R	0	0
Total	$400,000,000	

Payment rules:

1. For payment of periodic coupon interest: Disburse periodic coupon interest to tranches A, B, and C on the basis of the amount of principal outstanding at the beginning of the period. For tranche Z, accrue the interest based on the principal plus accrued interest in the previous period. The interest for tranche Z is to be paid to the earlier tranches as a principal pay down. Disburse periodic interest to the IO tranche based on the notional amount at the beginning of the period.

2. For disbursement of principal payments: Disburse principal payments to tranche A until it is completely paid off. After tranche A is completely paid off, disburse principal payments to tranche B until it is completely paid off. After tranche B is completely paid off, disburse principal payments to tranche C until it is completely paid off. After tranche C is completely paid off, disburse principal payments to tranche Z until the original principal balance plus accrued interest is completely paid off.

3. No principal is to be paid to the IO tranche. The notional amount of the IO tranche declines based on the principal payments to all other tranches.

Similarly, from tranche B with a par value of $36 million, the excess interest is 100 basis points (1%) and therefore an IO with a coupon rate of 1% and a notional amount of $36 million can be created. But this is equivalent to creating an IO with a notional amount of $4.8 million and a coupon rate of 7.5%. This procedure is shown below for all four tranches:

Tranche	Par amount	Excess interest (%)	Notional amount for a 7.5% coupon rate IO
A	$194,500,000	1.50	$38,900,000
B	36,000,000	1.00	4,800,000
C	96,500,000	0.50	6,433,333
Z	73,000,000	0.25	2,433,333
	Notional amount for 7.5% IO:		$52,566,667

Exhibit 8: FRR-09 – A Hypothetical Five Tranche Sequential Pay with an Accrual Tranche, a High-Coupon Tranche, and a Residual Class

Tranche	Par amount	Coupon rate (%)
A	$ 97,250,000	6.00
B	21,600,000	6.50
C	72,375,000	7.00
Z	62,571,429	7.25
H	146,203,571	9.00
R	0	0
Total	$400,000,000	

Payment rules:

1. For payment of periodic coupon interest: Disburse periodic coupon interest to tranches A, B, C, and H on the basis of the amount of principal outstanding at the beginning of the period. For tranche Z, accrue the interest based on the principal plus accrued interest in the previous period. The interest for tranche Z is to be paid to the earlier tranches as a principal pay down.

2. For disbursement of principal payments: Disburse 50% of principal payments to tranche A and 50% to tranche H until tranche A is completely paid off. After tranche A is completely paid off, disburse 60% of principal payments to tranche B and 40% to tranche H until tranche B is completely paid off. After tranche B is completely paid off, disburse 75% of principal payments to tranche C and 25% to tranche H until tranche H is completely paid off. After tranche C is completely paid off, disburse 85.711% of principal payments to tranche Z until the original principal balance plus accrued interest is completely paid off and 14.289% to Tranche H.

CREATION OF A HIGH-COUPON BOND

A high-coupon bond can be created from a CMO structure in which the coupon rate for each tranche is different. We will illustrate how this can be done for FRR-03. Suppose that a tranche with a coupon rate of 9% is sought. Exhibit 8 shows this structure, FRR-09. It includes four tranches, A, B, C, and Z, that are sequential pays, tranche H which is a 9% coupon tranche, and the residual class. Let's see how the par amount for all the tranche's is determined.

For each of the tranches A, B, C, and Z in FRR-03, the excess interest is stripped off to create the 9% coupon for tranche H. This requires splitting the par amount for each of the tranches as follows. Consider first tranche A in FRR-03. The par amount is $194.5 million. The excess interest for the tranche is 1.5%. To obtain a tranche with a 9% coupon, the par amount of tranche A in FRR-03 must be split evenly between tranche A and tranche H in FRR-09. That is, $97.25 million is allocated to the par amount of tranche A. In general, the formula for determining the percentage of a tranche's par amount allocated to the high coupon tranche is as follows:

$$1 - \frac{\text{Target coupon for high coupon tranche} - \text{Collateral coupon}}{\text{Target coupon} - \text{Tranche coupon}}$$

For example, the percentage of tranche A's par amount allocated to tranche H is:

$$1 - \frac{9.0\% - 7.5\%}{9.0\% - 6.0\%} = 0.5 = 50\%$$

Thus, 50% of the par amount of tranche A in FRR-03 of $195 million is allocated to tranche H.

For tranche B with a par amount of $36 million in FRR-03, the percentage allocated to tranche H is:

$$1 - \frac{9.0\% - 7.5\%}{9.0\% - 6.5\%} = 0.4 = 40\%$$

Therefore, $14.4 million which is 40% of the par amount of tranche B in FRR-03 of $36 million is allocated to tranche H.

The same procedure is followed for splitting the par amount of tranches C and Z. The par amount for tranche H is $146,203,571 as shown below:

Tranche	Par amount in FRR-03	Excess interest (%)	Percentage allocated to tranche H	Percentage allocated to tranche H	Par amount in FRR-09
A	$194,500,000	1.50	50.00000	$94,250,000	$97,250,000
B	36,000,000	1.00	40.00000	14,400,000	21,600,000
C	96,500,000	0.50	25.00000	24,125,000	72,375,000
Z	73,000,000	0.25	14.28572	10,428,571	62,571,429
		Total par amount for Tranche H:		$146,203,571	

The par amount for tranches A, B, C, and Z in FRR-09 are shown in the last column.

The principal payments between the current paying tranche and tranche H are divided according to the percentages above. For example, if the current paying tranche is B and the principal payment is $1 million, then $600,000 is paid to tranche B and $400,000 to tranche H.

Creation of an Inverse IO from a High Coupon Tranche

A high coupon tranche can be stripped to create either of the following:

    1. a floater and an inverse IO floater

    2. a floater, an inverse IO floater, and a two-tiered index bond IO

Floater/inverse IO floater combination: Since the coupon rate is 9% we can create a floater with a 9% coupon. Assuming that the margin is 50 basis points, we can create an inverse IO with an 8.5% cap (9% – 50 basis points). If the reference rate is one-month LIBOR, the formula for the inverse IO would be 8.5% – LIBOR. The notional amount will be $146,203,571.

Floater/inverse IO floater/TTIB IO combination: To see how this combination is created, we assume the floater will be the same as in the previous structure. But for the inverse IO we will assume an 8% cap rather than an 8.5% cap in the previous structure. The TTIB will be 8.5 – LIBOR with a 50 basis point cap. The strike for the TIBB will be 8%.

AN ACTUAL DEAL: FN92-059

Now we will look at an actual deal: FNMA REMIC Trust, Series 1992-59, which we will denote by FN92-059. Exhibit 9 provides summary information about the CMO structure and its collateral. The first panel describes the tranches in the structure. The second panel shows the average life and principal paydown window based on the prepayment rate assumed when the deal was offered. The third panel describes the collateral.

    There are six tranches in this structure: four regular interest bond classes (tranches F, S, A, and Z) and two residuals (R and RL). The par value is $200 million. The collateral is $200 million of Fannie Mae passthroughs with an 8.5% coupon rate and 118 WAM. The mortgage loans are 15-year loans with a 9.25% WAC with a maximum coupon rate of 11%.

    Tranche F is a sequential-pay class with the highest priority. It is a conventional floating-rate class. Assuming 195 PSA, the average life for this tranche is 3.53 years, with the principal paydown window shown in the second panel of Exhibit 9. Tranches S and A pay down simultaneously with tranche F. Thus, their average life and principal paydown windows are identical to that of tranche F. Tranche A is basically an inverse IOette. If one-month LIBOR is 4.3125%, for example, the coupon rate is 655.0779%. Tranche F is a principal-only class. After tranches F, S, and A are paid down, tranche Z is paid down. This is an accrual bond.

    Note that the average life for the collateral, assuming 195 PSA is 3.84. This structure allows the creation of tranches with slightly shorter average lives (3.53 years) and a tranche with a substantially greater average life (9.23 years). The variability of the average life over a wide range of prepayment scenarios for tranches F, S, A, and Z is reported in Exhibit 10.

Exhibit 9: Description of FNMA REMIC Trust, Series 1992-59

Bond Structure:

	Tranche	Balance ($000)	Coupon rate (%)	Type of bond
1	F	$164,900	1-month LIBOR + 0.4	sequential-pay floater
2	S	1,331	1189.4 - 123.89 x LIBOR	inverse IO that pays with F
3	A	27,769	0	PO that pays with F
4	Z	6,000	8.5	sequential-pay accrual
5	R	0	0	residual class
6	RL	0	0	residual class
	Total	$200,000,000		

Average Life and Principal Paydown at 195 PSA:

	Tranche	Average life	Principal pay window
1	F	3.53	6/92 - 1/01
2	S	3.53	6/92 - 1/01
3	A	3.53	6/92 - 1/01
4	Z	9.23	1/01 - 3/02
5	R	0	N/A
6	RL	0	N/A

Collateral:

Type	Balance	WAM	WAC (%)	P/T rate (%)
FNMA	$200,000,000	118	9.25	8.5

Average life of collateral at 195 PSA: 3.84 years

Exhibit 10: Average Life for FN92-059 for Various Prepayment Assumptions

Tranche	Average life assuming a PSA speed of								
	50	100	195	250	300	400	500	600	700
F,S,A	4.83	4.32	3.53	3.15	2.85	2.35	1.97	1.67	1.43
Z	9.58	9.49	9.23	9.02	8.79	8.23	7.56	6.84	6.12

Chapter 6

PLANNED AMORTIZATION CLASS BONDS

The CMO innovations discussed in the previous two chapters attracted many institutional investors who had previously either avoided investing in mortgage-backed securities or allocated only a nominal portion of their portfolio to this sector of the fixed-income market. While some traditional corporate bond buyers shifted their allocation to CMOs, a majority of institutional investors remained on the sidelines, concerned about investing in an instrument that they continued to perceive as posing significant prepayment risk despite the innovations designed to reduce this risk.

Potential demand for a CMO product with less uncertainty about the cash flow increased in the mid-1980s because of two trends in the corporate bond market. First was the increased event risk faced by investors, highlighted by the RJR Nabisco leveraged buyout in 1988.[1] The second trend was a decline in the number of triple-A rated corporate issues. Traditional corporate bond buyers sought a structure with both the characteristics of a corporate bond (either a bullet maturity or a sinking-fund type schedule of principal

---

[1] Event risk refers to the unexpected impairment of an issuer's ability to make interest and principal payments as the result of a takeover, corporate restructuring, or natural or industrial accident.

repayment) and high credit quality. While CMOs satisfied the second condition, they did not satisfy the first.

In March 1987, the M.D.C. Mortgage Funding Corporation CMO Series O included a class of bonds referred to as "stabilized mortgage reduction term bonds" or "SMRT" bonds; another class in its CMO Series P was referred to as "planned amortization class bonds" or "PAC" bonds. The Oxford Acceptance Corporation III Series C CMOs included a class of bonds referred to as a "planned redemption obligation bonds" or "PRO" bonds. These three bonds share a characteristic that, if the prepayments are within a specified range, a schedule of principal payments will be realized.

The greater predictability of the cash flow for these classes of bonds, now referred to exclusively as *PAC bonds*, occurs because there is a principal repayment schedule that must be satisfied. PAC bondholders have priority over all other classes in the CMO issue in receiving principal payments from the underlying collateral. The greater certainty of the cash flow for the PAC bonds comes at the expense of the non-PAC classes, called the *support bonds* or *companion bonds*.

The basic idea behind the PAC bond is as follows. Should the actual principal repayment be greater than the scheduled amount, the support bonds receive the excess. This means that the support bonds accept the contraction risk. Should the actual principal repayment be less than the scheduled amount, the PAC bondholders have priority on subsequent principal payments from the collateral. This reduces extension risk, again absorbed by the support bonds. Because PAC bonds have protection against both extension risk and contraction risk, they are said to provide *two-sided prepayment protection*.

This chapter describes the features of PAC bonds, the nature of the two-sided prepayment risk, and how the protection changes over time. The next chapter discusses support bond classes.

CREATION OF A PAC BOND

To illustrate how to create a PAC bond, we will use as collateral a $400 million passthrough with a coupon rate of 7.5%, an 8.125% WAC, and a WAM of 357 months. The second column of Exhibit 1 shows the principal payment (regularly scheduled principal repayment plus prepayments) for selected months assuming a prepayment speed of 90 PSA, and the next column shows the principal payments for selected months assuming that the passthrough prepays at 300 PSA.

Exhibit 1: Monthly Principal Payment for $400 Million 7.5% Coupon Passthrough with an 8.125% WAC and a 357 WAM Assuming Prepayment Rates of 90 PSA and 300 PSA

Month	At 90% PSA	At 300% PSA	Minimum principal payment — the PAC schedule
1	508,169.52	1,075,931.20	508,169.52
2	569,843.43	1,279,412.11	569,843.43
3	631,377.11	1,482,194.45	631,377.11
4	692,741.89	1,683,966.17	692,741.89
5	753,909.12	1,884,414.62	753,909.12
6	814,850.22	2,083,227.31	814,850.22
7	875,536.68	2,280,092.68	875,536.68
8	935,940.10	2,474,700.92	935,940.10
9	996,032.19	2,666,744.77	996,032.19
10	1,055,784.82	2,855,920.32	1,055,784.82
11	1,115,170.01	3,041,927.81	1,115,170.01
12	1,174,160.00	3,224,472.44	1,174,160.00
13	1,232,727.22	3,403,265.17	1,232,727.22
14	1,290,844.32	3,578,023.49	1,290,844.32
15	1,348,484.24	3,748,472.23	1,348,484.24
16	1,405,620.17	3,914,344.26	1,405,620.17
17	1,462,225.60	4,075,381.29	1,462,225.60
18	1,518,274.36	4,231,334.57	1,518,274.36
101	1,458,719.34	1,510,072.17	1,458,719.34
102	1,452,725.55	1,484,126.59	1,452,725.55
103	1,446,761.00	1,458,618.04	1,446,761.00
104	1,440,825.55	1,433,539.23	1,433,539.23
105	1,434,919.07	1,408,883.01	1,408,883.01
211	949,482.58	213,309.00	213,309.00
212	946,033.34	209,409.09	209,409.09
213	942,601.99	205,577.05	205,577.05
346	618,684.59	13,269.17	13,269.17
347	617,071.58	12,944.51	12,944.51
348	615,468.65	12,626.21	12,626.21
349	613,875.77	12,314.16	3,432.32
350	612,292.88	12,008.25	0
351	610,719.96	11,708.38	0
352	609,156.96	11,414.42	0
353	607,603.84	11,126.28	0
354	606,060.57	10,843.85	0
355	604,527.09	10,567.02	0
356	603,003.38	10,295.70	0
357	601,489.39	10,029.78	0

Exhibit 2: Graphical Presentation
of Monthly Principal Payment for Collateral
($400 Million 7.5% Coupon with an 8.125% WAC and a 357 WAM)
Assuming a Prepayment Rate of 90 PSA

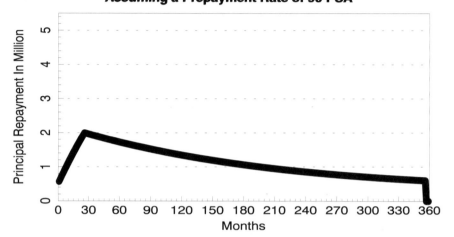

Exhibit 2 graphically presents the principal payments assuming a prepayment speed of 90 PSA. The horizontal axis shows the month in which a principal payment will be made and the vertical axis is the amount of the principal payment. Exhibit 3 graphically presents the principal payments over time assuming 300 PSA.

The last column of Exhibit 1 gives the minimum principal payment if the collateral speed is 90 PSA or 300 PSA for months 1 to 349.[2] For example, in the first month, the principal payment would be $508,169.52 if the collateral prepays at 90 PSA and $1,075,931.20 if the collateral prepays at 300 PSA. Thus, the minimum principal payment is $508,169.52, as reported in the last column of Exhibit 1. In month 103, the minimum principal payment is also the amount if the prepayment speed is 90 PSA, $1,446,761, compared to $1,458,618.04 for 300 PSA. In month 104, however, a prepayment speed of 300 PSA would produce a principal payment of $1,433,539.23, which is less than the principal payment of $1,440,825.55 assuming 90 PSA. So, $1,433,539.23 is reported in the last column of Exhibit 1. From month 104 on the minimum principal payment is the one that would result assuming a prepayment speed of 300 PSA.

---

[2] After month 346, the outstanding principal balance will be paid off if the prepayment speed is between 90 PSA and 300 PSA.

Exhibit 3: Graphical Presentation
of Monthly Principal Payment for Collateral
($400 Million 7.5% Coupon with an 8.125% WAC and a 357 WAM)
Assuming a Prepayment Rate of 300 PSA

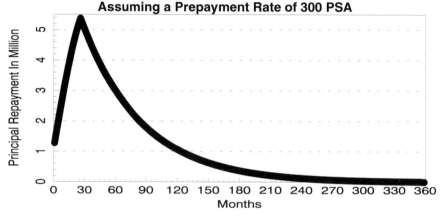

In fact, if the collateral prepays at any speed between 90 PSA and 300 PSA, the minimum principal payment would be the amount reported in the last column of Exhibit 1. For example, if we had included principal payment figures assuming a prepayment speed of 200 PSA, the minimum principal payment would not change: from month 1 through month 103, the minimum principal payment is that generated from 90 PSA, but from month 104 on, the minimum principal payment is that generated from 300 PSA.

This example is displayed graphically in Exhibit 4, which combines Exhibits 2 and 3. The principal payment at 300 PSA is less than that at 90 PSA for the months after the point where the two curves intersect. The curve in Exhibit 5 graphically shows the minimum principal payment, the lighter of the two curves up to month 104 in Exhibit 4 and the darker of the two curves after month 104 in Exhibit 4.

This characteristic of the collateral allows for the creation of a PAC bond, assuming that the collateral prepays over its life at a speed between 90 PSA to 300 PSA. A schedule of principal repayments that the PAC bondholders are entitled to receive before any other bond class in the CMO is specified. The monthly schedule of principal repayments is as specified in the last column of Exhibit 1, which shows the minimum principal payment. The two speeds used to create a PAC bond are called the *initial PAC collars* (or *initial PAC bands*); in our case 90 PSA is the lower collar and 300 PSA the upper collar. While there is no assurance that the collateral will prepay between these two speeds, a PAC bond can be structured to assume that it will.

Exhibit 4: Graphical Presentation
of Monthly Principal Payment for Collateral
($400 Million 7.5% Coupon with an 8.125% WAC and a 357 WAM)
Assuming a Prepayment Rate of 90 PSA and 300 PSA

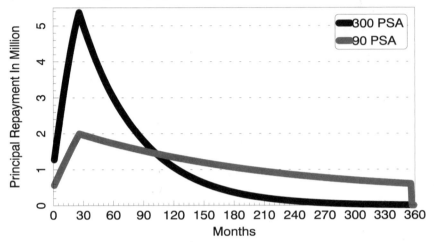

Exhibit 5: Graphical Presentation
of Minimum Monthly Principal Payment for Collateral
($400 Million, 7.5% Coupon with an 8.125% WAC and a 357 WAM)
Assuming a Prepayment Rate Between 90 PSA and 300 PSA

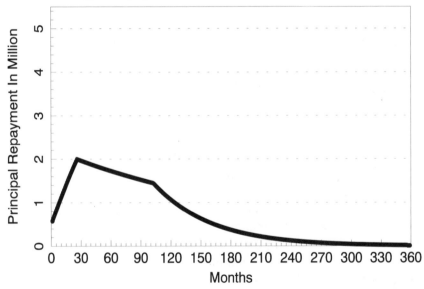

Average Life

Exhibit 6 shows a CMO structure, FRR-10, that we created from the $400 million, 7.5% coupon passthrough with a WAC of 8.125% and a WAM of 357 months. There are just two bond classes in this structure: a 7.5% coupon PAC bond with an initial collar of 90 to 300 PSA with a par value of $243.8 million, and a support (non-PAC) bond with a par value of $156.2 million.

Exhibit 7 reports the average life for the PAC bond and the support bond in FRR-10 assuming various prepayment speeds. Notice that between 90 PSA and 300 PSA, the average life for the PAC bond is stable at 7.26 years. However, at slower or faster PSA speeds, the schedule is broken, and the average life changes, lengthening when the prepayment speed is less than 90 PSA and shortening when it is greater than 300 PSA. Even so, there is much greater variability in the average life of the support bond.

While Exhibit 7 clearly indicates the stability of the average life for the PAC bond, it represents a rather naive analysis, as it assumes that prepayments will remain at one PSA speed for the life of the collateral. Vector analysis — that is, varying the PSA speed over time — can provide further insight into the effect of prepayments on the average life of a PAC bond. The importance of doing this will be illustrated later in this chapter.

Creating a Series of PAC Bonds

Most CMO PAC structures have more than one class of PAC bonds. To see how this is done graphically, look at Exhibit 8. The curve in the exhibit is the same as in Exhibit 5 except that there are six letters under the curve — P-A, P-B, P-C, P-D, P-E, and P-F — separated by a straight line from the horizontal axis to the curve. Each of these letters represents a PAC bond. The schedule of principal repayments for each PAC bond is revealed in the exhibit. For PAC P-A, the schedule of principal repayments is shown by the segment of the curve from the vertical axis to point 1 on the curve. For PAC P-B, the schedule of principal repayments is shown by the segment of the curve from point 1 to point 2 on the curve, and so on.

We created the six PAC bonds in Exhibit 8 from FRR-10, which we call FRR-11. Information about this CMO structure is reported in Exhibit 9. The total par value of the six PAC bonds is equal to $243.8 million, which is the amount of the single PAC bond in FRR-10. The schedule of principal repayments for selected months for each PAC bond is shown in Exhibit 10.

Exhibit 6: FRR-10 – CMO Structure
with One PAC Bond and One Support Bond

Tranche	Par amount	Coupon rate (%)
P (PAC)	$243,800,000	7.5
S (Support)	156,200,000	7.5
Total	$400,000,000	

Payment rules:

1. For payment of periodic coupon interest: Disburse periodic coupon interest to each tranche on the basis of the amount of principal outstanding at the beginning of the period.

2. For disbursement of principal payments: Disburse principal payments to tranche P based on its schedule of principal repayments. Tranche P has priority with respect to current and future principal payments to satisfy the schedule. Any excess principal payments in a month over the amount necessary to satisfy the schedule for tranche P are paid to tranche S. When tranche S is completely paid off, all principal payments are to be made to tranche P regardless of the schedule.

Exhibit 7: Average Life for PAC Bond and Support Bond
in FRR-10 Assuming Various Prepayment Speeds

Prepayment rate (PSA)	PAC Bond (P)	Support Bond (S)
0	15.97	27.26
50	9.44	24.00
90	7.26	18.56
100	7.26	18.56
150	7.26	12.57
165	7.26	11.16
200	7.26	8.38
250	7.26	5.37
300	7.26	3.13
350	6.56	2.51
400	5.92	2.17
450	5.38	1.94
500	4.93	1.77
700	3.70	1.37

Exhibit 8: Graphical Depiction
of a PAC CMO Structure with Six PAC Bonds

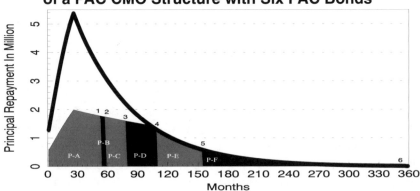

Exhibit 9: FRR-11 – CMO Structure
with Six PAC Bonds and One Support Bond

Tranche	Par amount	Coupon rate (%)
P-A	$85,000,000	7.5
P-B	8,000,000	7.5
P-C	35,000,000	7.5
P-D	45,000,000	7.5
P-E	40,000,000	7.5
P-F	30,800,000	7.5
S	156,200,000	7.5
Total	$400,000,000	

Payment rules:

1. For payment of periodic coupon interest: Disburse periodic coupon interest to each tranche on the basis of the amount of principal outstanding at the beginning of the period.

2. For disbursement of principal payments: Disburse principal payments to tranches P-A to P-F based on their respective schedules of principal repayments. Tranche P-A has priority with respect to current and future principal payments to satisfy the schedule. Any excess principal payments in a month over the amount necessary to satisfy the schedule for tranche P-A are paid to tranche S. Once tranche P-A is completely paid off, tranche P-B has priority, then tranche P-C, etc. When tranche S is completely paid off, all principal payments are to be made to the remaining PAC tranches in order of priority regardless of the schedule.

Exhibit 10: Mortgage Balance for Selected Months
for FRR-11 Assuming 165 PSA

				Tranche			
Month	A	B	C	D	E	F	Support
1	85,000,000	8,000,000	35,000,000	45,000,000	40,000,000	30,800,000	156,200,000
2	84,491,830	8,000,000	35,000,000	45,000,000	40,000,000	30,800,000	155,998,246
3	83,921,987	8,000,000	35,000,000	45,000,000	40,000,000	30,800,000	155,746,193
4	83,290,609	8,000,000	35,000,000	45,000,000	40,000,000	30,800,000	155,444,011
5	82,597,868	8,000,000	35,000,000	45,000,000	40,000,000	30,800,000	155,091,931
6	81,843,958	8,000,000	35,000,000	45,000,000	40,000,000	30,800,000	154,690,254
7	81,029,108	8,000,000	35,000,000	45,000,000	40,000,000	30,800,000	154,239,345
8	80,153,572	8,000,000	35,000,000	45,000,000	40,000,000	30,800,000	153,739,635
9	79,217,631	8,000,000	35,000,000	45,000,000	40,000,000	30,800,000	153,191,621
10	78,221,599	8,000,000	35,000,000	45,000,000	40,000,000	30,800,000	152,595,864
11	77,165,814	8,000,000	35,000,000	45,000,000	40,000,000	30,800,000	151,952,989
12	76,050,644	8,000,000	35,000,000	45,000,000	40,000,000	30,800,000	151,263,687
13	74,876,484	8,000,000	35,000,000	45,000,000	40,000,000	30,800,000	150,528,708
52	5,170,458	8,000,000	35,000,000	45,000,000	40,000,000	30,800,000	109,392,664
53	3,379,318	8,000,000	35,000,000	45,000,000	40,000,000	30,800,000	108,552,721
54	1,595,779	8,000,000	35,000,000	45,000,000	40,000,000	30,800,000	107,728,453

Exhibit 10 (Concluded)

55	0	7,819,804	35,000,000	45,000,000	40,000,000	30,800,000	106,919,692
56	0	6,051,358	35,000,000	45,000,000	40,000,000	30,800,000	106,126,275
57	0	4,290,403	35,000,000	45,000,000	40,000,000	30,800,000	105,348,040
58	0	2,536,904	35,000,000	45,000,000	40,000,000	30,800,000	104,584,824
59	0	790,826	35,000,000	45,000,000	40,000,000	30,800,000	103,836,469
60	0	0	34,052,132	45,000,000	40,000,000	30,800,000	103,102,817
61	0	0	32,320,787	45,000,000	40,000,000	30,800,000	102,383,711
62	0	0	30,596,756	45,000,000	40,000,000	30,800,000	101,678,995
78	0	0	3,978,669	45,000,000	40,000,000	30,800,000	92,239,836
79	0	0	2,373,713	45,000,000	40,000,000	30,800,000	91,757,440
80	0	0	775,460	45,000,000	40,000,000	30,800,000	91,286,887
81	0	0	0	44,183,878	40,000,000	30,800,000	90,828,046
82	0	0	0	42,598,936	40,000,000	30,800,000	90,380,792
83	0	0	0	41,020,601	40,000,000	30,800,000	89,944,997
108	0	0	0	3,758,505	40,000,000	30,800,000	82,288,542
109	0	0	0	2,421,125	40,000,000	30,800,000	82,030,119
110	0	0	0	1,106,780	40,000,000	30,800,000	81,762,929
111	0	0	0	0	39,815,082	30,800,000	81,487,234
112	0	0	0	0	38,545,648	30,800,000	81,203,294
113	0	0	0	0	37,298,104	30,800,000	80,911,362
153	0	0	0	0	1,715,140	30,800,000	65,030,732
154	0	0	0	0	1,107,570	30,800,000	64,575,431
155	0	0	0	0	510,672	30,800,000	64,119,075
156	0	0	0	0	0	30,724,266	63,661,761
157	0	0	0	0	0	30,148,172	63,203,587
158	0	0	0	0	0	29,582,215	62,744,644
347	0	0	0	0	0	29,003	1,697,536
348	0	0	0	0	0	16,058	1,545,142
349	0	0	0	0	0	3,432	1,394,152
350	0	0	0	0	0	0	1,235,674
351	0	0	0	0	0	0	1,075,454
352	0	0	0	0	0	0	916,910
353	0	0	0	0	0	0	760,026
354	0	0	0	0	0	0	604,789
355	0	0	0	0	0	0	451,182
356	0	0	0	0	0	0	299,191
357	0	0	0	0	0	0	148,801

Effect on Average Life

Exhibit 11 shows the average life for the six PAC bonds and the support bond in FRR-11 at various prepayment speeds. From a PAC bond in FRR-10 with an average life of 7.26, we have created six bonds with an average life as short as 2.58 years (P-A) and as long as 16.92 years (P-F) if prepayments stay within 90 PSA and 300 PSA.

As expected, the average lives are stable if the prepayment speed is between 90 PSA and 300 PSA. Notice that even outside this range the average life is stable for several of the PAC bonds. For example, the PAC P-A bond is stable even if prepayment speeds are as high as 400 PSA. For the PAC P-B, the average life does not vary when prepayments are in the initial collar until prepayments are greater than 350 PSA. Why is it that the shorter the PAC, the more protection it has against faster prepayments?

To understand this phenomenon, remember there are $156.2 million in support bonds that are protecting the $85 million of PAC P-A. Thus, even if prepayments are faster than the initial upper collar, there may be sufficient support bonds to assure the satisfaction of the schedule. In fact, as can be seen from Exhibit 11, even if prepayments are at 400 PSA over the life of the collateral, the average life is unchanged.

Now consider PAC P-B. The support bonds provide protection for both the $85 million of PAC P-A and $93 million of PAC P-B. As can be seen from Exhibit 11, prepayments could be 350 PSA and the average life is still unchanged. From Exhibit 11 it can be seen that the degree of protection against extension risk increases the shorter the PAC. Thus, while the initial collar may be 90 to 300 PSA, the *effective collar* is wider for the shorter PAC tranches.

PAC Window

As we explained in Chapter 4, the length of time over which expected principal repayments are made is referred to as the window. For a PAC bond it is referred to as the *PAC window*. In Exhibit 8, the PAC window for P-B is the number of months between point 1 and point 2; for P-D it is the number of months between point 3 and point 4. A PAC window can be wide or narrow. The narrower a PAC window, the more it resembles a corporate bond with a bullet payment. PAC buyers appear to prefer tight windows, although institutional investors facing a liability schedule are generally better off with a window that more closely matches the liabilities.

Investor demand dictates the PAC windows that issuers will create. Investor demand in turn is governed by the nature of investor liabilities.

Exhibit 11: Average Life for the Six PAC Bonds in FRR-11 Assuming Various Prepayment Speeds

Prepayment rate (PSA)	PAC Bonds					
	P-A	P-B	P-C	P-D	P-E	P-F
0	8.46	14.61	16.49	19.41	21.91	23.76
50	3.58	6.82	8.36	11.30	14.50	18.20
90	2.58	4.72	5.78	7.89	10.83	16.92
100	2.58	4.72	5.78	7.89	10.83	16.92
150	2.58	4.72	5.78	7.89	10.83	16.92
165	2.58	4.72	5.78	7.89	10.83	16.92
200	2.58	4.72	5.78	7.89	10.83	16.92
250	2.58	4.72	5.78	7.89	10.83	16.92
300	2.58	4.72	5.78	7.89	10.83	16.92
350	2.58	4.72	5.94	6.95	9.24	14.91
400	2.57	4.37	4.91	6.17	8.33	13.21
450	2.50	3.97	4.44	5.56	7.45	11.81
500	2.40	3.65	4.07	5.06	6.74	10.65
700	2.06	2.82	3.10	3.75	4.88	7.51

EFFECTIVE COLLARS AND ACTUAL PREPAYMENTS

As we have emphasized several times, the creation of a mortgage-backed security cannot make prepayment risk disappear. This is true for both a passthrough and a CMO. Thus, the reduction in prepayment risk (both extension risk and contraction risk) that a PAC offers must come from somewhere.

Where does the prepayment protection come from? It comes from the support bonds. It is the support bonds that forgo principal payments if the collateral prepayments are slow; support bonds do not receive any principal until the PAC bonds receive the scheduled principal repayment. This reduces the risk that the PAC bonds will extend. Similarly, it is the support bonds that absorb any principal payments in excess of the scheduled principal payments that are made. This reduces the contraction risk of the PAC bonds. Thus, the key to the prepayment protection offered by a PAC bond is the amount of support bonds outstanding. If the support bonds are paid off quickly because of faster-than-expected prepayments, then there is no longer any protection for the PAC bonds. In fact, in FRR-11, if the support bond is paid off, the structure is effectively reduced to a sequential-pay CMO.

The support bonds can be thought of as bodyguards for the PAC bondholders. When the bullets fly — i.e., prepayments occur — it is the bodyguards that get killed off first. The bodyguards are there to absorb the bullets. Once all the bodyguards are killed off (i.e., the support bonds paid off with faster-than-expected prepayments), the PAC bonds must fend for themselves: they are exposed to all the bullets.

**Exhibit 12: Average Life For PAC Tranches of FRR-11
One Year From Now Assuming Various Prepayment Speeds
for the First 12 Months**

First 12 mos.	Thereafter	Speed for: PAC					
		P-A	P-B	P-C	P-D	P-E	P-F
90 PSA	90 PSA	1.81	3.72	4.77	6.89	9.82	15.91
100 PSA	100 PSA	1.81	3.72	4.77	6.89	9.82	15.91
165 PSA	165 PSA	1.81	3.72	4.77	6.89	9.82	15.91
200 PSA	200 PSA	1.81	3.72	4.77	6.89	9.82	15.91
300 PSA	300 PSA	1.81	3.72	4.77	6.89	9.82	15.91
400 PSA	400 PSA	1.80	3.37	3.90	5.17	7.32	12.21
600 PSA	600 PSA	1.41	2.16	2.50	3.29	4.65	7.83
800 PSA	800 PSA	1.09	1.56	1.79	2.34	3.28	5.48
First 12 mos.	Thereafter	Speed for: PAC					
		P-A	P-B	P-C	P-D	P-E	P-F
42 CPR	90 PSA	2.73	6.17	8.26	12.78	18.86	25.42
42 CPR	100 PSA	2.52	5.69	7.63	11.92	17.93	24.92
42 CPR	165 PSA	1.70	3.77	5.06	8.08	12.91	21.07
42 CPR	200 PSA	1.46	3.19	4.28	6.83	11.03	18.94
42 CPR	300 PSA	1.05	2.24	2.96	4.69	7.61	13.97
42 CPR	400 PSA	0.84	1.74	2.28	3.55	5.72	10.67
42 CPR	600 PSA	0.60	1.23	1.57	2.37	3.73	6.92
42 CPR	800 PSA	0.47	0.97	1.22	1.77	2.71	4.92

The top panel of Exhibit 12 shows what happens to the average life for all PAC tranches of FRR-11 one year from now if prepayments for the first 12 months are the speed shown and the future speed is the same as the first 12 months. For example, if the collateral prepays at 165 PSA for the first 12 months and then prepays at the same speed thereafter, the average life one year from now will be 1.81 years. Notice that for all the PAC tranches the average life is still stable for the initial collar. In contrast, the second panel shows what will happen to the average life one year from now if the collateral pays at 42 CPR for the first 12 months and prepays at the indicated speed thereafter. We selected 42 CPR so the support bonds will be paid off by the end of the first year. The structure is now effectively a sequential-pay structure and, as indicated by the average lives reported in the exhibit, there is substantial average life variability for the original PAC tranches. A comparison of the lower and upper panel clearly demonstrates the role of the support bonds.

With the bodyguard metaphor for the support bonds in mind, let's consider two questions asked by CMO buyers:

1. Will the schedule of principal repayments be satisfied if prepayments are faster than the initial upper collar?

2. Will the schedule of principal repayments be satisfied as long as prepayments stay within the initial collar?

Actual Prepayments Greater than the Initial Upper Collar

Let's address the first question. The initial upper collar for FRR-11 is 300 PSA? Suppose that actual prepayments are 500 PSA for seven consecutive months; will this disrupt the schedule of principal repayments? The answer is: It depends!

There are two pieces of information we will need to answer this question. First, when does the 500 PSA occur? Second, what has been the actual prepayment experience up to the time that prepayments are 500 PSA? For example, suppose six years from now is when the prepayments reach 500 PSA, and also suppose that for the past six years the actual prepayment speed has been 90 PSA every month. What this means is that there are more bodyguards (i.e., support bonds) around than was expected when the PAC was structured at the initial collar. In establishing the schedule of principal repayments, it was assumed that the bodyguards would be killed off at 300 PSA. But the actual prepayment experience results in them being killed off at only 90 PSA. Thus, six years from now, when the 500 PSA is assumed to occur, there are more bodyguards than expected. In turn, a 500 PSA for seven consecutive months may have no effect on the ability of the schedule of principal repayments to be met.

In contrast, suppose that the actual prepayment experience for the first six years is 300 PSA (the upper collar of the initial PAC collar). In this case, there are no extra bodyguards around. As a result, any prepayment speeds faster than 300 PSA, such as 500 PSA in our example, jeopardize satisfaction of the principal repayment schedule and increase extension risk. This does not mean that the schedule will be "busted" — the term used in the CMO market when a PAC schedule is broken. What it does mean is that the prepayment protection is reduced.

It should be clear from these observations that the initial collars are not particularly useful in assessing the prepayment protection for a seasoned PAC bond. This is most important to understand, as it is common for CMO buyers to compare prepayment protection of PACs in different CMO structures, and conclude that the greater protection is offered by the one with the wider collar. This approach is inadequate because it is actual prepayment experience that determines the degree of prepayment protection, as well as the expected future prepayment behavior of the collateral.

The way to determine this protection is to calculate the effective collar for a seasoned PAC bond. An effective collar for a seasoned PAC is the lower and the upper PSA that can occur in the future and still allow maintenance of the schedule of principal repayments.

The effective collar changes every month. An extended period over which actual prepayments are below the upper range of the initial PAC collar will result in an increase in the upper range of the effective collar. This is because there will be more bodyguards around than anticipated. An extended period of prepayments slower than the lower range of the initial PAC collar will raise the lower range of the effective collar. This is because it will take faster prepayments to make up the shortfall of the scheduled principal payments not made plus the scheduled future principal payments.

Actual Prepayments within the Initial Collar

The PAC schedule may not be satisfied even if the actual prepayments never fall outside of the initial collar. This may seem surprising since our previous analysis indicated that the average life would not change if prepayments are at either extreme of the initial collar. However, recall that all of our previous analysis has been based on a single PSA speed for the life of the structure.

Let's use vector analysis to see what happens to the effective collar if the prepayments are at the initial upper collar for a certain number of months. Exhibit 13 shows the average life two years from now for the PAC bond in FRR-10 assuming that prepayments are 300 PSA for the first 24 months. Notice that the average life is stable at six years if the prepayments for the following months are between 115 PSA and 300 PSA. That is, the effective PAC collar is no longer the initial collar. Instead, the lower collar has shifted upward. This means that the protection from year 2 on is for 115 to 300 PSA, a narrower band than initially even though the earlier prepayments did not exceed the initial upper collar.

PROVIDING GREATER PROTECTION: LOCKOUTS AND REVERSE PAC STRUCTURES

There are two ways to provide greater protection for PAC bonds: lockout structures and reverse PAC structures.

Exhibit 13: Average Life Two Years from Now for PAC Bond of FRR-10 Assuming Prepayments of 300 PSA for First 24 Months

PSA from Year 2 on	Average Life
95	6.43
105	6.11
115	6.01
120	6.00
125	6.00
300	6.00
305	5.62

Lockout Structures

One obvious way to provide greater protection for PAC bonds is to issue fewer PAC bonds relative to support bonds. In FRR-11, for example, rather than creating the six PAC bonds with a total par value of $243.8 million, we could use only $158.8 million of the $400 million of collateral to create these bonds, by reducing the amount of each of the six PAC bonds. An alternative is not to issue one of the PAC bonds, typically the shorter-term one. For example, suppose that we create only the last five of the six PAC bonds in FRR-11. The $85 million for PAC P-A is then used to create more support bonds. Such a CMO structure with no principal payments to a PAC bond class in the earlier years is referred to as a *lockout structure*.

Exhibit 14 shows a lockout structure, which we create by not issuing Class P-A in FRR-11. We will call this CMO FRR-12. Exhibit 15 gives the average life for the five PAC bonds in FRR-12. Notice that at prepayment speeds less than 90 PSA, there is less variance in average lives within the PAC collar of 90 to 350 PSA than in FRR-11 (see Exhibit 11).

Reverse PAC Bond Structures

A lockout structure provides greater prepayment protection to all PAC bonds in the CMO structure. One way to provide greater prepayment protection to only some PAC bonds is to alter the principal payment rules for distributing principal once all the support bonds have been paid off.

In FRR-11, for example, once the support bond in this structure is paid off, the structure effectively becomes a sequential-pay structure. For PAC P-A this means that while there is protection against extension risk, as this tranche receives principal payments before the other five PAC bonds, there is no protection against contraction.

Exhibit 14: FRR-12 CMO Lockout Structure with Five PAC Bonds and One Support Bond

Tranche	Par amount	Coupon rate (%)
P-B	8,000,000	7.5
P-C	35,000,000	7.5
P-D	45,000,000	7.5
P-E	40,000,000	7.5
P-F	30,800,000	7.5
S	241,200,000	7.5
Total	$400,000,000	

Payment rules:

1. For payment of periodic coupon interest: Disburse periodic coupon interest to each tranche on the basis of the amount of principal outstanding at the beginning of the period.

2. For disbursement of principal payments: Disburse principal payments to tranches P-B to P-F based on their respective schedules of principal repayments. Tranche P-B has priority with respect to current and future principal payments to satisfy the schedule. Any excess principal payments in a month beyond the amount necessary to satisfy the schedule for tranche P-B are paid to tranche S. Once tranche P-B is completely paid off, tranche P-C has priority, then tranche P-D, etc. When tranche S is completely paid off, all principal payments are to be made to the remaining PAC tranches in order of priority, regardless of the schedule.

Exhibit 15: Average Life for the Five PAC Bonds in FRR-12 Assuming Various Prepayment Speeds

Prepayment rate (PSA)	PAC Bonds				
	P-B	P-C	P-D	P-E	P-F
0	5.34	9.00	13.91	17.64	29.46
50	4.81	6.30	9.17	12.32	17.07
90	4.72	5.78	7.89	10.83	16.92
100	4.72	5.78	7.89	10.83	16.92
150	4.72	5.78	7.89	10.83	16.92
165	4.72	5.78	7.89	10.83	16.92
200	4.72	5.78	7.89	10.83	16.92
250	4.72	5.78	7.89	10.83	16.92
300	4.72	5.78	7.89	10.83	16.92
350	4.72	5.94	6.95	9.24	14.91
400	4.39	4.95	6.17	8.33	13.21
450	3.97	4.44	5.56	7.45	11.81
500	3.65	4.07	5.06	6.74	10.65
700	2.82	3.10	3.75	4.88	7.51

To provide greater protection to PAC P-A, the payment rules after all support bonds have been paid off can be specified so that any principal payments in excess of the scheduled amount will be paid to the last PAC bond, P-F. Thus, PAC P-F is exposed to greater contraction risk, which provides the other five PAC bonds with more protection against contraction risk. The principal payment rules would also specify that once the support bond and PAC P-F bond are paid off, then all principal payments in excess of the scheduled amounts to earlier tranches are to be paid to the next to the last PAC bond, PAC P-E in our example.

A CMO structure requiring any excess principal payments to be made to the longer PAC bonds after all support bonds are paid off is called a *reverse PAC structure.*

THE WIDE VARIETY OF PAC BONDS

We have described how the collateral can be used to create a CMO with accrual bonds, floaters, inverse floaters, interest-only bonds, principal-only bonds, inverse interest-only bonds, and more. These same types of bond classes can be created from a PAC bond. The difference between the bond classes described in previous chapters and those created from a PAC bond is simply the prepayment protection offered by the PAC structure.

For example, in FRR-11, suppose that we want to create a floater and an inverse floater from the $30.8 million of PAC P-F. This can be done in the manner described in Chapter 5. We can call this structure FRR-13, summarized in Exhibit 16. There are now seven PAC bonds, with P-F being split into a floater (P-FF) with a par value of $23.1 million and an inverse floater (P-IFF) with a par value of $7.7 million. The coupon rate formula for the PAC floater and PAC inverse floater is shown in Exhibit 14. The schedule of principal repayments for these two PAC bonds is the same as for FRR-11 (see Exhibit 10), with each scheduled principal payment distributed in proportion to the par value of the two classes relative to the total of the PAC from which they are created. Since $23.1 million of the $30.8 million PAC P-F is used to create the floater and $7.7 million to create the inverse floater, the floater will receive 75% ($23.1/$30.8) of the amount indicated in the schedule of principal repayments for Class P-F in FRR-11, and the inverse floater will receive the balance, 25%. The average life is the same as for Class P-F in each prepayment rate scenario.

Exhibit 16: FRR-13 – CMO Structure with Seven PAC Bonds (Including a Floater and an Inverse Floater) and One Support Bond

Tranche	Par amount	Coupon rate (%)
P-A	$ 85,000,000	7.50
P-B	8,000,000	7.50
P-C	35,000,000	7.50
P-D	45,000,000	7.50
P-E	40,000,000	7.50
P-FF	23,100,000	One-month LIBOR + 0.5
P-IFF	7,700,000	$28.5 - 3 \times$ LIBOR
S	156,200,000	7.50
Total	$400,000,000	

Payment rules:

1. For payment of periodic coupon interest: Disburse periodic coupon interest to each tranche on the basis of the amount of principal outstanding at the beginning of the period. A maximum coupon rate is set for P-FF at 10%. A minimum coupon rate for P-IFF is set at 0%.

2. For disbursement of principal payments: Disburse principal payments to tranches P-A, P-B, P-C, P-D, P-E, P-FF, and P-IFF according to their respective schedules of principal repayments. Tranche P-A has priority with respect to current and future principal payments to satisfy the schedule. Any excess principal payments in a month over the amount necessary to satisfy the schedule for tranche P-A are paid to tranche S. Once tranche P-A is completely paid off, tranche P-B has priority, then tranche P-C, etc. When tranche S is completely paid off, all principal payments are to be made to the remaining PAC tranches in order of priority regardless of the schedule.

Creation of a PAC IO

Now let's consider how to create a PAC IO in a structure in which the coupon rate is not the same for each PAC tranche. A CMO structure with a PAC IO is FRR-14 described in Exhibit 17. This structure has the same six PAC tranches with different coupon rates, a PAC IO, and a residual class. The PAC IO is created from stripping the excess interest from the first five PAC tranches. In the previous chapter, we described how to strip off the excess interest from a sequential-pay tranches to create an IO class. The same procedure was followed here to create a PAC IO with a coupon rate of 7.5% and a notional amount of $27,333,333. The determination of the notional amount for the PAC IO is shown below:

Tranche	Par amount	Excess interest	Notional amount for a 7.5% coupon rate IO
P-A	$85,000,000	1.50%	$17,000,000
P-B	8,000,000	1.25%	1,333,333
P-C	35,000,000	1.00%	4,666,667
P-D	45,000,000	0.50%	3,000,000
P-E	40,000,000	0.25%	1,333,333
Notional amount for 7.5% PAC IO:			$27,333,333

Exhibit 17: FRR-14 – CMO Structure with Six PAC Bonds, a PAC IO, and One Support Bond

Tranche	Par amount	Coupon rate (%)
P-A	$ 85,000,000	6.00
P-B	8,000,000	6.25
P-C	35,000,000	6.50
P-D	45,000,000	7.00
P-E	40,000,000	7.25
P-F	30,800,000	7.50
P-IO	27,333,333 (notional)	7.50
S	156,200,000	7.50
R	0	0
Total	$400,000,000	

Payment rules:

1. For payment of periodic coupon interest: Disburse periodic coupon interest to each tranche on the basis of the amount of principal outstanding at the beginning of the period. Disburse periodic interest to the P-IO tranche based on the notional amount at the beginning of the period.

2. For disbursement of principal payments: Disburse principal payments to tranches P-A to P-F based on their respective schedules of principal repayments. Tranche P-A has priority with respect to current and future principal payments to satisfy the schedule. Any excess principal payments in a month over the amount necessary to satisfy the schedule for tranche P-A are paid to tranche S. Once tranche P-A is completely paid off, tranche P-B has priority, then tranche P-C, etc. When tranche S is completely paid off, all principal payments are to be made to the remaining PAC tranches in order of priority regardless of the schedule.

3. No principal is to be paid to the P-IO tranche. The notional amount of the IO tranche declines based on the principal payments to all other tranches.

To understand the prepayment protection afforded the PAC IO, it is important to identify the PAC tranche components that were used to create it. Shown below is the percentage of the notional amount of each PAC tranche as a percentage of the notional amount of the PAC IO:

PAC Tranche	$\dfrac{\text{Notional amount from PAC tranche}}{\text{Notional amount of PAC IO}}$
A	62.195%
B	4.878%
C	17.073%
D	10.976%
E	4.878%

An investor should recognize that a PAC IO is a combination of PAC IOs with different effective bands. The PAC IO in FRR-14 is heavily weighted on the short end.

Exhibit 18: FRR-15 – CMO Structure with Six PAC Bonds, a High Coupon PAC, One Support Bond, and a Residual

Tranche	Par amount	Coupon rate (%)
P-A	$ 42,500,000	6.00
P-B	4,363,636	6.25
P-C	21,000,000	6.50
P-D	33,750,000	7.00
P-E	34,800,000	7.25
P-F	30,800,000	7.50
P-H	77,100,650	9.00
S	156,200,000	7.50
R	0	0
Total	$400,000,000	

Payment rules:

1. For payment of periodic coupon interest: Disburse periodic coupon interest to each tranche on the basis of the amount of principal outstanding at the beginning of the period.

2. For disbursement of principal payments: Disburse principal payments to tranches P-A to P-F and P-H based on their respective schedules of principal repayments. Tranches P-A and P-H have priority with respect to current and future principal payments to satisfy the schedule. Any excess principal payments in a month over the amount necessary to satisfy the schedule for tranches P-A and P-H are paid to tranche S. Once tranche P-A is completely paid off, tranches P-B and P-H have priority, then tranches P-C and P-H, etc. When tranche S is completely paid off, all principal payments are to be made to the remaining PAC tranches in order of priority regardless of the schedule. When there is any shortfall of principal to be paid to a current paying PAC tranche, the amount is to be divided between a PAC tranche and P-H as follows:

P-A	50.000%	P-H	50.000%
P-B	54.545%	P-H	45.455%
P-C	60.000%	P-H	40.000%
P-D	75.000%	P-H	25.000%
P-E	85.714%	P-H	14.286%

Creation of a High Coupon PAC (Premium PAC)

In the previous chapter we described how to create a high coupon bond from sequential-pay tranches. The same procedure can be used to create a high coupon PAC. For example, suppose a high coupon PAC with a 9% coupon rate is sought. It can be created from the first five PACs: the structure is shown in Exhibit 18 (FRR-15). The high coupon bond is P-H and the par amount for this tranche is $77,100,650 as shown below:

Tranche	Par amount to be split	Excess interest	Percentage allocated to tranche P-H	Par amount in FRR-15 Tranche P-H	Tranche
P-A	$ 85,000,000	1.50%	50.000%	$42,500,000	$42,500,000
P-B	8,000,000	1.25%	45.455%	3,636,364	4,363,636
P-C	35,000,000	1.00%	40.000%	14,000,000	21,000,000
P-D	45,000,000	0.50%	25.000%	11,250,000	33,750,000
P-E	40,000,000	0.25%	14.286%	5,714,286	34,285,714
Total par amount for Tranche P-H:				$77,100,650	

The schedule of principal payments for tranche P-H is proportional to the principal payments of the original schedule prior to the creation of the high coupon tranche. The percentage shown in the table above indicates how the principal will be divided between the current paying PAC tranche and the high coupon tranche.

Also as explained in the previous chapter, a high coupon tranche can be stripped to create either (1) a floater and an inverse IO floater combination or (2) a floater, an inverse IO floater, and a TTIB IO combination. This can also be done for the high coupon PAC in FRR-15.

Chapter 7

TAC BONDS, VADM BONDS, AND SUPPORT BONDS

In this chapter, we discuss three bond classes: targeted amortization class bonds, very accurately determined maturity bonds, and support bonds.

TARGETED AMORTIZATION CLASS BONDS

A Targeted Amortization Class, or TAC, bond resembles a PAC bond in that both have a schedule of principal repayment. The difference between a PAC bond and a TAC bond is that the former has a wide PSA range over which the schedule of principal repayment is protected against contraction risk and extension risk. A TAC bond, in contrast, has a single PSA rate from which the schedule of principal repayment is protected. As a result, the prepayment protection afforded the TAC bond is less than that for a PAC bond. As we shall see, the creation of a bond with a schedule of principal repayments based on a single prepayment rate results in protection against contraction risk but not extension risk. Thus, while PAC bonds are said to have two-sided prepayment protection, TAC bonds have one-sided prepayment protection. Such a bond is acceptable to institutional investors who are not overly concerned with some extension risk but greatly concerned with contraction risk.

As an example of a CMO structure with a TAC bond, consider FRR-16, which has one TAC bond and one support bond. The collateral for this structure is the same $400 million passthrough that we have used throughout this book. The par value for the TAC bond is $350 of the $400 million, and the par value for the support bond is $50 million. The TAC bond schedule is generated for a prepayment rate of 165 PSA. The average life at this speed is 6.86 years. Exhibit 1 summarizes the structure of FRR-16; Exhibit 2 gives the principal repayment schedule and ending outstanding balance for selected months for the TAC bond.

Average Life

The TAC bond is designed to have protection against contraction risk but not extension risk. To see this, let's look at four scenarios for the prepayment speeds for the collateral:

Scenario 1: The collateral pays at exactly 165 PSA for its entire life.

Scenario 2: The collateral pays at less than 165 PSA for its entire life.

Scenario 3: The collateral pays faster than 165 PSA but slower than 235 PSA for its entire life.

Scenario 4: The collateral pays faster than 235 PSA for its entire life.

Exhibit 3 reports the average life for the TAC bond and the support bond for these scenarios.

Scenario 1: In this scenario, the schedule of principal repayments will be met because the TAC bond was created assuming a prepayment rate of 165 PSA. The average life is 6.86 years.

Scenario 2: The principal payments from the collateral will not be sufficient to satisfy the schedule in the earlier years. Usually, the principal payments in later years will be sufficient to make up the shortfall and to get back on schedule. In FRR-16, for example, there would be a shortfall in the principal payments from months 1 to 273 if the collateral prepays at 100 PSA.

As can be seen from Exhibit 3, the average life of the TAC bond extends to 9.62 years at 100 PSA. The extension is greater at slower speeds.

Exhibit 1: FRR-16 – CMO Structure with One TAC Bond and One Support Bond

Tranche	Par amount	Coupon rate (%)
T (TAC)	$350,000,000	7.50
S (Support)	50,000,000	7.50
Total	$400,000,000	

Payment rules:

1. For payment of periodic coupon interest: Disburse periodic coupon interest to each tranche based on the amount of principal outstanding at the beginning of the period.

2. For disbursement of principal payments: Disburse principal payments to tranche T based on its schedule of principal repayments. Tranche T has priority with respect to current and future principal payments to satisfy the schedule. Any excess principal payments in a month over the amount necessary to satisfy the schedule for tranche T are paid to tranche S. When tranche S is completely paid off, all principal payments are to be made to tranche T regardless of the schedule.

Exhibit 2: Schedule of Principal Repayments for TAC Tranche and Corresponding End of Month Outstanding Balance for Selected Months for FRR-16 (Based on 165 PSA)

Month	Repayment schedule	Ending balance
1	709,923	349,290,076
2	821,895	348,468,180
3	933,559	347,534,621
4	1,044,821	346,489,799
5	1,155,586	345,334,213
6	1,265,759	344,068,454
7	1,375,246	342,693,207
8	1,483,954	341,209,253
9	1,591,789	339,617,464
10	1,698,659	337,918,804
11	1,804,472	336,114,332
12	1,909,138	334,205,193
207	647,483	1,394,761
208	641,500	753,261
209	635,570	117,690
210	117,690	0
211	0	0
212	0	0
213	0	0
353	0	0
354	0	0
355	0	0
356	0	0
357	0	0

Exhibit 3: Average Life for the TAC Bond in FRR-16 For Various Assumed Prepayment Rates

Prepayment Rate (PSA)	TAC Bond	Support Bond
0	19.14	29.06
50	13.28	28.07
90	10.21	26.56
100	9.62	26.07
150	7.36	23.15
165	6.86	22.21
200	7.00	12.58
220	7.15	7.39
230	7.27	4.67
235	7.36	3.07
250	7.10	2.43
300	6.21	1.71
350	5.49	1.40
400	4.92	1.21
450	4.46	1.08
500	4.08	0.98
700	3.08	0.73

Scenario 3: If the prepayment speed is greater than 165 PSA but less than 235 PSA, the schedule of principal repayments can be satisfied until all the support bonds are paid off. At that time, the principal payments available from the remaining collateral will be insufficient to meet the schedule of principal repayments for a period of time. After that time, however, the principal payments from the remaining collateral will be sufficient to meet the schedule of principal repayments for the TAC bond. As can be seen in Exhibit 3, the average life assuming various prepayment rates between 165 PSA and 235 PSA reported in Exhibit 3 indicates that the extension could be as long as 7.36 years.

Scenario 4: If the prepayment speed is greater than 235 PSA over the life of the collateral, the average life will shorten. The average life would shorten from 6.86 years assuming 165 PSA to 3.08 years if the collateral speed is 700 PSA.

These scenarios clearly indicate how, assuming a constant PSA speed over the life of the collateral, the TAC bond is protected against contraction risk but exposed to extension risk. The drawback of this analysis, as we noted elsewhere, is that it assumes the PSA speed will be constant. Vector prepayment analysis — i.e., sets of prepayment speeds — provides better insight into what might occur.

As in the case of PAC bonds where the effective collar changes each month depending on the actual prepayment experience, the PSA rate at which the TAC bond is protected also changes each month when the actual prepayment experience is different from the initial PSA rate used to create the TAC bond. It is possible for there to be a narrow collar for the TAC bond. To understand why, once again consider what happens to the support bonds when prepayments are slower than the 165 PSA rate used to create the TAC bond in FRR-16. There are more bodyguards — the support bonds — than would exist if the prepayment speed is 165 PSA. It is therefore possible that the prepayments can be slightly slower or faster than 165 PSA and still meet the schedule of principal repayments.

Creating a Series of TACs

In the PAC bond CMO structure FRR-11, we carved up the PAC bond and created a series of PAC bonds in which each individual PAC bond has a different average life. The same can be done with the TAC bond in FRR-12. We have done this in FRR-17, which has six TAC bonds, T-A, T-B, T-C, T-D, T-E, and T-F. This structure is summarized in Exhibit 4. Exhibit 5 shows the average life for the six TAC bonds under the same scenarios as used in Exhibit 3. The exhibit shows how the average life stability differs for each TAC bond.

Reverse TAC Bond Structures

Some institutional investors are interested in protection against extension risk but are willing to accept contraction risk. This is the opposite protection from that sought by the buyers of TAC bonds. The structures created to provide such protection are referred to as *reverse TAC bonds*.

For example, a reverse TAC structure can be created by splitting the collateral as follows: $250 million to create the reverse TAC tranche and $150 million for the support bond. The principal repayment schedule is generated assuming a prepayment speed of 90 PSA. The average life assuming 90 PSA is 6.85 years. Exhibit 6 reports the average life for various prepayment speeds for the resulting reverse TAC structure.

There are four scenarios here:

Scenario 1: The collateral pays at exactly 90 PSA for its entire life. In this scenario, the average life is 6.85 years.

Exhibit 4: FRR-17 – CMO Structure
with Six TAC Bonds and One Support Bond

Tranche	Par amount	Coupon rate (%)
T-A	$135,000,000	7.50
T-B	8,000,000	7.50
T-C	55,000,000	7.50
T-D	40,000,000	7.50
T-E	75,000,000	7.50
T-F	37,000,000	7.50
S	50,000,000	7.50
Total	$400,000,000	

Payment rules:

1. For payment of periodic coupon interest: Disburse periodic coupon interest to each tranche based on the amount of principal outstanding at the beginning of the period.

2. For disbursement of principal payments: Disburse principal payments to tranches T-A to T-F based on their respective schedule of principal repayments. Tranche T-A has priority with respect to current and future principal payments to satisfy the schedule. Any excess principal payments in a month over the amount necessary to satisfy the schedule for tranche T-A are paid to tranche S. Once tranche T-A is completely paid off, tranche T-B has priority, then tranche T-C, etc. When tranche S is completely paid off, all principal payments are to be made to the remaining classes with a schedule in order of priority regardless of the schedule.

Exhibit 5: Average Life for FRR-17
Assuming Various Prepayment Rates

Prepayment rate (PSA)	T-A	T-B	T-C	T-D	T-E	T-F
0	11.41	18.66	20.64	23.18	25.65	27.69
50	5.34	10.45	12.80	16.41	20.79	24.97
90	3.76	7.25	9.05	12.04	16.43	21.58
100	3.52	6.74	8.41	11.23	15.47	20.66
150	2.72	5.03	6.24	8.35	11.75	16.45
165	2.56	4.69	5.81	7.75	10.92	15.38
200	2.56	4.69	5.81	7.75	11.04	16.43
220	2.56	4.69	5.81	7.75	11.17	17.60
230	2.56	4.69	5.81	7.75	11.25	18.58
235	2.56	4.69	5.81	7.75	11.30	19.42
250	2.56	4.69	5.64	7.38	10.75	18.64
300	2.45	4.08	4.89	6.32	9.17	16.23
350	2.28	3.63	4.30	5.54	7.99	14.24
400	2.13	3.29	3.87	4.95	7.07	12.61
450	2.00	3.03	3.53	4.48	6.35	11.27
500	1.89	2.81	3.26	4.10	5.76	10.16
700	1.58	2.26	2.56	3.12	4.22	7.18

Exhibit 6: Average Life for Reverse TAC Structure Assuming Various Prepayment Rates (Created Assuming 90 PSA)

Prepayment rate (PSA)	Reverse TAC	Support Bond
0	16.17	27.39
50	9.54	24.44
85	7.10	21.68
90	6.85	21.28
100	6.85	19.71
150	6.86	13.45
165	6.87	11.96
200	6.92	9.00
250	7.08	5.57
300	7.27	2.94
310	7.11	2.80
350	6.52	2.41
400	5.87	2.10
450	5.33	1.88
500	4.88	1.72
700	3.66	1.34

Scenario 2: The collateral pays at less than 85 PSA for its entire life. If this occurs, the reverse TAC bond would extend, with the maximum extension being 16.17 years at 0 PSA.

Scenario 3: The collateral pays faster than 90 PSA but slower than 310 PSA for its entire life. The maximum extension is to 7.27 years if the speed is 300 PSA.

Scenario 4: The collateral pays faster than 310 PSA for its entire life. The average life will decline below 6.85 years.

These scenarios indicate how a reverse TAC bond can contract while providing protection against extension risk.

TAC Bonds as Support Bonds

TAC bonds in a CMO structure were used quite differently in the earlier deals. Today TAC and reverse TAC bonds are created from support bonds and thereby provide support for PAC bonds.

VERY ACCURATELY DETERMINED MATURITY BONDS

Accrual or Z-bonds have been used in CMO structures as support for bonds called *very accurately determined maturity* (VADM) or *guaranteed final maturity* bonds. In this case, the interest accruing (i.e., not being paid out) on a Z bond is used to pay the interest and principal on a VADM bond. This effectively provides protection against extension risk even if prepayments slow down, since the interest accruing on the Z bond will be sufficient to pay off the scheduled principal and interest on the VADM bond. Thus, the maximum final maturity can be determined with a high degree of certainty. If prepayments are high, resulting in the supporting Z bond being paid off faster, however, a VADM bond can shorten.

A VADM is similar in character to a reverse TAC. For structures with similar collateral, however, a VADM bond offers greater protection against extension risk. Moreover, most VADMs will not shorten significantly if prepayments speed up. Thus, they offer greater protection against contraction risk compared to a reverse TAC with the same underlying collateral. Compared to PACs, VADM bonds have greater absolute protection against extension risk, and while VADM bonds do not have as much protection against contraction risk, as noted previously, the structures that have included these bonds are such that contraction risk is generally not significant.

As an illustration of a plain vanilla CMO structure with a VADM, consider FRR-18 in Exhibit 7. The speed assumed is 165 PSA. There are four tranches, V, B, C, and Z. The interest accruing to the Z-bond, or accrual bond, is used to pay down tranche V, the VADM bond. Exhibit 8 shows the outstanding balance for the first 31 months assuming 165 PSA. The final maturity is in month 30. The maximum extension can be determined by determining the mortgage balance assuming no prepayments, that is, 0 PSA. The final maturity in this case would be 83 months.

Exhibit 9 shows a VADM created from a PAC structure. There are five tranches in this structure FRR-19: V, B, C, Z, and S. Tranches V, B, C, and Z are the PAC bonds, and tranche S is the support bond. The VADM bond is tranche V, and the accrual bond from which the interest will be used to pay down the VADM is tranche Z. The PAC bonds are created with a PAC band of 90 to 300 PSA. The corresponding mortgage balances for selected months for each PAC tranche if the prepayment speed is between 90 and 300 PSA are shown in Exhibit 10. The final maturity for the VADM can be seen to be seven years (84 months).

Exhibit 7: FRR-18 –
CMO Sequential-Pay Structure with a VADM

Tranche	Par amount	Coupon rate (%)
V (VADM)	$ 77,000,000	7.50
B	88,000,000	7.50
C	165,000,000	7.50
Z (Accrual)	70,000,000	7.50
Total	$400,000,000	

Payment rules:

1. For payment of periodic coupon interest: Disburse periodic coupon interest to tranches V, B and C based on the amount of principal outstanding at the beginning of the period. The interest earned by tranche Z is to be paid to tranche V as a paydown of principal and accrued as interest to tranche Z.

2. For disbursement of principal payments: Disburse principal payments to tranche V until it is completely paid off. The interest from tranche Z is to be paid to tranche V as a paydown of principal. After tranche V is completely paid off, disburse principal payments to tranche B until it is completely paid off. After tranche B is completely paid off, disburse principal payments to tranche C until it is completely paid off. After tranche C is completely paid off, disburse principal payments to tranche Z until the original mortgage balance plus accrued interest is completely paid off.

Exhibit 8: Mortgage Balance for Months 1-31
for FRR-18 Assuming 165 PSA

	Tranche			
Month	V (VADM)	B	C	Z (Accrual)
1	77,000,000	88,000,000	165,000,000	70,000,000
2	75,852,577	88,000,000	165,000,000	70,437,500
3	74,590,446	88,000,000	165,000,000	70,877,734
4	73,213,901	88,000,000	165,000,000	71,320,720
5	71,723,325	88,000,000	165,000,000	71,766,475
6	70,119,198	88,000,000	165,000,000	72,215,015
7	68,402,095	88,000,000	165,000,000	72,666,359
8	66,572,684	88,000,000	165,000,000	73,120,524
9	64,631,727	88,000,000	165,000,000	73,577,527
10	62,580,078	88,000,000	165,000,000	74,037,387
11	60,418,685	88,000,000	165,000,000	74,500,120
12	58,148,586	88,000,000	165,000,000	74,965,746
27	12,024,369	88,000,000	165,000,000	82,309,747
28	8,225,769	88,000,000	165,000,000	82,824,183
29	4,452,903	88,000,000	165,000,000	83,341,834
30	705,500	88,000,000	165,000,000	83,862,721
31	0	84,983,291	165,000,000	84,386,863

Exhibit 9: FRR-19 – CMO PAC Structure with a VADM

Tranche	Par amount	Coupon rate (%)
V (VADM)	$ 75,000,000	7.5
B	92,800,000	7.5
C	10,000,000	7.5
Z (Accrual)	66,000,000	7.5
S	156,200,000	7.5
Total	$400,000,000	

Payment rules:

1. For payment of periodic coupon interest: Disburse periodic coupon interest to tranches V, B, C, and S on the basis of the amount of principal outstanding at the beginning of the period. The interest earned by tranche Z is to be paid to tranche V as a paydown of principal and accrued as interest to tranche Z.

2. For disbursement of principal payments: Disburse principal payments to tranches V, B, C, and Z based on their respective schedules of principal repayments. Tranches V, B, C, and Z have priority with respect to current and future principal payments to satisfy the schedule. Any excess principal payments in a month over the amount necessary to satisfy the schedule for tranche V are paid to tranche S. Once tranche V is completely paid off, tranche B has priority, then tranche C, etc. When tranche S is completely paid off, all principal payments are to be made to the remaining classes with a schedule in order of priority regardless of the schedule.

Exhibit 11 shows the same information assuming no prepayments (i.e., 0 PSA). As can be seen from this exhibit, the VADM has a final maturity of seven years if no prepayments are made. If the prepayment speed is outside the upper PAC band, the VADM's final maturity will be less than seven years. This can be seen in Exhibit 12, which shows the monthly mortgage balance for selected months for each tranche assuming a prepayment speed of 500 PSA. In this case, the final maturity is 57 months.

The average life for all five tranches assuming a wide range of prepayment scenarios is shown in Exhibit 13. Note the stability of the average life of the VADM bond.

SUPPORT BONDS

The support bonds — or bodyguards — are the bonds that provide prepayment protection for bond classes in a structure providing a schedule of principal repayments — PAC and TAC bonds. Consequently, they are exposed to the greatest level of prepayment risk. We saw this in Chapter 6 for structures with PAC bonds, and earlier in this chapter for structures with TAC bonds, where the average life variability for the support bond was significant. This is the same as saying that the timing of the principal payment or cash flow of support bonds is much less certain than the bond classes they are designed to protect. Because of this, investors must be particularly careful in assessing the cash flow characteristics of support bonds to reduce the likelihood of adverse portfolio consequences due to prepayments.

Exhibit 10: Mortgage Balance for Selected Months for FRR-19 Assuming 90 to 300 PSA

Month	V (VADM)	Tranche B	C	Z (Accrual)
1	75,000,000	92,800,000	10,000,000	66,000,000
2	74,319,965	92,559,365	10,000,000	66,412,500
3	73,635,541	92,258,868	10,000,000	66,827,578
4	72,946,698	91,898,661	10,000,000	67,245,250
5	72,253,409	91,478,925	10,000,000	67,665,533
6	71,555,645	90,999,871	10,000,000	68,088,443
7	70,853,377	90,461,736	10,000,000	68,513,996
8	70,146,575	89,864,789	10,000,000	68,942,208
9	69,435,211	89,209,324	10,000,000	69,373,097
10	68,719,255	88,495,666	10,000,000	69,806,679
11	67,998,676	87,724,168	10,000,000	70,242,971
12	67,273,447	86,895,209	10,000,000	70,681,989
71	15,059,365	4,060,751	10,000,000	102,083,716
72	13,992,276	2,837,012	10,000,000	102,721,740
73	12,918,294	1,623,114	10,000,000	103,363,750
74	11,837,374	419,042	10,000,000	104,009,774
75	10,749,472	0	9,224,783	104,659,835
76	9,654,543	0	8,040,323	105,313,959
77	8,552,541	0	6,865,651	105,972,171
78	7,443,420	0	5,700,752	106,634,497
79	6,327,135	0	4,545,615	107,300,963
80	5,203,639	0	3,400,228	107,971,594
81	4,072,884	0	2,264,578	108,646,416
82	2,934,825	0	1,138,655	109,325,456
83	1,789,415	0	22,447	110,008,740
84	636,604	0	0	109,612,237
85	0	0	0	108,683,625
86	0	0	0	107,124,919
87	0	0	0	105,572,694
345	0	0	0	55,873
346	0	0	0	42,272
347	0	0	0	29,003
348	0	0	0	16,059
349	0	0	0	3,432
350	0	0	0	0

Exhibit 11: Mortgage Balance for Selected Months for FRR-19 Assuming No Prepayments (0 PSA)

Month	V (VADM)	Tranche B	C	Z (Accrual)
1	75,000,000	92,800,000	10,000,000	66,000,000
2	74,319,965	92,800,000	10,000,000	66,412,500
3	73,635,541	92,800,000	10,000,000	66,827,578
4	72,946,698	92,800,000	10,000,000	67,245,250
5	72,253,409	92,800,000	10,000,000	67,665,533
6	71,555,645	92,800,000	10,000,000	68,088,443
7	70,853,377	92,800,000	10,000,000	68,513,996
8	70,146,575	92,800,000	10,000,000	68,942,208
9	69,435,211	92,800,000	10,000,000	69,373,097
10	68,719,255	92,800,000	10,000,000	69,806,679
11	67,998,676	92,800,000	10,000,000	70,242,971
12	67,273,447	92,800,000	10,000,000	70,681,989
80	5,203,639	92,800,000	10,000,000	107,971,594
81	4,072,884	92,800,000	10,000,000	108,646,416
82	2,934,825	92,800,000	10,000,000	109,325,456
83	1,789,415	92,800,000	10,000,000	110,008,740
84	636,604	92,800,000	10,000,000	110,696,295
85	0	92,276,346	10,000,000	111,388,147
86	0	91,108,593	10,000,000	112,084,323
146	0	5,302,864	10,000,000	162,891,520
147	0	3,573,053	10,000,000	163,909,592
148	0	1,832,059	10,000,000	164,934,027
149	0	79,811	10,000,000	165,964,864
150	0	0	8,316,236	167,002,145
151	0	0	6,541,260	168,045,908
152	0	0	4,754,809	169,096,195
153	0	0	2,956,810	170,153,046
154	0	0	1,147,188	171,216,503
155	0	0	0	171,612,472
156	0	0	0	170,856,168
157	0	0	0	170,094,742
158	0	0	0	169,328,161
346	0	0	0	42,272
347	0	0	0	29,003
348	0	0	0	16,059
349	0	0	0	3,432
350	0	0	0	0

Exhibit 12: Mortgage Balance for Selected Months for FRR-19 Assuming 500 PSA

Month		Tranche		
	V (VADM)	B	C	Z (Accrual)
1	75,000,000	92,800,000	10,000,000	66,000,000
2	74,319,965	92,559,365	10,000,000	66,412,500
3	73,635,541	92,258,868	10,000,000	66,827,578
4	72,946,698	91,898,661	10,000,000	67,245,250
5	72,253,409	91,478,925	10,000,000	67,665,533
6	71,555,645	90,999,871	10,000,000	68,088,443
7	70,853,377	90,461,736	10,000,000	68,513,996
8	70,146,575	89,864,789	10,000,000	68,942,208
9	69,435,211	89,209,324	10,000,000	69,373,097
10	68,719,255	88,495,666	10,000,000	69,806,679
11	67,998,676	87,724,168	10,000,000	70,242,971
12	67,273,447	86,895,209	10,000,000	70,681,989
41	25,208,976	51,640,155	10,000,000	84,679,770
42	19,505,934	51,640,155	10,000,000	85,209,019
43	13,954,519	51,640,155	10,000,000	85,741,575
44	8,550,096	51,640,155	10,000,000	86,277,460
45	3,288,165	51,640,155	10,000,000	86,816,694
46	0	49,804,516	10,000,000	87,359,298
47	0	44,814,602	10,000,000	87,905,294
48	0	39,954,464	10,000,000	88,454,702
49	0	35,220,113	10,000,000	89,007,544
50	0	30,607,674	10,000,000	89,563,841
51	0	26,113,388	10,000,000	90,123,615
52	0	21,733,607	10,000,000	90,686,888
53	0	17,464,791	10,000,000	91,253,681
54	0	13,303,503	10,000,000	91,824,016
55	0	9,246,407	10,000,000	92,397,916
56	0	5,290,266	10,000,000	92,975,403
57	0	1,431,940	10,000,000	93,556,500
58	0	0	7,668,379	94,141,228
59	0	0	3,996,624	94,729,610
60	0	0	413,802	95,321,671
61	0	0	0	92,834,557
62	0	0	0	90,020,806
63	0	0	0	87,291,615
64	0	0	0	84,644,459
350	0	0	0	1,049
351	0	0	0	894
352	0	0	0	746
353	0	0	0	606
354	0	0	0	472
355	0	0	0	345
356	0	0	0	224
357	0	0	0	109

Exhibit 13: Average Life of Each Tranche
of FRR-19 Assuming 0 to 700 PSA

PSA	V	B	C	Z	S
			Average Life		
0	3.83	9.88	12.61	19.52	27.26
50	3.83	5.10	8.59	13.80	24.00
90	3.83	3.35	6.51	11.54	20.06
100	3.83	3.35	6.51	11.54	18.56
150	3.83	3.35	6.51	11.54	12.57
165	3.83	3.35	6.51	11.54	11.16
200	3.83	3.35	6.51	11.54	8.38
250	3.83	3.35	6.51	11.54	5.37
300	3.83	3.35	6.51	11.54	3.13
350	3.60	3.41	6.26	10.27	2.51
400	3.26	3.39	5.70	9.24	2.17
450	2.98	3.30	5.24	8.38	1.94
500	2.74	3.19	4.85	7.65	1.77
700	2.16	2.71	3.76	5.64	1.37

Types of Support Bonds

In the CMO structures we created in this and the previous chapter, there was only one support bond. In actual deals the support bond typically is divided into different bond classes. All the bond classes we have discussed in previous chapters are available, including sequential-pay support bond classes, floater and inverse floater support bond classes, accrual support bond classes, deep discount and premium support bond classes, interest-only and principal-only support bond classes.

The support bond can even be partitioned so as to create support bond classes with a schedule of principal repayments. That is, support bond classes that are PAC bonds or TAC bonds can be created. In a structure with a PAC bond and a support bond with a PAC schedule of principal repayments, the former is called a PAC I bond or Level I PAC bond and the latter a PAC II bond or Level II PAC bond. While PAC II bonds have greater prepayment protection than the support bond classes without a schedule of principal repayments, the prepayment protection is less than that provided PAC I bonds.

Exhibit 14: FRR-20 – CMO Structure with a PAC I Bond, a PAC II Bond, and a Support Bond Class without a Principal Repayment Schedule

Tranche	Par amount	Coupon rate (%)
P-I (PAC I)	$243,800,000	7.50
P-II (PAC II)	50,330,000	7.50
S	105,870,000	7.50
Total	$400,000,000	

Payment rules:

1. For payment of periodic coupon interest: Disburse periodic coupon interest to each tranche based on the amount of principal outstanding at the beginning of the period.

2. For disbursement of principal payments: Disburse principal payments to tranche P-I based on its schedule of principal repayments. Tranche P-I has priority with respect to current and future principal payments to satisfy the schedule. Any excess principal payments in a month over the amount necessary to satisfy the schedule for tranche P are paid to tranches P-II and S. Priority is given to tranche P-II to satisfy its schedule of principal repayments. Any excess principal payments in a month are paid to tranche S. When tranche S has completely paid off its original balance, then any excess is to be paid to tranche P-II regardless of its schedule. After tranche P-II has completely paid off its original mortgage balance, any excess is paid to tranche P-I regardless of its schedule.

Support Bonds with PAC Schedules

As an illustration of a PAC II bond and its average life variability, consider FRR-10. This structure has one PAC bond with a par value of $243.8 million and one support bond with a par value of $156.2 million. Let's divide the $156.2 million support bond into two bond classes. From $50.33 million a PAC II bond with an initial collar of 100 PSA and 225 PSA will be created. The new structure is FRR-20, summarized in Exhibit 14. There are three bond classes in this structure: a PAC I bond (P-I), and two support bond classes, a PAC II bond (P-II) and a support bond class without a schedule of principal repayments (S).

The principal repayment schedule is determined according to several steps.

Step 1: Generate the minimum principal repayment schedule possible using the PAC II prepayment band. This is done by determining the principal payment assuming 100 PSA and 225 PSA for the amount from which both the PAC I and PAC II are to be created. In FRR-20, $294.13 million ($243.8 million for PAC I plus $50.33 million for PAC II) is used to create the two bond classes with schedules. This is what was done in Exhibit 15 for selected months. The fourth column gives the minimum principal repayment that can be supported with the PAC II prepayment band of 100 PSA and 225 PSA.

Exhibit 15: Generating the Principal Repayment Schedule for a PAC I and PAC II for FRR-20

	$294.13 million of par value Principal Repayment			$248.3 million of par value Principal Repayment		PAC I	PAC II
Month	100 PSA	225 PSA	Minimum	90 PSA	300 PSA	schedule	schedule
1	535,005	872,138	535,005	508,170	1,075,931	508,170	26,836
2	603,364	1,024,624	603,364	569,843	1,279,412	569,843	33,520
3	671,562	1,176,643	671,562	631,377	1,482,194	631,377	40,185
4	739,564	1,328,019	739,564	692,742	1,683,966	692,742	46,822
5	807,335	1,478,576	807,335	753,909	1,884,415	753,909	53,426
6	874,841	1,628,139	874,841	814,850	2,083,227	814,850	59,990
7	942,045	1,776,533	942,045	875,537	2,280,093	875,537	66,508
8	1,008,913	1,923,584	1,008,913	935,940	2,474,701	935,940	72,973
9	1,075,410	2,069,120	1,075,410	996,032	2,666,745	996,032	79,378
10	1,141,502	2,212,970	1,141,502	1,055,785	2,855,920	1,055,785	85,717
11	1,207,155	2,354,964	1,207,155	1,115,170	3,041,928	1,115,170	91,985
12	1,272,333	2,494,935	1,272,333	1,174,160	3,224,472	1,174,160	98,173
60	1,846,060	2,815,961	1,846,060	1,731,345	3,059,085	1,731,345	114,715
61	1,837,061	2,780,945	1,837,061	1,724,031	3,007,151	1,724,031	113,030
62	1,828,109	2,746,357	1,828,109	1,716,753	2,956,086	1,716,753	111,356
63	1,819,203	2,712,190	1,819,203	1,709,510	2,905,876	1,709,510	109,694
64	1,810,345	2,678,440	1,810,345	1,702,301	2,856,506	1,702,301	108,044
65	1,801,532	2,645,102	1,801,532	1,695,127	2,807,963	1,695,127	106,405
66	1,792,766	2,612,171	1,792,766	1,687,988	2,760,232	1,687,988	104,778
67	1,784,046	2,579,641	1,784,046	1,680,883	2,713,301	1,680,883	103,162
68	1,775,371	2,547,508	1,775,371	1,673,813	2,667,155	1,673,813	101,558
69	1,766,742	2,515,767	1,766,742	1,666,776	2,621,782	1,666,776	99,965
70	1,758,157	2,484,414	1,758,157	1,659,774	2,577,170	1,659,774	98,384
300	621,923	115,305	115,305	704,536	37,571	37,571	77,734
301	619,449	113,589	113,589	702,412	36,787	36,787	76,803
302	616,990	111,897	111,897	700,299	36,017	36,017	75,880
303	614,545	110,226	110,226	698,199	35,262	35,262	74,964
304	612,113	108,577	108,577	696,110	34,520	34,520	74,057
305	609,695	106,950	106,950	694,034	33,793	33,793	73,157
345	523,432	56,776	56,776	620,308	13,600	13,600	43,176
346	521,520	55,835	55,835	618,685	13,269	13,269	42,565
347	519,618	54,906	54,906	617,072	12,945	12,945	41,961
348	517,727	53,989	53,989	615,469	12,626	12,626	41,363
349	515,848	53,085	53,085	613,876	12,314	3,432	49,653
350	513,979	52,194	52,194	612,293	12,008	0	52,194
351	512,121	51,314	51,314	610,720	11,708	0	51,314
352	510,274	50,446	50,446	609,157	11,414	0	50,446
353	508,437	49,590	49,590	607,604	11,126	0	49,590
354	506,612	48,746	48,746	606,061	10,844	0	48,746
355	504,797	47,913	47,913	604,527	10,567	0	47,913
356	502,992	47,091	47,091	603,003	10,296	0	47,091
357	501,199	46,281	46,281	601,489	10,030	0	45,638

Exhibit 16: Average Life for FRR-20
For Various Assumed Prepayment Rates

Prepayment rate	Average life			
	PAC I bond	PAC II bond	Bond S	Support bond in FRR-10
0	15.973	25.44	28.13	27.26
50	9.44	20.32	25.77	24.00
90	7.26	15.69	22.14	20.06
100	7.26	13.77	20.84	18.56
150	7.26	13.77	12.00	12.57
165	7.26	13.77	9.91	11.16
200	7.26	13.77	5.82	8.38
225	7.26	13.77	3.42	6.75
250	7.26	10.75	2.81	5.37
300	7.26	5.07	2.20	3.13
350	6.56	3.85	1.88	2.51
400	5.92	3.24	1.66	2.17
450	5.38	2.85	1.51	1.94
500	4.93	2.58	1.39	1.77
700	3.70	1.99	1.08	1.37

Step 2: Determine the minimum principal repayment for each month, on the basis of the amount of PAC I bonds to be created and the PAC I prepayment band. This is then the PAC I principal repayment schedule. In FRR-20, the prepayment band is 90 PSA and 300 PSA, and the amount of PAC I bonds to be created is $243.8 million. This is shown in the sixth column of Exhibit 15.

Step 3: For each month subtract the repayment schedule for the PAC I bonds from the minimum principal repayment found in Step 1. The resulting value is the principal repayment schedule for PAC II. For FRR-20, this result is given in the last column of Exhibit 15.

Exhibit 16 indicates the average life for all the bond classes in FRR-20 under various prepayment scenarios. Also shown in the exhibit is the average life for the support bond in FRR-10. The PAC I enjoys the same prepayment protection in the structure with a PAC II as it does in the structure without a PAC II. The PAC II has considerably more average life variability than the PAC I but less variability than the support bond class S. Comparison of the support bond class S in FRR-20 with the support bond in FRR-10 shows that the presence of a PAC II increases the average life variability. Now the support bond class is providing protection for not only a PAC I but also a support bond with a schedule.

There is more that can be done with the PAC II bond. A series of PAC IIs can be created just as we did with the PACs in FRR-11. PAC IIs can also be used to create any other type of bond class, such as a PAC II inverse floater or accrual bond, for example.

The support bond without a principal repayment schedule can be used to create any type of bond class. In fact, a portion of the non-PAC II support bond can be given a schedule of principal repayments. This bond class would be called a PAC III bond or a Level III PAC bond. While it provides protection against prepayments for the PAC I and PAC II bonds and is therefore subject to considerable prepayment risk, such a bond class has greater protection than the support bond class without a schedule of principal repayments.

Chapter 8

WHOLE-LOAN CMO STRUCTURES

All the cash flow structures found in agency CMOs as described in the previous four chapters are also applicable to whole-loan CMO structures. The major additional element in structuring whole-loan CMOs is credit enhancement. The investor in a whole-loan CMO is exposed to both prepayment risk and credit risk. Other elements include compensating interest payments and clean-up call provisions.

In this chapter, we will discuss various credit enhancement structures, compensating interest payments, and clean-up call provisions. In addition, we will discuss the factors that affect default rates and delinquencies for mortgage loans and the PSA Standard Default Assumption benchmark and assesment of whole-loan prepayments.

CREDIT ENHANCEMENTS

There are four nationally recognized companies that rate whole-loan CMOs: Standard & Poor's Corporation, Moody's Investors Service, Fitch Investors Service, and Duff & Phelps Credit Rating Company. The primary factors considered by these rating agencies in assigning a rating are the type of property (single family residences, condominiums), the type of loan (fixed-rate level payment, adjustable rate, balloon), the term of the loans, the geographical dispersion of the loans, the loan size (conforming loans, jumbo loans), the amount of seasoning of the loans, and the purpose of the loans (purchase or refinancing). Typically, a double A or triple A rating is sought for the most senior tranche. The amount of credit enhancement necessary depends on rating agency requirements.

There are two general types of credit enhancement structures: external and internal. We will describe each type below.

External Credit Enhancements

External credit enhancements come in the form of third-party guarantees that provide for first loss protection against losses up to a specified level, for example, 10%. The most common forms of external enhancements are (1) a corporate guarantee, (2) a letter of credit, (3) pool insurance, and (4) bond insurance.

Pool insurance policies cover losses resulting from defaults and foreclosures. Policies are typically written for a dollar amount of coverage that continues in force throughout the life of the pool. However, some policies are written so that the dollar amount of coverage declines as the pool seasons as long as two conditions are met: (1) the credit performance is better than expected and (2) the rating agencies that rated the issue approve. The three major providers of pool insurance are GEMICO, PMI Mortgage Insurance Corp., and United Guarantee Insurance. Since only defaults and foreclosures are covered, additional insurance must be obtained to cover losses resulting from bankruptcy (i.e., court mandated modification of mortgage debt), fraud arising in the origination process, and special hazards (i.e., losses resulting from events not covered by a standard homeowner's insurance policy).

Bond insurance provides the same function as in municipal bond structures. The major insurers are FGIC, AMBAC, and MBIA. Typically, bond insurance is not used as primary protection but to supplement other forms of credit enhancement.

A CMO issue with external credit support is subject to the credit risk of the third-party guarantor. Should the third-party guarantor be downgraded, the CMO issue itself could be subject to downgrade even if the structure is performing as expected. For example, in the early 1990s, mortgage-backed securities issued by Citibank Mortgage Securities Inc. were downgraded when Citibank, the third-party guarantor, was downgraded. This is the chief disadvantage of third-party guarantees. Therefore, it is imperative that investors perform credit analysis on both the collateral (the loans) and the third-party guarantor.

External credit enhancements do not materially alter the cash flow characteristics of a CMO structure except in the form of prepayment. In case of a default resulting in net losses within the guarantee level, investors will receive the principal amount as if a prepayment has occurred. If the net losses exceed the guarantee level, investors will have a shortfall in the cash flow.

Internal Credit Enhancements

Internal credit enhancements come in more complicated forms than external credit enhancements and may alter the cash flow characteristics of the loans even in the absence of default. The most common forms of internal credit enhancements are reserve funds (cash reserve funds or excess servicing spread accounts) and senior/subordinated structures.

Reserve funds: Reserve funds come in two forms, cash reserve funds and excess servicing spread accounts. *Cash reserve funds* are straight deposits of cash generated from issuance proceeds. In this case, part of the underwriting profits from the deal are deposited into a hypothecated fund which typically invests in money market instruments. Cash reserve funds are typically used in conjunction with letters of credit or other kinds of external credit enhancements. For example, a CMO may have 10% credit support, 9% of which is provided by a letter of credit and 1% from a cash reserve fund.

Excess servicing spread accounts involve the allocation of excess spread or cash into a separate reserve account after paying out the net coupon, servicing fee, and all other expenses on a monthly basis. For example, suppose that the gross weighted average coupon (gross WAC) is 7.75%, the servicing and other fees is 0.25%, and the net weighted average coupon (net WAC) is 7.25%. This means that there is excess servicing of 0.25%. The amount in the reserve account will gradually increase and can be used to pay for possible future losses.

The excess spread is analogous to the guarantee fee paid to an agency, except that this is a form of self-insurance. This form of credit enhancement relies on the assumption that defaults occur infrequently in the initial stages of the loans but gradually increase in the following two to five years. This assumption is consistent with the PSA's Standard Default Assumption (SDA) curve that we will describe later in the chapter.

Senior/subordinated structure: The most widely used internal credit support structure is by far the senior/subordinated structure. The subordinated class is the first loss piece absorbing all losses on the underlying collateral thus protecting the senior class. For example, a $100 million deal can be divided into two classes: a $92.25 million senior class and a $7.75 million subordinated class. The subordination level in this hypothetical structure is 7.75%. The subordinated class will absorb all losses up to $7.75 million, and the senior class will start to experience losses thereafter. So, if there is $5 million of losses, the subordinated class will realize this loss. Thus, it would realize a 64.5% loss ($5/$7.75). If, instead, there is $10 million of losses, the subordinated class will experience $7.75 million of losses or a 100% loss and the senior class will experience a loss of $2.25 million ($10 million minus $7.75 million) or a 2.4% loss ($2.25/$92.25).

The subordinated class holder would obviously require a yield premium to take on the greater default risk exposure relative to the senior class. This setup is another form of self-insurance wherein the senior class holder is giving up yield spread to the subordinated class holder. This form of credit enhancement does not affect cash flow characteristics of the senior class except in the form of prepayment. To the extent that losses are within the subordination level, the senior class holder will receive principal as if a prepayment has occurred. Exhibit 1 shows the average life of both classes at 165 PSA before any default assumption for a hypothetical $100 million structure with a 7.75% subordination level.

Almost all existing senior/subordinated structures also incorporate a *shifting interest structure*. A shifting interest structure redirects prepayments disproportionally from the subordinated class to the senior class according to a specified schedule. An example of such a schedule would be as follows:

Months	Percentage of prepayments directed to senior class
1-60	100
61-72	70
73-84	60
85-96	40
97-108	20
109+	pro rata

Exhibit 1: Average Life for Senior/Subordinated Structure Assuming No Defaults

Structure Gross WAC = 8.125% New WAC = 7.50% WAM = 357 Months	Average Life at 165 PSA assuming no defaults
No shifting interest	
Senior class (92.25%)	8.77
Subordinate class (7.75%)	8.77
With shifting interest	
Senior class (92.25%)	8.41
Subordinate class (7.75%)	13.11
With shifting interest	
Senior class (84.5%)	7.98
Subordinate class (15.5%)	13.11

The rationale for the shifting interest structure is to have enough insurance outstanding to cover future losses. Because of the shifting interest structure, the subordination amount may actually grow in time, especially in a low default and fast prepayment environment. This is sometimes referred to as "riding up the credit curve." Using the same example of our previous $100 million deal with 7.75% initial subordination and assuming a cumulative pay-down (prepayments and regular repayments) of $20 million by year 3, the subordination will actually increase to 10.7% [$7.75/($92.25 − $20)] without any net losses. Even if the subordinated class has experienced some losses, say, $1 million, the subordination will still increase to 9.3% [($7.75 − $1)/($92.25 − 20)].

While the shifting interest structure is beneficial to the senior class holder from a credit standpoint, it does alter the cash flow characteristics of the senior class even in the absence of defaults. As Exhibit 1 indicates, a 7.75% subordination with the shifting interest structure will shorten the average life of the senior class to 8.41 years at the same 165 PSA, assuming no default. The size of the subordination also matters. A larger subordinated class redirects a higher proportion of prepayments to the senior class, thereby shortening the average life even further. A 15.5% subordination in the same example shortens the average life to 7.98 (see Exhibit 1).[1]

It may be counter-intuitive that the size of the subordination should affect the average life and cash flow of the senior class more than the credit quality. This is because the size of the subordination is already factored into the rating. The rating agency typically requires more subordination for lower credit quality loans to obtain a triple A rating and less

It may be counter-intuitive that the size of the subordination should affect the average life and cash flow of the senior class more than the credit quality. This is because the size of the subordination is already factored into the rating. The rating agency typically requires more subordination for lower credit quality loans to obtain a triple A rating and less subordination for better credit quality loans. From a credit standpoint, the investor may be indifferent between a 5% subordination on a package of good quality loans and a 10% subordination on a package of lower quality loans as long as the rating agency gives them the same rating. However, the quality of the underlying loans will determine the default rate and therefore the timing of the cash flow.

COMPENSATING INTEREST

An additional factor to consider which is unique to whole loan CMO structures is compensating interest. Mortgage passthroughs and CMOs pay principal and interest on a monthly basis (with the exception of some early quarterly-pay CMOs), and principal paydown factors are also calculated only once a month. While homeowners may prepay their mortgage on any day throughout the month, the agencies guarantee and pay the investors a full month of interest as if all the prepayments occur on the last day of the month. Unfortunately, this guarantee does not apply to whole-loan mortgages and, consequently, not to whole-loan CMOs. If a homeowner pays off a mortgage on the tenth day of the month, he will stop paying interest for the rest of the month. Because of the payment delay (for example, 25 days) and the once-a-month calculation of principal paydown, the investor will receive full principal but only 10 days of interest on the 25th of the following month.

This phenomenon is known as *payment interest shortfall* or *compensating interest* and is handled differently by different issuers and services. Some issuers will only pay up to a specified amount and some will not pay at all. Exhibit 2 is a list of issuers who *generally* pay and those who do not *generally* pay compensating interest. The economic value of compensating interest depends on the level of prepayment and the types of CMO tranches. Generally, the faster the prepayment and the higher the coupon tranche, the higher the economic value of compensating interest.

Exhibit 2: Treatment of Compensating Interest By Some Issuers

Issuers who generally pay compensating interest	Issuers who generally do not pay compensating interest
Chase	GE
Citicorp	RFC
Capstead	Ryland
PruHome	SecPac
RTC	Sears

CLEAN-UP CALL PROVISIONS

All whole-loan CMO structures are issued with "clean-up" call provisions. The clean-up call provides the servicers or the residual holders (typically the issuers) the right, but not the obligation, to call back all the outstanding tranches of the CMO structure when the CMO balance is paid down to a certain percentage of the original principal balance. The servicers typically find it more costly than the servicing fee to service the CMO when the balance is paid down to a small amount. For example, suppose a $100 million CMO was originally issued with a 10% clean-up call. When the entire CMO balance is paid down to $10 million or less, the servicer can exercise the call to pay off all outstanding tranches like a balloon payment regardless of the percentage balance of the individual tranches.

The call provision, when exercised, shortens the principal payment window and the average life of the back-end tranches of a CMO. This provision is not unique to whole-loan CMO structures. It is mandatory, however, for all whole-loan CMO structures while agency CMOs may or may not have clean-up calls. Typically, FHLMC CMOs have 1% clean-up calls, and FNMA CMOs do not have clean-up calls.

ASSESSING PREPAYMENT RATES OF WHOLE-LOAN CMOs

We have discussed the prepayment conventions in Chapter 3 using both the PSA and CPR models. While analyzing whole-loan prepayments is beyond the scope of this chapter, there are implications for using the PSA and CPR conventions on whole loans. Traditionally, the agencies only reported the WAM of the CMO with the implied age being the loan term minus the WAM. For example, a group of 30-year loans is assumed to be 10 months old if they have a reported WAM of 350 months, and a group of 15-year loans is assumed to be 10 months old if they have a reported WAM of 170.

Recently, the agencies started to report loan age as well as WAM. FHLMC calls it WALA (weighted average loan age), and FNMA calls it CAGE (calculated loan age). These are critical measures because WALA and WAM may not add up to 360 or 180 months. This is due to partial prepayments (curtailments). Partial prepayments do not impact the age of the loans but shortens the WAM of the loans.

Partial prepayment is not a new phenomenon but is more noticable recently for two reasons. The first reason is the steepness of the yield curve. Homeowners find that partial prepayment on a 7% mortgage is a higher yielding investment than a 3% certificate of deposit. The second reason is the recent changes in the Internal Revenue Code that limit tax deductions on mortgage interest payments for higher income taxpayers. Both reasons impact jumbo mortgages more than conforming mortgages.

Partial prepayment can distort the reported prepayment speeds. For example, if the loan age is not available and the loans backing the whole loan have a WAM of 350 and the prepayment speed is 2% CPR, this converts to 100 PSA.[2] If the WALA is known to be three months due to partial prepayments, 2% CPR converts to 333 PSA.[3]

DEFAULT AND DELIQUENCY RATES

There have been several studies of mortgage loan defaults.[4] These studies suggest that the key factor affecting defaults is the loan-to-value ratio

---

[2] This is found as follows when the seasoning is assumed to be 10 months:

$$\frac{2\% \text{ CPR} \times 100 \text{ PSA}}{10\,(0.2\% \text{ CPR})} = 100 \text{ PSA}$$

[3] This is found as follows when the seasoning is three months:

$$\frac{2\% \text{ CPR} \times 100 \text{ PSA}}{3\,(0.2\% \text{ CPR})} = 333 \text{ PSA}$$

[4] See, for example, Helen F. Peters, Scott M. Pinkus, and David J. Askin, "Default: The Last Resort," *Secondary Mortgage Markets* (August 1984), pp. 16-22; Robert Van Order, "The Hazards of Default," *Secondary Mortgage Markets* (Fall 1990), pp. 29-32; and, Scott Brown, et al, *Analysis of Mortgage Servicing Portfolios* (New York: Financial Strategies Group, Prudential-Bache Capital Funding, December 1990).

at origination. There is also a seasoning affect in default rates and geographical differences in default rates. Geographical differences in default rates are affected by local economies, the trend of housing values in a region, and state foreclosure laws. We will describe the affect of LTVs, seasoning, and state foreclosure laws on deliquencies and defaults below.

Surprising, characteristics of the borrower have not been found to materially affect default rates. For example, the payment-to-income (PTI) ratio is a measure of the burden of the mortgage payments. It is expected that the higher this ratio at origination, the greater the probability of default. One study found that the probability of default increased only slightly the higher this burden.[5] This conclusion is only tentative because the study's sample did not include many observations with high PTIs. No other borrower characteristics examined in the study appeared to significantly affect default rates.

Loan-to-Value Ratio

All studies of defaults on mortgage loans have found that the loan-to-value ratio at the time of origination, or *original LTV*, is the most significant variable affecting the likelihood of default. Approaches by the rating agenies and private mortgage insurers emphasize original LTV as the best predictor of future deliquency and default. For example, FHA/VA insured/guaranteed loans in which borrowers have little or no equity have long been known to have higher default rates than conventional loans.

Unfortunately, many deliquency models using original LTV have underestimated the level of deliquencies in portfolios in recent years. Mismeasurement of the amount of equity borrowers have in their home is the chief cause. Such mismeasurement is due to two factors: declining home prices and removal of equity via second mortgages or home equity lines of credit.

Exhibit 3 shows the effects of changing property values on the distribution of LTVs. Almost all original LTVs fall under 80% in a large (100,000 plus) portfolio of securitized loans and none above 90%.[6] Adjusted for declines in property values, however, nearly 40% have current LTVs above 80% and about 15% have current LTVs above 90%.

---

[5] Van Order, "The Hazards of Default."

[6] The data reported in Exhibits 3 through 6 are from an issuer of nonagency securities. The authors thank Doug Bendt of Mortgage Risk Assessment Corp. for furnishing the data.

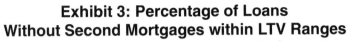

Exhibit 3: Percentage of Loans
Without Second Mortgages within LTV Ranges

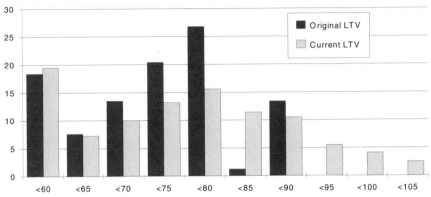

Source: Mortgage Risk Assessment Corporation

Exhibit 4 shows that borrowers with second mortgages behind their first mortgage become delinquent twice as often as borrowers without second mortgages. This pattern is due to high *combined LTV* — borrowers act according to how much equity they have in the property, as indicated in Exhibit 5. As Exhibit 6 shows, even adjusting for the higher combined LTVs, borrowers with second mortgages have higher deliquency rates compared to a borrowers with the same combined LTV without any seconds. On average, deliquency rates are about 25% higher — possibly because the combined monthly payments on a first and second mortgage would be higher than the same sized first mortgage.

Seasoning

Empirical studies suggest that there is a seasoning effect for default rates. That is, default rates tend to decline as mortgage loans become seasoned.[7] The reason for the seasoning effect on default rates is twofold. First, since a borrower typically knows shortly after moving into a home whether or not he or she can afford to make the mortgage payments, default rates are higher in the earlier years. Second, the longer a borrower remains in a home, the lower the LTV ratio (i.e., the greater the equity in the home), and therefore the incentive to default declines.

---

[7] For conventional mortgage loans, the maximum default rate appears to be three to four years after origination. For FHA/VA mortgage loans, it seems to be two to three years after origination. (See: Brown et al, *Analysis of Mortgage Servicing Portfolios*, p. 8.)

Exhibit 4: Percentage Delinquencies

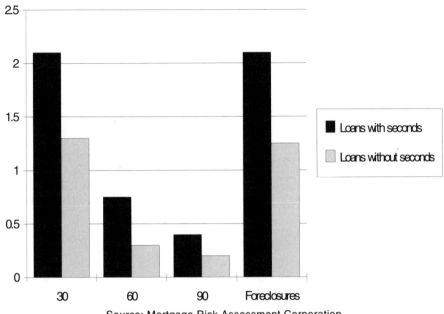

Source: Mortgage Risk Assessment Corporation

Exhibit 5: Percentage of Loans
with Second Mortgages Within LTV Ranges

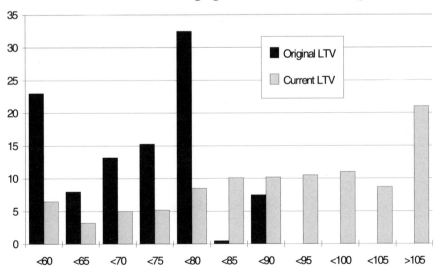

Source: Mortgage Risk Assessment Corporation

Exhibit 6: Percentage Delinquencies by LTV Range

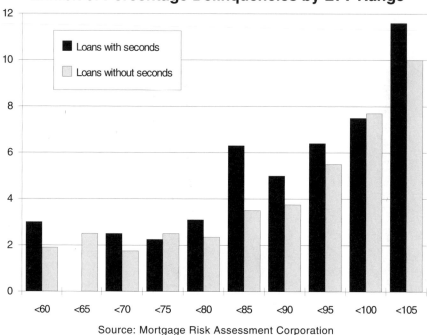

Source: Mortgage Risk Assessment Corporation

State Foreclosure Laws and Default Losses

State foreclosure laws significantly affect default losses. These state laws differ in three primary ways: (1) foreclosure procedures, (2) statutory right of redemption, and (3) deficiency judgment.[8] Foreclosure procedures can be either judicial or nonjudicial. The former is done under court supervision, resulting in a lengthening of the time to sell the property. This delay increases the losses associated with a foreclosure because of the opportunity loss on funds that could have been reinvested, additional taxes and insurance that must be paid, and legal expenses. Moreover, the property value might decline in the interim due to lack of maintenance or downturn in property values. In a nonjudicial foreclosure,[9] a sale can be made faster because there is no court proceeding; therefore, the costs associated with foreclosure are reduced. There are 23 states that only permit judicial foreclosure.[10]

---

[8] Terrence M. Clauretie and Thomas N. Herzog, "How State Laws Affect Foreclosure Costs," *Secondary Mortgage Markets* (Spring 1989), pp. 26-27.

[9] Such foreclosure procedures are also called power of sale procedures, foreclosures by advertisement, or a trustee's sale.

A statutory right of redemption is a right granted to the borrower to redeem the property by paying any deficiencies, including legal expenses, for a specified period *after* a foreclosure;[11] 29 states grant this right to borrowers.[12] If this right allows the borrower the right to occupy the property after foreclosure, there is the standard moral hazard problem which could result in deterioration of the property, as well as reluctance of potential buyers to bid on property where moral hazard exists. This will result in the receipt of lower bid prices.

A deficiency judgment allows the lender to recover any deficiencies from the borrower's personal assets. While the costs of recovery and the limited personal assets of the borrower may make pursuit of this right by the lender uneconomic, its existence may discourage a default in some instances. This would occur in cases where the borrower has the capacity to pay and sufficient personal assets to satisfy any judgment, but whose property value has declined so that no equity remains in the property (i.e., the LTV is 1 or higher). Only six states do not allow deficiency judgments.[13]

An empirical study by Clauretie and Herzog, based on data from private mortgage insurance and FHA claims, investigated the effect of state laws on losses.[14] A statistical analysis of the data found that losses are significantly lower in states with nonjudicial foreclosure procedures and a deficiency judgment right;[15] losses are greater where states grant a statutory right of redemption. These researchers found that on a $100,000 loan, lenders are exposed to potential additional losses of $500 to $1,000 if a property is located in a state with only a judicial foreclosure process and statutory right of redemption.

---

[10] Clauretie and Herzog, "How State Laws Affect Foreclosure Costs," p. 26.

[11] An equitable right of redemption gives the borrower the right to redeem the property by paying all deficiencies and legal costs before a foreclosure. This right is granted to borrowers in all states.

[12] Clauretie and Herzog, "How State Laws Affect Foreclosure Costs," p. 26.

[13] Clauretie and Herzog, "How State Laws Affect Foreclosure Costs," p. 27.

[14] Clauretie and Herzog, "How State Laws Affect Foreclosure Costs," pp. 27-28.

[15] The deficiency judgment was not found to be statistically significant for the FHA data. The low default rates in California in the study period and the fact that California was one of only six states which did not have a deficiency judgment may have caused this result.

Exhibit 7: PSA Standard Default Assumption Benchmark (100 SDA)

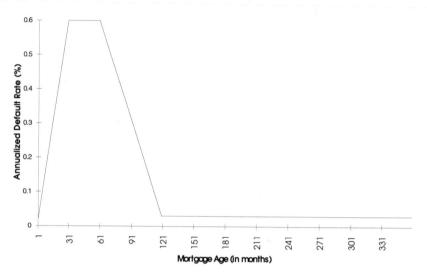

PSA STANDARD DEFAULT ASSUMPTION BENCHMARK

With the increase in whole-loan CMO issuance, the Public Securities Association introduced a standardized benchmark for default rates. The PSA standard default assumption (SDA) benchmark gives the annual default rate for a
mortgage pool as a function of the seasoning of the mortgages. The PSA
SDA benchmark, or 100 SDA, specifies the following:

(1) the default rate in month 1 is 0.02% and increases by 0.02% up to
month 30 so that in month 30 the default rate is 0.60%;

(2) from month 30 to month 60, the default rate remains at 0.60%;

(3) from month 61 to month 120, the default rate declines linearly
from 0.60% to 0.03%;

(4) from month 120 on, the default rate remains constant at 0.03%.

This pattern is illustrated in Exhibit 7.

As with the PSA prepayment benchmark, multiples of the benchmark are found by multiplying the default rate by the assumed multiple. For example, 200 SDA means the following pattern:

(1) the default rate in month 1 is 0.04% and increases by 0.04% up to month 30 so that in month 30 the default rate is 1.20%;

(2) from month 30 to month 60, the default rate remains at 1.20%;

(3) from month 61 to month 120, the default rate declines from 1.20% to 0.06%;

(4) from month 120 on, the default rate remains constant at 0.06%.

A 0 SDA means that no defaults are assumed.

SECTION III:
ANALYSIS OF CMOs

Chapter 9

STATIC CASH FLOW YIELD ANALYSIS

In Section II our focus was on the various CMO structures and the effects on the tranches in a structure. Our analysis was confined to the variability of a tranche's average life over a range of prepayment scenarios. We did not consider price or any measure of yield or return under various prepayment scenarios.

Our purpose in Section III is to explain the analysis of CMO bond classes. In this chapter, we look at the conventional framework for evaluating CMOs: static cash flow analysis. In the next chapter we discuss a more advanced technology, the option-adjusted spread analysis. The static cash flow yield methodology is the simplest of the two valuation technologies to apply, although it may offer little insight into the relative value of a CMO. In Chapter 10, we discuss how to apply the total return framework to assess the potential performance of a CMO tranche or portfolio.

CASH FLOW YIELD

The yield on any financial instrument is the interest rate that makes the present value of the cash flow equal to its market price plus accrued interest if any.[1] The starting point for calculating the yield is the estimation of the cash flow from the financial instrument. For example, for a noncallable Treasury security, the cash flow is known with certainty. So, for example, if a 30-year Treasury bond has a coupon rate of 7.5%, we know its cash flow per $100 of par value will be $3.75 every six months for the next 59 six-month periods and $103.75 after the 60th six-month period from now. Suppose the price of this Treasury bond is $95.43 per $100 of par value. The yield then is found by trial-and-error (or by using a search algorithm) by trying different discount rates. The interest rate we are looking for is the one that will make the present value of the cash flow equal to $95.43. The six-month interest rate that will give this value is 3.95%. The market convention for annualizing a six-month yield is to double it; the resulting annualized yield then is said to be calculated on a *bond-equivalent yield basis*, abbreviated as BEY. Thus, for our hypothetical Treasury, the yield is 7.9% BEY.

In the case of the hypothetical 30-year Treasury security, the yield calculated is referred to as the *yield to maturity*. This terminology is adopted because the cash flow used to calculate the yield is to the maturity date. The yield to maturity for all noncallable bonds is calculated in the same way. For a callable security, another yield measure is also calculated, the *yield to call*. The yield to call is simply the interest rate that will make the present value of the bond's cash flow equal to its price, assuming it is called. Various yield to call measures arecalculated for a callable bond according to different assumptions as to when the bond will be called.

For mortgage-backed securities, a yield is calculated in the same manner, with the resulting yield measure called a *cash flow yield*.[2] The problem, of course, in calculating an MBS cash flow yield is that prepayments mean that the cash flow is unknown. Consequently, to determine a cash flow yield some assumption about the prepayment rate must be made.

The cash flow for a CMO bond class may be monthly, quarterly, or semiannually, and therefore must be annualized. The convention is to compare the yield on a CMO with that of Treasury coupon securities and corporate bonds by calculating the CMO's bond-equivalent yield. Recall

---

[1] Another name used to describe the yield is the *internal rate of return*.

[2] Some market participants also refer to the cash flow yield as the yield to maturity. This practice will not be followed in this book.

that the bond-equivalent yield for a Treasury coupon security and a corporate bond is found by doubling the semiannual yield. However, it is incorrect to do this for a CMO that pays more frequently than semiannually because the investor has the opportunity to generate greater interest by reinvesting the more frequent cash flows.

The market practice is to calculate a yield so as to make it comparable to the yield to maturity on a bond-equivalent yield basis. The formula for annualizing the periodic cash flow yield for a CMO bond class is as follows:

$$\text{For a monthly-pay CMO: Bond-equivalent yield} = 2\left[(1 + i_M)^6 - 1\right]$$

where i_M is the monthly interest rate that will equate the present value of the projected monthly cash flow to the price of the CMO bond class.

$$\text{For a quarterly-pay CMO: Bond-equivalent yield} = 2\left[(1 + i_Q)^2 - 1\right]$$

where i_Q is the quarterly interest rate that will equate the present value of the projected quarterly cash flow to the price of the CMO bond class.

To illustrate the cash flow yield, we'll use one of the CMO structures we developed in Chapter 4, FRR-03. Exhibit 1 summarizes cash flow yields according to various constant PSA prepayment assumptions for the four regular tranches assuming different purchase prices. Notice that the greater the discount assumed to be paid for the tranche, the more a tranche will benefit from faster prepayments. The converse is true for a tranche for which a premium is paid. The faster the prepayments, the lower the cash flow yield.

Exhibit 2 reports the cash flow yield using vector analysis. The top panel shows the cash flow yield for the four regular interest classes and the collateral assuming 165 PSA. Nine vectors are then shown assuming that the PSA is constant from months 1 to 36, and then changes for months 37 through 138, and again changes for months 139 through 357.

Once the cash flow yield is calculated according to some prepayment assumption, a yield spread is determined. As explained in Chapter 2, the yield spread is typically measured relative to a comparable Treasury security, where comparable is defined as having either (1) an average life similar to the Treasury's maturity, or (2) a Macaulay duration close to that of the Treasury.

Exhibit 1: Price/Cash Flow Yield Table for the Four Regular Interest Classes in FFR-03

Tranche 1:
Orig Par: $194,500,000;
Type: SEQ;
Coupon: 6.0% (Fixed)

If price paid is	50 PSA	100 PSA	165 PSA	250 PSA	400 PSA	500 PSA	700 PSA	1000 PSA
95-25	6.78	7.06	7.39	7.76	8.30	8.61	9.14	9.85
96-25	6.59	6.79	7.03	7.31	7.70	7.93	8.31	8.84
97-25	6.40	6.53	6.69	6.86	7.11	7.26	7.50	7.84
98-25	6.22	6.28	6.35	6.42	6.53	6.60	6.71	6.85
99-25	6.04	6.03	6.01	5.99	5.96	5.95	5.92	5.89
100-25	5.86	5.78	5.68	5.56	5.40	5.31	5.15	4.93
101-25	5.69	5.53	5.35	5.14	4.85	4.68	4.39	4.00
102-25	5.51	5.29	5.03	4.73	4.30	4.06	3.64	3.08
103-25	5.34	5.06	4.71	4.32	3.76	3.45	2.90	2.17
Average life:	7.48	4.90	3.48	2.62	1.94	1.69	1.38	1.11
Mod duration:	5.56	3.99	2.98	2.32	1.76	1.55	1.28	1.04

Tranche 2:
Orig Par: $36,000,000;
Type: SEQ;
Coupon: 6.50% (Fixed)

If price paid is	50 PSA	100 PSA	165 PSA	250 PSA	400 PSA	500 PSA	700 PSA	1000 PSA
97-01	6.85	6.93	7.03	7.17	7.39	7.52	7.75	8.01
98-01	6.75	6.79	6.85	6.94	7.07	7.15	7.28	7.44
99-01	6.64	6.66	6.68	6.71	6.75	6.78	6.82	6.88
100-01	6.54	6.53	6.50	6.48	6.44	6.41	6.37	6.32
101-01	6.44	6.39	6.33	6.25	6.13	6.05	5.92	5.77
102-01	6.34	6.27	6.16	6.03	5.82	5.70	5.48	5.23
103-01	6.24	6.14	6.00	5.81	5.52	5.35	5.05	4.69
104-01	6.14	6.01	5.83	5.60	5.22	5.00	4.62	4.17
Average life:	15.98	10.86	7.49	5.37	3.70	3.12	2.47	1.97
Mod duration:	9.66	7.57	5.75	4.40	3.19	2.75	2.21	1.80

Exhibit 1 (Concluded)

Tranche 3:
Orig Par: $96,500,000;
Type: SEQ;
Coupon: 7.00 (Fixed)

If price paid is	50 PSA	100 PSA	165 PSA	250 PSA	400 PSA	500 PSA	700 PSA	1000 PSA
96-09	7.41	7.46	7.55	7.66	7.87	8.01	8.26	8.59
97-09	7.32	7.35	7.41	7.49	7.63	7.72	7.90	8.13
98-09	7.22	7.24	7.27	7.31	7.39	7.44	7.54	7.66
99-09	7.12	7.13	7.13	7.14	7.16	7.17	7.18	7.21
100-09	7.03	7.02	7.00	6.97	6.92	6.89	6.83	6.76
101-09	6.94	6.91	6.87	6.81	6.69	6.62	6.49	6.31
102-09	6.85	6.81	6.74	6.64	6.47	6.36	6.15	5.88
103-09	6.76	6.70	6.61	6.48	6.24	6.09	5.81	5.44
104-09	6.67	6.60	6.48	6.32	6.02	5.83	5.48	5.01
Average life:	21.02	15.78	11.19	7.97	5.31	4.38	3.30	2.49
Mod duration:	10.67	9.22	7.48	5.89	4.29	3.65	2.85	2.22

Tranche 4:
Orig Par: $73,000,000;
Type: SEQ;
Coupon: 7.35% (Fixed)

If price paid is	50 PSA	100 PSA	165 PSA	250 PSA	400 PSA	500 PSA	700 PSA	1000 PSA
96-20	7.62	7.63	7.65	7.69	7.79	7.85	8.00	8.22
97-20	7.53	7.53	7.55	7.58	7.64	7.68	7.77	7.92
98-20	7.44	7.44	7.45	7.46	7.49	7.51	7.55	7.62
99-20	7.35	7.35	7.35	7.35	7.34	7.34	7.33	7.32
100-20	7.26	7.26	7.25	7.23	7.20	7.17	7.12	7.03
101-20	7.18	7.17	7.15	7.12	7.06	7.01	6.91	6.74
102-20	7.10	7.08	7.06	7.01	6.92	6.84	6.70	6.46
103-20	7.01	7.00	6.97	6.91	6.78	6.68	6.49	6.18
104-20	6.93	6.92	6.87	6.80	6.64	6.53	6.28	5.90
Average life:	27.24	24.58	20.27	15.47	10.34	8.35	5.95	4.09
Mod duration:	11.57	11.14	10.22	8.86	6.91	5.96	4.62	3.40

Source: Calculated using SFW Software Copyright(c) 1989 by Wall Street Analytics, Inc.

Exhibit 2: Vector Analysis of Cash Flow Yield for the Four Regular Interest Classes of FRR-03 and Collateral

	Assumptions:		
	Coupon (%)	Price	Cash flow yield at 165 PSA (%)
Tranche A	6.00	99-25	6.00
Tranche B	6.50	100-01	6.50
Tranche C	7.00	100-09	7.00
Tranche Z	7.25	100-20	7.25
Collateral	7.50	100-04	7.50

	PSA Vector Scenario								
Months	(1)	(2)	(3)	(4)	(5)	(6)	(7)	(8)	(9)
1- 36	165	165	165	165	165	165	165	165	165
37-138	50	50	300	400	400	400	400	500	600
139-357	250	400	400	200	700	500	165	200	1000
Tranche A:									
Cash flow yield	6.03	6.03	6.00	6.00	6.00	6.00	6.00	6.00	5.99
Average life	5.03	5.03	3.04	2.90	2.90	2.90	2.90	2.81	2.75
Modified duration	3.97	3.97	2.67	2.56	2.56	2.56	2.56	2.49	2.44
Tranche B:									
Cash flow yield	6.53	6.53	6.48	6.47	6.47	6.47	6.47	6.46	6.45
Average life	12.20	11.95	5.51	4.86	4.86	4.86	4.86	4.45	4.17
Modified duration	8.19	8.08	4.50	4.04	4.04	4.04	4.04	3.75	3.55
Tranche C:									
Cash flow yield	7.02	7.01	6.97	6.95	6.95	6.95	6.95	6.93	6.92
Average life	14.60	13.48	7.68	6.46	6.46	6.46	6.46	5.70	5.18
Modified duration	8.87	8.47	5.74	5.03	5.03	5.03	5.03	4.55	4.21
Tranche D:									
Cash flow yield	7.25	7.24	7.22	7.21	7.21	7.21	7.21	7.19	7.17
Average life	20.97	18.07	13.51	12.29	10.91	11.21	12.53	10.18	8.29
Modified duration	10.42	9.73	8.25	7.65	7.25	7.35	7.71	6.78	5.98
Collateral:									
Cash flow yield	7.54	7.53	7.50	7.49	7.49	7.49	7.49	7.48	7.47
Average life	10.89	10.07	6.29	5.65	5.40	5.45	5.69	5.00	4.48
Modified duration	6.46	6.25	4.49	4.13	4.06	4.08	4.14	3.81	3.55

Source: Calculated using SFW Software Copyright (c) 1989 by Wall Street Analytics, Inc.

Limitations of Cash Flow Yield Measure

All yield measures suffer from problems that limit their use in assessing the performance of a bond. The yield to maturity has two major shortcomings as a measure of a bond's potential return. To realize the stated yield to maturity, the investor must: (1) reinvest the coupon payments at a rate equal to the yield to maturity, and; (2) hold the bond to the maturity date. The importance of reinvesting the coupon payments should not be minimized.

For example, consider a 10% coupon bond with 30 years to maturity selling at par and paying interest semiannually. The yield to maturity for this bond is 10%. Suppose that an investor buys this bond for $1,000 expecting to earn a 10% yield for 30 years. A 10% yield (compounded semiannually) on any investment of $1,000 means that at the end of 30 years the investor should have $18,679.[3] This means $17,679 will come from interest and $1,000 from the return of principal. With the bond, however, only $3,000 is paid in interest ($100 of coupon interest per year for 30 years), and $1,000 is paid in principal repayment. That is, the issuer pays only $3,000 of the $17,679 in interest to generate a yield of 10% for 30 years; the balance must come from reinvesting the semiannual coupon payments. In fact, this example shows very clearly that the reinvestment of the coupon payments is the major source of return through time for this bond. If the coupon payments indeed can be reinvested at a 10% yield (BEY), the interest generated from the reinvestment will add up to $14,679. If interest rates decline, the coupon interest payments will be reinvested at a lower rate than the stated yield to maturity, and the investor comes up short. The risk that investors will realize a lower rate when they reinvest the coupon payments is called *reinvestment risk*. Reinvestment risk is greater, the longer the maturity of the security, and the higher the coupon rate.

These shortcomings are equally applicable to the cash flow yield measure: (1) the projected cash flows are assumed to be reinvested at the cash flow yield, and (2) the mortgage-backed security is assumed to be held until the final payout based on some prepayment assumption. The importance of reinvestment risk, the risk that the cash flow will have to be reinvested at a rate lower than the cash flow yield, is particularly important for many mortgage-backed securities, because payments are monthly and include both interest and principal that must be reinvested. Moreover, the cash flow yield is dependent on realization of the projected cash flow according to some prepayment assumption. If the prepayment

---

[3] This is simply an application of the compound interest formula: $1,000 $(1.05)^{60}$ = $18,679$.

experience is different from the prepayment rate assumed, the cash flow yield may not be realized.

PRICE VOLATILITY:
EFFECTIVE DURATION AND CONVEXITY

Investors want to know more than just the yield on their holdings. They also want to know how sensitive the price of the security is to changes in interest rates. In this section we discuss the price volatility characteristics of mortgage-backed securities and how to measure price volatility.

Price/Yield Relationship for a Passthrough Security

A fundamental property of an option-free bond (i.e, a bond that is not callable or putable) is that the price of a bond is inversely related to its yield. The reason for this is that the current market value is the present value of the future cash flow. As the required yield used in discounting the cash flow rises, the present value must fall; hence, the price falls. The opposite occurs when the required yield falls: the present value of the cash flow increases, and therefore the price of the bond increases.

If we graphed the price/yield relationship for any option-free bond, we would find that it has the "bowed" shape shown in Exhibit 3. This shape is referred to as *convex*. The convexity of the price/yield relationship has important implications for the investment characteristics of a bond, as we will see.

While the price/yield relationship for an option-free bond is convex, the price/yield relationship for a passthrough security takes a different shape. Exhibit 4 shows the price/yield relationship for both a hypothetical noncallable passthrough security (i.e, one whose underlying mortgage loans do not give the homeowner the right to prepay) and a passthrough security with the same coupon. The convex curve a-a' is the price/yield relationship for the hypothetical noncallable passthrough security. The unusual shaped curve denoted by a-b is the price/yield relationship for the passthrough security.

The price/yield relationship for the passthrough security takes this shape because if prevailing mortgage rates are higher than the rate paid by homeowners whose mortgage loan is the collateral for the passthrough security, it is unlikely that homeowners will refinance and thereby prepay. Therefore, at high yield levels relative to the mortgage rate homeowners are paying, the passthrough security will have the same price/yield relationship as the hypothetical noncallable passthrough security.

Exhibit 3: Price/Yield Relationship for an Option-Free Bond

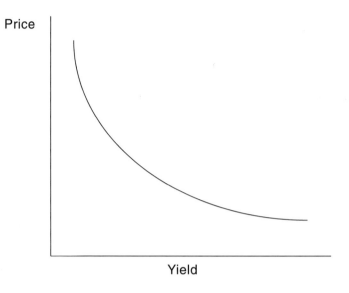

Exhibit 4: Price/Yield Relationship for a Passthrough Security and a Hypothetical Noncallable Passthrough Security

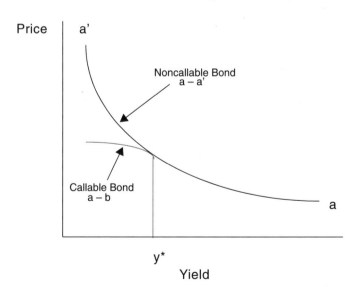

As yields in the market decline, however, the likelihood that homeowners will benefit from refinancing their mortgages increases. We may not know the exact yield level at which homeowners begin to view refinancing favorably, but we do know that there is some level. In Exhibit 4, at yield levels below y*, the price/yield relationship for the passthrough security diverges from the price/yield relationship for the hypothetical noncallable passthrough security. Suppose, for example, that the market yield is such that a hypothetical noncallable passthrough security would be selling for 109. Since it is callable at 100 (i.e., the homeowner pays par to retire the loan), investors would not pay 109. If they did and homeowners prepaid, investors would receive 100 for a security they purchased for 109. Notice that for a range of yields below y*, there is price compression — that is, there is limited price appreciation as yields decline. For the reasons to be discussed later, the portion of the passthrough price/yield relationship below y* is said to exhibit *negative convexity* (another term for price compression).

Bond Price Volatility Properties for Noncallable Securities

There are two fundamental properties of price volatility:

- For small changes in yield, the absolute change in price is approximately the same whether yields increase or decrease.

- When yields change by a large amount, a given change in basis points will produce more of a price increase if yields decline than a price decline if yields increase.

An investment implication of this second property is that the capital gain that will be realized on a bond if yield decreases is greater than the capital loss that will be realized if yield increases by the same number of basis points. For example, consider a 9%, 20-year Treasury security selling at par ($100). The yield to maturity for this security is 9%. If the required yield falls from 9% to 6% (a decline of 300 basis points), the price would rise to $134.67, an increase of 34.67%. If the required yield rises from 9% to 12% (an increase of 300 basis points), however, the price would fall to $77.43, a decline of 22.57%. Thus, the increase in price when the yield falls by 300 basis points, 34.67%, is greater than the price decline when the yield rises by the same number of basis points, 22.57%.

Two characteristics of an option-free bond determine its price volatility: coupon and term to maturity.

• For a given term to maturity and initial yield, the lower the coupon rate, the greater the price volatility of a bond.

• For a given coupon rate and initial yield, the longer the term to maturity, the greater the price volatility.

An investment implication of the first characteristic is that, holding maturity constant, bonds selling at a deep discount will have greater price volatility than bonds selling near or above par. Zero-coupon bonds thus have the greatest price volatility for a given maturity.

As we shall see, the collateral for a CMO may have undesirable convexity features. Yet it is possible to create CMO bond classes with more suitable convexity features for institutional investors seeking asset/liability matching or betting on the direction of interest rate changes or volatility.

Measuring Price Volatility

While there are several measures of price volatility, and all are related, the most commonly one used in the bond market is duration.[4]

Modified Duration: We have mentioned duration as some measure of the "time" to maturity of a bond, which is called Macaulay duration. The main reason for focusing on duration is that it is related to the price sensitivity of a bond to interest rate changes. More specifically, the *modified duration* of a bond measures the *approximate* percentage change in a bond's price for a 100-basis point change in interest rates. The modified duration of a bond is found as follows:

$$\text{Modified Duration} = \frac{\text{Macaulay Duration}}{1 + \text{yield}/f}$$

where f is the frequency of cash flow payments (i.e., 2 for a Treasury coupon security and 12 for a passthrough security).

So, for example, if a bond has a modified duration of 4, this means that the price of that bond will change by approximately 4% for a 100-basis point change in interest rates. For the same bond, a 50-basis point change in

---

[4] See Frank J. Fabozzi, Mark Pitts, and Ravi E. Dattatreya, "Price Volatility Characteristics of Fixed Income Securities," Chapter 7 in Frank I. Fabozzi (ed.), *The Handbook of Fixed Income Securities* (Homewood, IL: Business One Irwin, 1991), p. 128.

interest rates would result in a price change of about 2%.

Convexity: For small changes in yield, modified duration does a good job of estimating the actual percentage price change for an option-free bond. However, for large changes in yield it does not. In fact, the larger the yield change, the poorer the approximation. The reason is that duration is a linear approximation of the convex price/yield relationship. Exhibit 5 demonstrates the increase in the error in projecting a new price when yields change by a large amount. The line tangent to the price/yield relationship at y* represents the approximation using duration.[5]

The approximation can be improved by supplementing duration with another measure, *convexity*. How this measure is calculated for an option-free bond is not essential to our discussion.[6] What is important is how to interpret the convexity measure. It can be demonstrated that the percentage price change not explained by duration (i.e., the percentage price change due to convexity) is equal to:[7]

$$\text{Convexity} \times (\text{Yield change in decimal})^2 \times 100$$

For example, a convexity of 80 means that if yields change by 100 basis points (0.01 in decimal form), the percentage price change in addition to duration would be

$$80 \times (0.01)^2 \times 100 = 0.8\%$$

---

[5] Actually, the tangent line is the dollar duration (i.e., the dollar price change) estimate, but there is no loss of generality in our discussion if we refer to the tangent line as the modified duration estimate.

[6] The formula for convexity for a semiannual-pay bond whose next coupon payment is six months from now is:

$$\frac{\dfrac{(1)\ (2)\ C}{(1+y)^1} + \dfrac{(2)\ (3)\ C}{(1+y)^2} + \dfrac{(3)\ (4)\ C}{(1+y)^3} + \dots + \dfrac{(n)\ (n+1)\ (C+M)}{(1+y)^n}}{(1+y)^2\ P}$$

where C is the semiannual coupon payment, y is the semiannual yield to maturity, n is the number of semiannual periods to maturity, M is the maturity value, and P is the price.

[7] Some market participants refer to this as the *convexity gain*.

Exhibit 5: Error in Estimating Price Using Duration

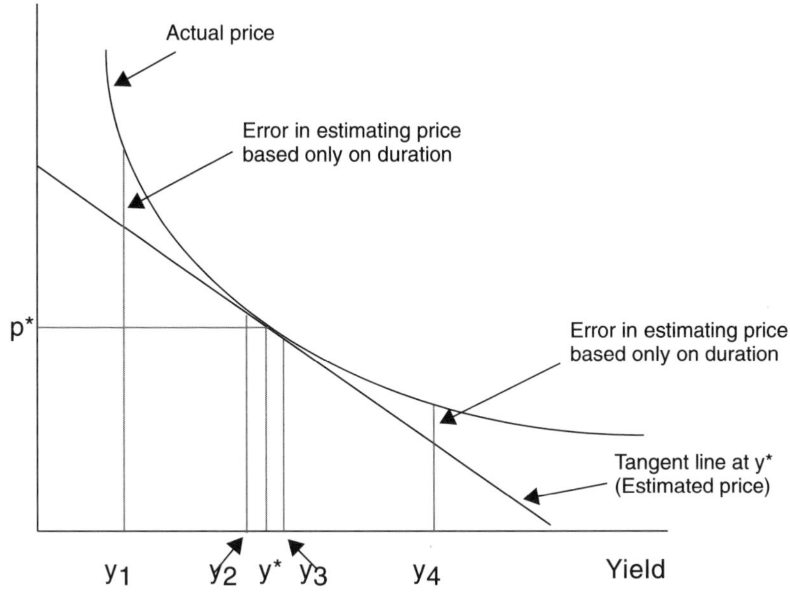

For duration, the percentage price change is proportional to the change in basis points; this is not true for convexity, because the change in yield is squared. So, for example, if a bond has a modified duration of 4, the percentage price change will be approximately 4% for a 100-basis point change in yield, 1% for a 25-basis point change in yield, and 8% for a 200-basis point change in yield. In contrast, if a bond has a convexity of 80, the percentage price change due to convexity is 0.8% for a 100-basis point change in yield, 0.05% for a 25-basis point change in yield, and 3.2% for a 200-basis point change in yield.

An important property of the convexity of an option-free bond is that as the yield increases (decreases), the modified duration of a bond decreases (increases). This property of convexity has interesting implications for bond investors. As yield declines, a bondholder would want a bond's price to increase as much as possible — hence, an investor wants duration to increase. The opposite is true if yield increases, when an investor wants the duration to decline. For this reason, investors commonly refer to the shape of the price/yield relationship for an option-free bond as having "positive" convexity — "positive" indicating that it is a good attribute of a bond. Later we will find that passthroughs exhibit "negative" convexity, which means that duration may not change in the desired direction as yield declines.

Without going into details, convexity measures the rate of change of duration as yield changes. The greater the rate of change of duration, the greater the convexity of a bond. Since the duration of all option-free bonds always changes in the "right" direction, greater convexity is a desirable property. Two bonds may have the same duration but different convexities. The more convex bond will perform better than the less convex bond when interest rates change.

The desirable nature of convexity, however, does not necessarily imply that a more convex security will outperform a less convex one. The fact that convexity is desirable means that it is reflected in the market price, and bonds with higher convexity typically sell for higher prices and lower yields than less convex bonds. Thus, the investor pays for higher convexity in the form of a lower yield.

Consequently, to obtain greater convexity, the investor must pay for it. The performance of a bond over some investment horizon will depend on actual market volatility. The greater actual market volatility, the greater the benefit from improving convexity. Thus, the yield giveup that an investor would be willing to pay to obtain higher convexity depends on the investor's expectations of future interest rate volatility.

Effective Duration: Modified duration is a measure of the sensitivity of a bond's price to interest rate changes, *assuming that the expected cash flow does not change with interest rates.* Consequently, modified duration is not an appropriate measure for mortgage-backed securities because projected cash flows shift as interest rates change and expected prepayments change. When interest rates fall, prepayments are expected to increase. As a result, when interest rates fall, duration may decrease rather than increase. This property is referred to as *negative convexity.*

The impact of negative convexity on the price performance of a mortgage-backed security is the same as for a callable bond. When interest rates fall, a bond with an embedded call option such as a mortgage-backed security will not perform as well as an option-free bond.

While Macaulay duration and modified duration are inappropriate as measures of interest rate sensitivity, there are ways to revise these measures to allow for changing prepayment rates as interest rates change. The same holds true for the standard convexity measure for an option-free bond. Since duration and convexity measure price responsiveness to changes in interest rates, it is possible to calculate these two measures by letting interest rates change by a small number of basis points above and below the prevailing yield, and see how the prices change. In general, the duration for *any* bond can be *approximated* as follows:

$$\text{Duration} = \frac{P_- - P_+}{(P_0)\,(y_+ - y_-)}$$

where P_- = price if yield is decreased by x basis points
P_+ = price if yield is increased by x basis points
P_0 = initial price (per \$100 of par value)
y_+ = initial yield plus x basis points
y_- = initial yield minus x basis points

Application of this formula to an option-free bond gives the modified duration because the cash flow does not change when yields change. For example, consider a 20-year 7% coupon bond selling at \$74.26. The yield to maturity for this bond is 10%. The Macaulay duration for this bond using the formula for Macaulay duration presented in Chapter 3 is 9.64. Therefore, modified duration is 9.18, as shown below:

$$\text{Modified Duration} = \frac{9.64}{(1 + 0.10/2)} = 9.18$$

Suppose, instead, we used the formula given above to approximate duration evaluating the price changes for a 20-basis point change up and down. Then,

P_- =   75.64
P_+ =   72.92
P_0 =   74.26
y_+ =   0.102
y_- =   0.098

substituting into the formula:

$$\frac{75.64 - 72.92}{(74.26)\,(0.102 - 0.098)} = 9.16$$

The approximation of 9.16 is close to the 9.18 modified duration calculated using the exact formula.

When the approximate duration formula is applied to a mortgage-backed security, the new prices at the higher and lower yield levels should reflect the change in the cash flow as a result of the change in expected prepayments. Duration calculated in this way is called *effective duration*. In such a computation, the price at the higher and lower interest rates will depend on the prepayment rate assumed. Typically a higher prepayment rate is assumed at the lower interest rate than at the higher interest rate. Thus, calculation of effective duration requires a prepayment model to determine how prepayments are expected to change as interest rates change.

To illustrate calculation of effective duration for CMO bond classes, consider FRR-03, a hypothetical sequential-pay CMO structure with five tranches. We introduced this structure in Chapter 4. The collateral for this structure is $400 million of passthroughs with a 7.5% passthrough rate and a 357 WAM. All the underlying mortgages are assumed to have a mortgage rate of 8.125%. The structure is summarized in the top panel of Exhibit 6. The second panel provides all the data necessary to calculate modified duration and effective duration of the four regular interest classes and the collateral. This panel shows the assumed cash flow yield and the corresponding initial price for the four regular interest classes assuming a prepayment speed of 165 PSA. The two columns following the initial prices give the new prices if the cash flow yield is changed by 25 basis points and assuming no change in the prepayment speed. The last two columns show new prices if the cash flow yield changes by 25 basis points and the prepayment speed is assumed to change; it decreases to 150 PSA if the cash flow yield increases by 25 basis points, and it increases to 200 PSA if the cash flow yield decreases by 25-basis points.

Exhibit 6 reports the modified duration and effective duration. To illustrate the calculation, consider tranche C. The data for calculating modified duration using the approximation formula are

$$P_- = 102.1875$$
$$P_+ = 98.4063$$
$$P_0 = 100.2813$$
$$y_+ = 0.0725$$
$$y_- = 0.0675$$

Substituting into the formula:

$$\frac{102.1875 - 98.40634}{(100.2813)\,(0.0725 - 0.0675)} = 7.54$$

Exhibit 6: Calculation of Effective Duration and Convexity for FRR-03

Structure of FRR-03

Tranche	Par amount	Coupon rate (%)
A	$194,500,000	6.00
B	36,000,000	6.50
C	96,500,000	7.00
Z (Accrual)	73,000,000	7.25
R	0	0
Collateral	$400,000,000	7.50

Tranche	Cash flow yield (%)	Initial price	New price: 165% PSA CFY change (bp) +25bp	-25bp	New price: CFY change (bp)/new PSA +25/150	-25/200
A	6.00	99.7813	99.0625	100.5313	99.0313	100.4375
B	6.50	100.0313	98.6250	101.5000	98.5625	101.2813
C	7.00	100.2813	98.4063	102.1875	98.3438	101.9063
Z	7.25	100.6250	98.0625	103.2500	98.0313	103.0313
Collateral	7.50	100.1250	98.7500	101.5000	98.7188	101.3438

Tranche	Modified duration	Effective duration	Standard convexity	Effective convexity
A	2.94	2.82	25.055	- 75.164
B	5.75	5.44	49.984	-174.945
C	7.54	7.11	24.930	-249.299
Z	10.31	9.94	49.689	-149.068
Collateral	5.49	5.24	0	-149.813

The effective duration for the same bond class is calculated as follows:

P_- = 101.9063 (at 200 PSA)

P_+ = 98.3438 (at 150 PSA)

P_0 = 100.2813

y_+ = 0.0725

y_- = 0.0675

Substituting into the formula:

$$\frac{101.9063 - 98.3438}{(100.2813)(0.0725 - 0.0675)} = 7.11$$

Notice that for all four tranches and the collateral the effective duration is less than the modified duration.

The divergence between modified duration and effective duration is much more dramatic for tranches trading at a substantial discount from par or at a substantial premium over par. To demonstrate this, we can create another hypothetícal CMO structure that differs from FRR-03 by including a PO class and an IO class created from tranche C. Let's look at the duration for the PO class. Assuming that the cash flow yield for the PO class is 7%, based on 165 PSA, the following prices are obtained:

Initial Price	New Price		New Price	
165 PSA	165 PSA	165 PSA	150 PSA	200 PSA
7.00% CFY	7.25% CFY	6.75% CFY	7.25% CFY	6.75% CFY
60.3125	59.2500	61.3750	57.6563	64.5938

The modified duration for this PO is 7.05. The effective duration of 23.01 is dramatically different.

Effective Convexity: The convexity of *any* bond can be *approximated* using the formula:

$$\frac{P_+ + P_- - 2(P_0)}{(P_0)\,[0.5\,(y_+ - y_-)]^2}$$

When the prices used in this formula assume that the cash flows do not change when yields change, the resulting convexity is a good approximation of the standard convexity for an option-free bond.When the prices used in the formula are derived by changing the cash flows (by changing prepayment rates) when yields change, the resulting convexity is called *effective convexity.*

Exhibit 6 reports the standard convexity and the effective convexity for the four regular interest classes in FRR-03 and the collateral. To illustrate the convexity formula, consider once again tranche C in FRR-03. The standard convexity is approximated as follows:

$$\frac{98.4603 + 102.1875 - 2\,(100.2813)}{(100.2813)\,[0.5\,(0.0725 - 0.0675)]^2} = 24.929$$

The effective convexity is:

$$\frac{98.3438 + 101.9063 - 2\,(100.2813)}{(100.2813)\,[0.5\,(0.0725 - 0.0675)\,]^2} = -249.29$$

Note the significant difference in the two convexity measures here and in Exhibit 6. The standard convexity indicates that the four regular interest classes have positive convexity, while the effective convexity indicates they have negative convexity. The difference is even more dramatic for tranches not trading near par. For a PO created from tranche C, the standard convexity is close to zero, while the effective convexity is 2,155! This means that if yields change by 100 basis points, the percentage change in price due to convexity would be:

$$2,155 \times (0.01)^2 \times 100 = 21.6\%$$

SUMMARY

This chapter discusses one of two methodologies that are used to value mortgage-backed securities: the static cash flow yield methodology. The static cash flow yield is the interest rate that will make the present value of the projected cash flow from an MBS equal to its market price (plus accrued interest). The periodic interest rate is annualized on a bond-equivalent basis. The cash flow yield assumes that (1) all the cash flows can be reinvested at a rate equal to the cash flow yield, (2) the MBS is held to the maturity date, and (3) the prepayment speed used to project the cash flow will be realized. The risk that the reinvestment rate will be less than the cash flow yield is reinvestment risk.

Option-free bonds have well-known price volatility properties, but MBS are securities with embedded call options. As a result, these securities may exhibit negative convexity. The duration of a bond measures its price volatility characteristics. More specifically, duration measures the approximate percentage change in price for a 100-basis point change in yield. Modified duration is not a good measure of price volatility for passthroughs because it assumes that the cash flow of an MBS does not change as yield changes. Effective duration does take into consideration how yield changes will affect prepayments and therefore cash flow. Convexity measures the percentage price change not explained by duration. The standard convexity measure for an option-free bond does not take into consideration how cash flow changes as yield changes. Effective convexity does, so it is therefore more suitable for measuring the convexity of an MBS.

$$\boxed{Chapter\ 10}$$

OPTION-ADJUSTED SPREAD ANALYSIS

A superior approach to the static cash flow yield framework for the valuation of CMO tranches is popularly referred to as the *option-adjusted spread analysis* (OAS analysis). The approach is complicated and computer-intensive, and dealer firms and software vendors use various proprietary OAS models. Despite the diversity of OAS models available, there are basic similarities. The purpose of this chapter is to explain the fundamentals of the OAS model, its critical assumptions, and interpretation and limitations of the model's output. We begin with an explanation of the limitations of the static cash flow yield spread analysis.

DRAWBACKS OF THE STATIC CASH FLOW YIELD SPREAD ANALYSIS

The traditional approach to yield spread analysis for a non-Treasury bond involves calculating the difference between the yield to maturity (or yield to call) of the bond and the yield to maturity of a comparable-maturity coupon Treasury. As we explained in the previous chapter, the yield spread for mortgage-backed securities is calculated as the difference between the cash flow yield on the MBS and the yield on a comparable maturity Treasury, where comparable means a Treasury with either the same average life or Macaulay duration as the MBS. The yield on the Treasury security is obtained from the Treasury yield curve.

There are two drawbacks of calculating the yield spread in this way. First, the yield is not a proper measure for either bond, because the calculation fails to take into consideration the term structure of interest rates. More specifically, the proper valuation of any security should be based on the Treasury spot rates. Spot rate means the theoretical rate that the U.S. government would have to pay if it issued a zero-coupon Treasury security with a specific maturity. In essence, this is equivalent to creating a package of zero-coupon Treasury instruments that has the same cash flow as that projected for the mortgage-backed security. The second drawback is that the Treasury security is option-free, while an MBS is a security with an embedded option. Thus, the value of an MBS should reflect the option granted to homeowners. The value of this option depends on future interest rate volatility.

The option-adjusted spread analysis overcomes these two drawbacks. We begin our discussion of the OAS framework by focusing on the first problem: failure to incorporate the term structure of interest rates.

STATIC SPREAD

The proper procedure to compare an MBS to a Treasury is to compare it to a portfolio of Treasury securities that have the same cash flow. The value of the MBS is then equal to the present value of all of the cash flows. The MBS's value, assuming the cash flows are default-free, will equal the present value of the replicating portfolio of Treasury securities. In turn, these cash flows are valued at the Treasury spot rates.

The *static spread* is a measure of the spread that the investor would realize over the entire Treasury spot rate curve if the mortgage-backed security is held to maturity. It is not a spread off one point on the Treasury yield curve, as is the cash flow yield spread. The static spread is the spread that will make the present value of the cash flow from the MBS when discounted at the Treasury spot rate plus the spread equal to the price of the MBS. A trial-and-error procedure (or search algorithm) is required to determine the static spread.

In general, the shorter the average life of the MBS, the less the static spread will differ from the cash flow yield spread. The magnitude of the difference between the cash flow yield spread and the static spread also depends on the shape of the yield curve. The steeper the yield curve, the greater the difference.

OPTION-ADJUSTED SPREAD

The second drawback to the static cash flow yield spread analysis is its failure to take into account future interest rate volatility that would affect the expected cash flow for a mortgage-backed security.

To understand the second drawback, consider a passthrough with a 9.5% rate, a WAM of ten years, and underlying mortgages with mortgage rates between 10% and 11%. The likelihood that homeowners will refinance falls as mortgage rates increase. If mortgage rates fall and refinancing occurs, the cash flows will change. A small drop in rates will not be sufficient to justify refinancing. Mortgage rates must drop enough so that it is economic for the homeowner to refinance.

Refinancing opportunities depend on how mortgage rates change over the life of the mortgage. For purposes of our illustration, we assume that the mortgage payments are due every six months rather than monthly. Suppose that the six-month interest rate (which we refer to as the short-term rate) is now 7%. Consider the ten possible interest rate paths for six-month forward interest rates for the subsequent 19 six-month periods shown in Exhibit 1, assuming that the six-month forward interest rates can rise or fall by 10% every six months.

The refinancing opportunity for the homeowners will be based not on the short-term forward rate but on a longer-term rate that reflects how much the homeowner would have to pay to refinance the mortgage. Let's make the simple assumption that the refinancing rate is 100 basis points higher than the short-term forward rate. Exhibit 2 shows the ten possible paths for the refinancing rate, each rate in the exhibit 100 basis points higher than in Exhibit 1.

The next step is to translate the interest rate paths into six-month cash flows. More specifically, each interest rate path determines the refinancing opportunity. A prepayment model can be used to project the cash flow for the MBS for each six-month period for a given interest rate path.

Exhibit 1: Ten Possible Paths for Six-Month Forward Rates Assuming an Initial Forward Rate of 7% and 10% Volatility

	Path of short-term forward rates (%)									
Period	1	2	3	4	5	6	7	8	9	10
1	7.0	7.0	7.0	7.0	7.0	7.0	7.0	7.0	7.0	7.0
2	7.7	7.7	7.7	6.3	6.3	6.3	7.7	6.3	7.7	7.7
3	8.5	6.9	6.9	6.9	5.7	5.7	8.5	5.7	8.5	8.5
4	7.6	6.2	6.2	7.6	5.1	6.2	9.3	6.2	9.3	9.3
5	6.9	6.9	5.6	8.4	4.6	6.9	8.4	6.9	8.4	8.4
6	7.5	7.5	5.1	9.2	4.1	6.2	7.5	7.5	7.5	7.5
7	8.3	8.3	4.5	10.1	4.5	5.6	6.8	8.3	6.8	6.8
8	9.1	9.1	5.0	11.2	5.0	5.0	6.1	9.1	6.1	6.1
9	10.0	10.0	5.5	12.3	5.5	4.5	5.5	8.2	6.7	6.7
10	9.0	9.0	6.1	13.5	6.1	4.1	5.0	7.4	6.1	7.4
11	9.9	8.1	6.7	12.2	6.7	4.5	4.5	8.1	5.4	6.7
12	8.9	8.9	7.3	10.9	7.3	4.0	4.0	8.9	4.9	6.0
13	8.1	9.8	8.1	9.8	8.1	4.4	3.6	9.8	4.4	5.4
14	8.9	8.9	7.2	8.9	7.2	4.0	3.2	10.8	4.0	4.9
15	9.7	8.0	6.5	8.0	6.5	4.4	2.9	9.7	4.4	5.3
16	8.8	7.2	7.2	8.8	7.2	3.9	3.2	10.7	4.8	4.8
17	7.9	6.5	7.9	9.6	7.9	3.5	3.5	9.6	5.3	4.3
18	7.1	7.1	8.7	10.6	8.7	3.2	3.9	10.6	5.8	4.8
19	7.8	7.8	7.8	11.7	9.6	2.9	4.3	11.7	6.4	5.2
20	8.6	7.0	8.6	10.5	8.6	3.2	4.7	12.8	7.0	4.7

Exhibit 2: Ten Possible Paths for the Refinancing Rate Assuming It is 100 Basis Points Higher than the Short-term Forward Rate

	Path of refinancing rate (%)									
Period	1	2	3	4	5	6	7	8	9	10
1	8.0	8.0	8.0	8.0	8.0	8.0	8.0	8.0	8.0	8.0
2	8.7	8.7	8.7	7.3	7.3	7.3	8.7	7.3	8.7	8.7
3	9.5	7.9	7.9	7.9	6.7	6.7	9.5	6.7	9.5	9.5
4	8.6	7.2	7.2	8.6	6.1	7.2	10.3	7.2	10.3	10.3
5	7.9	7.9	6.6	9.4	5.6	7.9	9.4	7.9	9.4	9.4
6	8.5	8.5	6.1	10.2	5.1	7.2	8.5	8.5	8.5	8.5
7	9.3	9.3	5.5	11.1	5.5	6.6	7.8	9.3	7.8	7.8
8	10.1	10.1	6.0	12.2	6.0	6.0	7.1	10.1	7.1	7.1
9	11.0	11.0	6.5	13.3	6.5	5.5	6.5	9.2	7.7	7.7
10	10.0	10.0	7.1	14.5	7.1	5.1	6.0	8.4	7.1	8.4
11	10.9	9.1	7.7	13.2	7.7	5.5	5.5	9.1	6.4	7.7
12	9.9	9.9	8.3	11.9	8.3	5.0	5.0	9.9	5.9	7.0
13	9.1	10.8	9.1	10.8	9.1	5.4	4.6	10.8	5.4	6.4
14	9.9	9.9	8.2	9.9	8.2	5.0	4.2	11.8	5.0	5.9
15	10.7	9.0	7.5	9.0	7.5	5.4	3.9	10.7	5.4	6.3
16	9.8	8.2	8.2	9.8	8.2	4.9	4.2	11.7	5.8	5.8
17	8.9	7.5	8.9	10.6	8.9	4.5	4.5	10.6	6.3	5.3
18	8.1	8.1	9.7	11.6	9.7	4.2	4.9	11.6	6.8	5.8
19	8.8	8.8	8.8	12.7	10.6	3.9	5.3	12.7	7.4	6.2
20	9.6	8.0	9.6	11.5	9.6	4.2	5.7	13.8	8.0	5.7

There are obviously an enormous number of interest rate paths. Let's imagine for the moment that we can analyze each path. For each path, we can calculate the present value of the cash flow of the MBS. The discount rate used to calculate the cash flow along a path is based on the Treasury spot rate at each period plus a spread, and spot rates can be calculated from the forward rates. Exhibit 3 shows the spot rates for each period given the short-term forward rates in Exhibit 1. The spot rate for a six-month period is calculated as follows from the six-month forward rates:

$$z_j = [(1+f_1)(1+f_2)(1+f_3) ... (1+f_j)]^{1/j} - 1$$

where

z_j = the spot rate for six-month period j

f_j = the six-month forward rate for period j

For example, for interest rate path 1 in Exhibit 2, the six-month spot rate for period 4 of 7.7% in Exhibit 3 is found as follows:

$$f_1 = 0.070 \quad f_2 = 0.077 \quad f_3 = 0.085 \quad f_4 = 0.076$$

$$z_4 = [(1.070)(1.077)(1.085)(1.076)]^{1/4} - 1$$

$$= (1.34536)^{1/4} - 1 = 1.077 - 1 = 0.077$$

A present value for each path can be calculated using the spot rate plus some assumed spread. An average of all the present values for all the paths can then be computed. If the average present value is equal to the market price of the MBS, the spread added to the Treasury spot rates is called the *option-adjusted spread*. If it is not, the present value along each path is calculated again using a different spread. Once again, if the average present value is equal to the market price of the MBS, this new spread is the option-adjusted spread. If not, the process continues until the spread is found that satisfies this condition.

Mathematically, the option-adjusted spread is the spread that satisfies the following condition:

$$PV_k = \frac{CF_{1k}}{(1+z_1+OAS)^1} + \frac{CF_{2k}}{(1+z_2+OAS)^2} + ... + \frac{CF_{Tk}}{(1+z_T+OAS)^T}$$

Exhibit 3: Treasury Spot Rate on Each Path Constructed from Six-Month Forward Rates

Period	Treasury Spot Rate (%)									
	1	2	3	4	5	6	7	8	9	10
1	7.00%	7.00	7.00	7.00	7.00	7.00	7.00	7.00	7.00	7.00
2	7.35	7.35	7.35	6.65	6.65	6.65	7.35	6.65	7.35	7.35
3	7.72	7.21	7.21	6.74	6.32	6.32	7.72	6.32	7.72	7.72
4	7.70	6.97	6.97	6.96	6.02	6.30	8.12	6.30	8.12	8.12
5	7.53	6.95	6.69	7.25	5.73	6.41	8.17	6.41	8.17	8.17
6	7.53	7.05	6.42	7.57	5.46	6.37	8.07	6.60	8.07	8.07
7	7.64	7.22	6.15	7.94	5.33	6.26	7.89	6.84	7.89	7.89
8	7.83	7.46	6.01	8.34	5.29	6.10	7.66	7.13	7.66	7.66
9	8.07	7.75	5.95	8.77	5.31	5.92	7.42	7.25	7.56	7.56
10	8.17	7.88	5.96	9.24	5.39	5.73	7.17	7.26	7.41	7.54
11	8.33	7.90	6.02	9.51	5.50	5.62	6.93	7.34	7.23	7.46
12	8.38	7.99	6.13	9.62	5.65	5.48	6.68	7.48	7.03	7.34
13	8.36	8.13	6.28	9.64	5.84	5.40	6.44	7.66	6.83	7.19
14	8.39	8.18	6.35	9.59	5.94	5.30	6.21	7.88	6.63	7.02
15	8.48	8.17	6.36	9.48	5.98	5.24	5.99	8.01	6.47	6.91
16	8.50	8.11	6.41	9.43	6.05	5.15	5.82	8.17	6.37	6.78
17	8.46	8.01	6.50	9.45	6.16	5.06	5.68	8.26	6.31	6.63
18	8.39	7.96	6.62	9.51	6.30	4.95	5.58	8.39	6.28	6.53
19	8.36	7.95	6.68	9.62	6.47	4.84	5.51	8.56	6.28	6.46
20	8.37	7.90	6.78	9.67	6.58	4.76	5.47	8.77	6.32	6.37

$$\text{Price} = (1/k)\,[PV_1 + PV_2 + \ldots + PV_k]$$

where

PV_k = Present value on path k

CF_{tk} = Projected cash flow at month t for path k

z_t = Spot rate for month t

K = Number of paths

Price = Observed market price

T = Number of months remaining for the passthrough

The option-adjusted spread can be interpreted as the average spread over the Treasury spot rate curve that equates the average present value over potential future interest rate paths to the observed market price. The spread is called "option-adjusted" because cash flows on the potential paths are adjusted to reflect the right of homeowners to prepay their mortgage loan.

Some Technical Issues

A number of technique issues are important in developing an option-adjusted spread model. In this section, we address six of them.

1. Our simplified illustration used only ten possible paths. This is too small a sample to provide any real indication of the potential cash flows that the investor could realize. The number of paths is determined using a technique called *variance reduction* which allows quite accurate results with a reasonable number of paths.

2. In practice, paths can be generated using Monte Carlo simulation, which requires specifying how the term structure will shift each period. This is accomplished by specifying a probability distribution for the short-term Treasury rate. A change in the short-term Treasury rate will determine how the entire term structure will shift. The assumed probability distribution must be consistent with the existing term structure of interest rates. This means that if an on-the-run Treasury security is evaluated, the OAS model should produce an OAS of zero. This is accomplished by adding a drift term to the short-term return generating process.[1]

3. Specification of the relationship between short-term rates and refinancing rates is necessary. In our simplified illustration, we conveniently assume that the spread between the two is 100 basis points. Empirical evidence on the relationship is necessary. More specifically, the correlation between the short-term and long-term rates must be estimated.

4. Restrictions on interest rate movements must be built into the model to prevent interest rates from reaching unreasonable levels. This is done by incorporating mean reversion into the model.

5. A prepayment model is needed to project the cash flow along each interest rate path. The OAS model will be only as good as the prepayment model used. Dealer firms and vendors have their

---

[1] For an explanation of how this is done, see Lakhbir S. Hayre and Kenneth Lauterbach, "Stochastic Valuation of Debt Securities," in Frank J. Fabozzi (ed.), *Managing Institutional Assets* (New York: Harper & Row, 1990), pp. 321-364.

own prepayment models, often varying considerably in the projections.

6. The volatility of interest rates assumed in the model will have an impact on the option-adjusted spread. The volatility assumption is incorporated with selection of a probability distribution for the short-term Treasury rate. One parameter that must be specified in selecting a probability distribution is the variance (or standard deviation). The larger the variance assumed, the greater the volatility assumed for interest rates. Our illustration assumes constant volatility for the short-term forward rate of 10% per period, but a constant volatility is not a requirement. The volatility may be different for different periods. We discuss the importance of the volatility assumption later.

The impact of these technical issues can cause option-adjusted spreads reported by different dealers to vary considerably.

Summary of Option-Adjusted Spread Calculation

We can summarize the procedure to calculate the option-adjusted spread as follows:

1. From the Treasury yield curve, estimate the term structure of interest rates (spot rates) and the implied forward rates.

2. Select a probability distribution for the short-term Treasury rate. The probability distribution should be selected so that it is consistent with (a) the current term structure of interest rates, and (b) the historical behavior of interest rates. This will prevent the possibility of arbitrage along the yield curve.

3. Use the probability distribution and Monte Carlo simulation to determine randomly a large number of interest rate paths.

4. For each path found in (3), determine the cash flows according to some prepayment model.

5. For an assumed spread and the term structure along a path, calculate a present value for each path.

6. Calculate the average present value for all paths.

7. Compare the average present value to the market price of the mortgage-backed security. If they are equal, the assumed spread used in (5) is the option-adjusted spread. If they are not, try another spread, and repeat (6) and (7).

Determining The Theoretical Value Given the OAS

Given the OAS, the model described above can determine the theoretical value of a mortgage-backed security that is consistent with that OAS. This is depicted in panels in A and B of Exhibit 4. Panel A shows that given the market price, the OAS can be calculated. This is the procedure described above. Given an OAS, the theoretical value can be determined. The theoretical value is the average present value of the paths, where the rates used to discount the cash flows on a path is the spot rates on the path plus the OAS.

Average Life

The average life reported in an OAS model is the average of the average lives along the interest rate paths. That is, for each interest rate path, there is an average life. The average of these average lives is the average life reported in an OAS model.

Additional information is conveyed by the distribution of the average life. The greater the range and standard deviation of the average life, the more the uncertainty about the tranche's average life.

Option Cost

The implied cost of the option embedded in an MBS can be obtained by calculating the difference between the option-adjusted spread at the assumed volatility of interest rates and the static spread. That is,

Option cost = Static spread − Option-adjusted spread

The option cost measures the prepayment (or option) risk embedded in the MBS. Note that the cost of the option is a by-product of the option-adjusted spread methodology, not valued explicitly with some option pricing model.

Exhibit 4: MBS Valuation

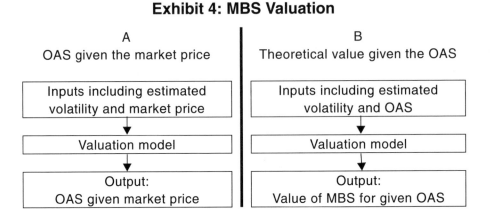

A OAS given the market price	B Theoretical value given the OAS
Inputs including estimated volatility and market price	Inputs including estimated volatility and OAS
Valuation model	Valuation model
Output: OAS given market price	Output: Value of MBS for given OAS

ILLUSTRATIONS

We use two illustrations to show how CMOs can be analyzed using the OAS methodology.[2] Exhibit 5 shows the OAS for a plain vanilla sequential-pay structure, FNMA 89-97. The structure included five bond classes, A, B, C, D, and Z, and a residual class. Class Z is an accrual bond, and the D class is an IOette. The focus of our analysis is on the A, B, C, and Z classes.

The top panel of Exhibit 5 shows the OAS and the option cost for the collateral and classes A, B, C, and Z. The OAS for the collateral is 70 basis points. Since the option cost is 45 basis points, the static spread is 115 basis points (70 basis points plus 45 basis points).

Notice that the classes did not share the OAS equally.[3] Class A did not receive a significant portion of the OAS, only 23 basis points. The longer maturity classes, particularly the Z class, received much of the OAS. The option cost was also distributed unequally among the four classes. The Z class, which was exposed to the greatest prepayment risk, had the highest option cost, a cost that was greater than for the collateral.

---

[2] These illustrations are drawn from Frank J. Fabozzi and Scott F. Richard, "Valuation of CMOs," in Frank J. Fabozzi (ed.), *CMO Portfolio Management* (Summit, NJ: Frank J. Fabozzi Associates, 1994).

[3] The OAS of the classes do not sum up to the OAS for the collateral for two reasons. First, Class D, the IOette, is not included in the exhibit. Second, the OAS's must be weighted by their par value.

Exhibit 5: OAS Analysis of FNMA 89-97
Classes A, B, C, and Z (As of 4/27/90)

	Base case (assumes 12% interest rate volatility)	
	Option-adjusted spread (in basis points)	Option cost (in basis points)
Collateral	70	45
Class		
A	23	29
B	46	41
C	59	36
Z	74	50

	Prepayments at 80% and 120% of Prepayment Model (assumes 12% interest rate volatility)			
	New option-adjusted spread (in basis points)		Change in price per $100 par (holding OAS constant)	
	80%	120%	80%	120%
Collateral	70	71	$0.00	$0.04
Class				
A	8	40	−0.43	0.48
B	31	65	−0.86	1.10
C	53	73	−0.41	0.95
Z	72	93	−0.28	2.70

	Interest rate volatility of 8% and 16%			
	New option-adjusted spread (in basis points)		Change in price per $100 par (holding OAS constant)	
	8%	16%	8%	16%
Collateral	92	46	$1.03	−$1.01
Class				
A	38	5	0.42	−0.51
B	67	21	1.22	−1.45
C	77	39	1.22	−1.36
Z	99	50	3.55	−3.41

The next panel of Exhibit 5 shows for the collateral and the four classes: (1) how the OAS changes if prepayments are 80% and 120% of the prepayment speed assumed in estimating the OAS in the base case (the top panel), and (2) the change in the dollar price if the prepayments are 80% and 120% of the prepayment speed assuming that the OAS is constant. For example, consider the collateral. If the prepayment speed is 80% of the assumed prepayment speed in the base case, the OAS will not change and there will be no change in the collateral price. Note, however, the dramatic change for the four classes.

To see how an investor might use the information in the second panel, consider Class A. At 80% of the prepayment speed, the OAS for this class declines from 23 basis points to 8 basis points. As explained earlier, a theoretical value can be determined given the OAS. Exhibit 5 shows that for a buyer of Class A, if the OAS is held constant, the panel indicates that the bondholder would lose $0.43 per $100 par value. The reason for the adverse effect of a slowdown in prepayment speed on Class A is obvious. If prepayments slow down, Class A (the class with the shortest stated maturity) extends. The OAS for the two longer classes (C and Z) does not change materially.

Should the prepayment speed be 120% greater than in the base case, the second panel in Exhibit 5 indicates that the collateral's OAS will increase only slightly (one basis point), but the OAS for the classes does not change equally. If prepayments are faster, the OAS of Class Z rises dramatically, and its price increases substantially ($2.70 per $100 par) assuming OAS is held constant at the base case of 74 basis points.

The third panel shows what happens if interest rate volatility is less or greater than the 12% assumed in the base case. Less interest rate volatility (8%) results in an increase in the collateral's OAS to 92 basis points (assuming price is held constant) and an increase in the collateral price (assuming a constant OAS of 70 basis points) of $1.03 per $100 par value. Thus, if actual volatility is less than that used to model the deal, the collateral and the classes would be underpriced. The greatest increase in value resulting from reduced future interest rate volatility would be for Class Z.

If volatility is greater instead of less (16%), there will be more scenarios in which the homeowner will be likely to prepay. Consequently, the OAS and the change in price (holding OAS constant) will decline for the collateral and the four classes.

Exhibit 6 shows how to apply the OAS methodology to a more complicated CMO structure, FHLMC Series 120. There are 14 classes in this structure: nine PAC bonds (including two PAC PO bonds and a PAC IO bond), a TAC support bond, an accrual support bond, a coupon-paying support bond, and a residual bond. Basic information about this structure is summarized in Exhibit 7.[4]

---

[4] Notice that for the PAC IO (the I bond) the coupon rate shown is 857%. Prior to 1992, all classes of a REMIC had to have some principal allocated. In this case, the original balance for the PAC IO class is $100,000.

Exhibit 6: OAS Analysis of FHLMC 120

	Base Case (assumes 12% interest rate volatility)	
	OAS (in basis points)	Option Cost (in basis points)
Collateral	72	34
Class		
A (PAC)	52	4
B (PAC PO)	48	−1
C (PAC PO)	64	−7
D (PAC)	67	5
E (PAC)	68	8
F (PAC)	73	9
G (PAC)	75	9
H (PAC)	85	9
J (Support TAC)	17	62
K (Support)	61	58
Z (Support Z)	78	83

	Prepayments at 80% and 120% of Prepayment Model (assumes 12% interest rate volatility)				
	Base Case OAS	New OAS (in basis points)		Change in Price per $100 par (holding OAS constant)	
		80%	120%	80%	120%
Collateral	72	69	77	$0.15	$0.22
Class					
A (PAC)	52	65	42	0.43	−0.35
B (PAC PO)	48	17	54	−0.71	0.12
C (PAC PO)	64	14	86	−1.52	0.67
D (PAC)	67	61	62	−0.24	−0.20
E (PAC)	68	65	61	−0.13	−0.37
F (PAC)	73	76	63	0.16	−0.59
G (PAC)	75	80	64	0.33	−0.68
H (PAC)	85	93	75	0.56	−0.69
J (Support TAC)	17	4	56	−0.43	1.34
K (Support)	61	64	75	0.17	0.82
Z (Support Z)	78	85	114	0.75	3.77

	Interest Rate Volatility of 8% and 16%				
	Base Case OAS	New OAS (in basis points)		Change in Price per $100 par (holding OAS constant)	
		8%	16%	8%	16%
Collateral	72	91	51	$0.88	−$0.91
Class					
A (PAC)	52	57	43	0.14	−0.31
B (PAC PO)	48	47	51	−0.02	0.07
C (PAC PO)	64	57	75	−0.15	0.35
D (PAC)	67	72	59	0.13	−0.34
E (PAC)	68	74	56	0.21	−0.59
F (PAC)	73	80	60	0.26	−0.80
G (PAC)	75	82	60	0.26	−0.88
H (PAC)	85	92	75	0.27	−0.69
J (Support TAC)	17	47	−17	0.54	−0.31
K (Support)	61	94	26	0.95	−1.98
Z (Support Z)	78	126	28	2.58	−5.30

Exhibit 7: Information about FHLMC 120 Classes

Total Issue: $300,000,000			Original Rating: S&P NR, Moody's NR,
Issue Date: 12/8/89			Fitch NR, D&P NR
Structure Type: REMIC CMO			Original Settlement Date: 1/30/90
Issuer Class: Agency			Days Delay: 30
Dated Date: 1/15/90			Payment Frequency: Monthly; 15th day of month

| | | | | Original Issue Pricing (180% PSA Assumed) | |
Tranche	Original Balance ($)	Coupon (%)	Stated Maturity	Average Life (yr)	Expected Maturity
120-A(PAC Bond)	37,968,750	16.0	11/15/13	4.0	12/15/95
120-B(PAC Bond)	20,500,000	0.0	2/15/11	3.4	10/15/94
120-C(PAC Bond)	9,031,250	0.0	11/15/13	5.3	12/15/95
120-D(PAC Bond)	12,000,000	9.0	2/15/15	6.3	9/15/96
120-E(PAC Bond)	40,500,000	9.0	5/15/18	7.9	7/15/99
120-F(PAC Bond)	10,000,000	9.0	1/15/19	10.0	8/15/00
120-G(PAC Bond)	6,500,000	9.0	6/16/19	10.9	6/15/01
120-H(PAC Bond)	33,000,000	9.0	2/15/21	15.5	4/15/18
120-I(PAC Bond)	100,000	857.0	2/15/21	7.9	4/15/18
120-J(PAC Bond)	99,600,000	9.5	2/15/21	3.2	10/15/99
120-K	15,700,000	9.5	7/15/15	8.3	7/15/01
120-R	90,000	9.5	2/15/21	8.1	4/15/19
120-S	10,000	9.5	2/15/21	8.1	4/15/19
120-Z (Accrual)	15,000,000	9.5	2/15/21	18.8	4/15/19

The top panel of Exhibit 6 shows the base case OAS and the option cost for the collateral and all but the residual and PAC IO classes. The collateral OAS is 72 basis points and the option cost is 34 basis points. Thus the static spread of the collateral to the Treasury spot rate curve is 106 basis points.

Several interesting observations about this structure are noteworthy. First, notice that Class J, a support TAC bond, did not realize a good OAS allocation. It has a low OAS and a high option cost. It would be expected that, given the prepayment uncertainty associated with this support bond, its OAS would be higher. The reason for the effect is that the bond was priced at issuance so that its static cash flow yield was high. Consequently, "yield buyers" in the market were probably willing to bid aggressively for this bond and thereby drive down its OAS, despite our warning in the previous chapter that yield is not a meaningful measure of potential return. Such buyers are willing to trade off "yield" for OAS. The support K bond did not get a good OAS allocation either, although, its allocation was more than three times greater than the J bond's. The K bond was also offered at a price that provided a high relative yield. This analysis indicates that the OAS for the K bond was higher than that for the J bond.

Second, notice that the B and C bonds have a negative option cost. These two bonds are PAC POs. Greater prepayment risk would mean a speeding up of prepayments, resulting in faster repayment of principal. Since PAC POs benefit from fast prepayments, they benefit from such a scenario, resulting in a negative option cost.

The next two panels in Exhibit 6 show the sensitivity of the OAS and the price (holding OAS constant at the base case) to changes in the prepayment speed (80% and 120% of the base case speed) and to changes in volatility (8% and 16%). This analysis once again shows that the change in the prepayment speed does not affect the collateral significantly, while the change in the OAS (holding price constant) and price (holding OAS constant) for each class is significant. For example, a slower prepayment speed, which increases the time period over which a PAC PO bondholder can recover the principal, significantly reduces the OAS and price. The opposite effect results if prepayments are faster than the base case. Class A, which is a high coupon bond (as can be seen from the information in Exhibit 7), benefits from a slowing of prepayments, as the bondholder will receive the higher coupon for a longer time. Faster prepayments represent an adverse scenario. This is supported by the results reported in the last panel of the exhibit.[5]

Other illustrations of the OAS methodology to CMOs appear in Exhibits 8 and 9. Exhibit 8 shows the OAS methodology applied to a four-class sequential-pay CMO structure, as well as to the underlying collateral (a GNMA 9%). The effect of interest rate volatility can be seen in the last three columns of the exhibit. Notice that the OAS for the CMO classes is much more sensitive to changes in interest rate volatility than the collateral, GNMA passthroughs. Thus, while a CMO class may have less prepayment risk than a passthrough, it is exposed to greater risk in terms of the effect of changes in interest rate volatility.

---

[5] A somewhat surprising result involves the effect that the change in prepayments has on the accrual bond (the Z-bond). Notice that whether prepayment speeds are slower or faster, the OAS and the price increase. Without the use of an OAS framework, this would not be intuitively obvious.

Exhibit 8: OASs for a GNMA 9 CMO

Class	Par amount ($)	Price	Coupon (%)	Average life (years)	B-E yield (%)	Treasury spread (bp)	OAS (bp) at volatility of: 10%	15%	20%
GNMA 9	100.0	96.65625	9.0	11	10.48	123	104	88	71
A	35.1	98.37792	8.0	2	9.10	100	67	48	21
B	19.0	95.50843	8.5	5	9.85	115	83	59	25
C	18.0	94.74840	9.0	7	10.27	125	103	80	52
Z	27.9	80.99889	9.0	17	10.87	150	102	79	52

Assumption: The GNMA 9 has a remaining term of 28 years; the CMO is priced assuming a projected prepayment speed of 100%PSA.
Source: Lakhbir S. Hayre and Kenneth Lauterbach, "Stochastic Valuation of Debt Securities," in Frank J. Fabozzi (ed.), *Managing Institutional Assets* (New York: Harper & Row, 1990), pp. 340

Exhibit 9: OASs for Several Types of MBS

Issue	Base case assumptions				20% increase in volatility		Yield Curve steepens	Mortgage spreads widen 20%
	Price	Yield (%)	Effective duration	OAS (bp)	OAS (bp)	% change in price	% change in price	% change in price
Fannie Mae CMO:								
90108-3 PAC 5-yr	97.344	9.12	4.5	58	55	-0.16	0.55	-0.51
90108-5 PAC 10-yr	93.500	9.54	6.8	72	68	-0.23	-0.47	-0.90
90108-6 PAC 18-yr	177.438	9.77	8.7	89	88	-0.12	-0.97	-1.49
Freddie Mac CMO:								
171-2 Pl Van 5-yr	98.531	9.37	3.6	58	46	-0.44	0.22	-0.48
169-3 Pl Van 20-yr	94.406	9.94	6.4	71	59	-0.73	-0.60	-0.93

Yield curve assumptions:

Maturity (years)	Base Case (%)	50% steeper (%)
2	7.91	7.59
3	8.07	7.83
4	8.23	8.07
5	8.32	8.20
7	8.56	8.56
10	8.69	8.76
30	8.82	8.95

Source: Greg Parseghian of the First Boston Corporation, November 1990.

Exhibit 9 shows the OAS methodology applied to IOs, POs, PACs, and plain vanilla CMO classes. This exhibit shows not only what might happen to the OAS and price if there is a 20% change in expected interest rate volatility, but also what happens if the yield curve changes and the spread between MBS and Treasuries widens.

EFFECTIVE DURATION AND CONVEXITY

Effective duration and convexity can be computed as part of the OAS methodology by increasing and decreasing the short-term Treasury rate by a small amount, keeping the option-adjusted spread constant. This produces two average total present values: one when the short-term interest rate is increased, and one when the short-term interest rate is decreased. These average total present values can be viewed as the theoretical prices under small interest rate changes. These prices are then substituted into the effective duration and convexity formulas given in Chapter 9.

Effective duration and effective convexity calculated in this way are sometimes referred to as *option-adjusted duration* and *option-adjusted convexity.*

EMPIRICAL EVIDENCE

Thomas Ho has quantified the risks associated with the different types of CMO bond classes in an analysis of all agency CMOs (Fannie Mae and Freddie Mac CMOs) as of December 15, 1991 (1,033 observations).[6] Exhibit 10 reports Ho's findings for the average and standard deviation of the average life, effective duration, effective convexity, and option-adjusted spread for floating-rate, inverse floating-rate, IOs, PACs, POs, and Z bonds.

SUMMARY

This chapter has explained the option-adjusted spread approach to valuing a CMO bond class. This approach takes into account (1) the term structure of interest rates, (2) the prepayment option embedded in a CMO bond, and (3) the expected volatility of interest rates. The static cash flow yield spread approach does not take these factors into account.

---

[6] Thomas S.Y. Ho, "CMO Yield Attribution and Option Spread," *Journal of Portfolio Management* (Spring 1993), pp. 57-68.

Exhibit 10: Risk Profiles for All Agency CMOs by Tranche Type (as of December 15, 1991)

Type of tranche	Average life Avg.	Std. dev.	Effective duration Avg.	Std. dev.	Effective convexity Avg.	Std. dev.	OAS Avg.	Std. dev.
Floaters	10.44	6.09	2.31	2.46	2.03	4.31	-4.07	21.35
Inverse floaters	11.01	6.20	6.90	11.65	-6.29	6.31	143.01	113.32
IOs	5.82	1.99	-17.90	14.33	-3.89	20.52	141.26	136.71
PACs	6.31	4.98	3.77	2.26	-0.10	0.67	6.53	8.23
POs	8.81	5.95	36.50	19.82	11.67	51.65	-32.41	304.38
Accruals (Zs)	12.36	5.40	9.98	3.98	-0.64	2.41	43.26	17.36

Source: Thomas S. Y. Ho, "CMO Yield Attribution and Option Spread," *Journal of Portfolio Management* (Spring 1993), Exhibit 10, p. 66.

The static spread measures the spread over the Treasury spot rate curve assuming that interest rates will not change in the future. The option-adjusted spread is the spread over the Treasury spot rate curve, taking into account the option granted to homeowners to prepay their mortgage as interest rates change. It is an average spread, because it is based on a large number of potential paths for interest rates. The cost of the embedded option is a by-product of the model, not specifically estimated with an option pricing model.

Different decisions on the many technical considerations incorporated into an option-adjusted spread model can result in considerable differences in the values for CMO tranches reported by dealer firms. A portfolio manager using an option-adjusted spread reported by a dealer or produced by a model developed by a vendor firm must recognize why these differences may occur.

Chapter 11

TOTAL RETURN FRAMEWORK

The first main step in the investment management process is setting investment objectives. Investment objectives will vary by type of financial institution and are essentially dictated by the nature of an institution's liabilities. For institutions such as banks and thrifts, the objective is to earn a return on invested funds that is higher than the cost of acquiring those funds. For institutions such as pension funds, the investment objective will be to generate sufficient cash flow from the investment portfolio to satisfy its pension obligations. Life insurance companies sell a variety of products guaranteeing a dollar payment or a stream of dollar payments at some time in the future. Premiums charged policyholders depend on the interest rate the company can earn on its investments. To realize a profit, the company must earn a higher return on the premium it invests than the implicit (or explicit) interest rate it has guaranteed policyholders.

Neither the static cash flow yield methodology nor the option adjusted spread methodology will tell a money manager whether investment objectives can be satisfied. We explain why in our discussion of the limitations of each methodology. The performance evaluation of an individual MBS or an MBS portfolio requires specification of an investment horizon, whose length for most financial institutions is dictated by the nature of its liabilities. For example, a life insurance company issuing a four-year guaranteed investment contract (GIC) would use a four-year investment horizon. For money managers who face no liabilities but are instead evaluated in terms of some benchmark index, the relevant investment horizon is typically one year.

The measure that should be used to assess the performance of a security or a portfolio over some investment horizon is the *total return*.[1] The purpose of this chapter is to discuss the total return framework and to show how total return is measured for CMOs. We also show how to incorporate static cash flow yield and option-adjusted spread methodologies into the total return framework.

TOTAL RETURN MEASURE

The total dollars received from investing in a CMO tranche consist of:

(1) the projected cash flow of the tranche from:
 (a) the projected interest payments,
 (b) the projected principal repayment (scheduled plus pre-payments).

(2) the interest earned on reinvestment of the projected interest payments and the projected principal repayments.

(3) the projected price of the CMO at the end of the investment horizon.

To obtain the cash flow, a prepayment rate over the investment horizon must be assumed. The second step requires assumption of a reinvestment rate. Finally, either of the methodologies described in the two previous chapters — static cash flow yield or option-adjusted spread — can be used to calculate the CMO price at the end of the investment horizon under a particular set of assumptions. Either approach requires assumption of the prepayment rate and the Treasury rates (i.e., the yield curve) at the end of the investment horizon. The static cash flow yield approach uses an assumed spread to a comparable Treasury to determine the required cash flow yield, which is then used to compute the projected price. The OAS methodology

---

[1] The total return is also called the *horizon return*.

requires an assumption of what the OAS will be at the investment horizon. From this assumption, the OAS methodology can produce the price. In practice, a constant OAS is assumed (i.e., it is assumed that the OAS will not change over the investment horizon).

For a monthly-pay CMO, the monthly total return is then found using the formula:

$$\text{Monthly total return} = \left(\frac{\text{Total future dollars}}{\text{Total proceeds paid}} \right)^{1/\text{Number of months in horizon}} - 1$$

where total proceeds paid is the purchase price plus accrued interest.

The monthly total return can be annualized on a bond-equivalent yield basis as follows:

$$\text{Bond-equivalent annual return} = 2 \left[(1 + \text{Monthly total return})^6 - 1 \right]$$

or, by computing the effective annual return as follows:

$$\text{Effective annual return} = (1 + \text{Monthly total return})^{12} - 1$$

To illustrate how to calculate total return for a CMO, we will use tranche C of FRR-03 described in Chapter 4. This tranche is a sequential-pay with a coupon rate of 7%. The assumptions are:

(1) the investment horizon is one-year.

(2) the amount purchased of this tranche is $9.65 million of the original par value at the issue date for a price of 100-09 and a cash flow yield of 7% assuming 165 PSA.

(3) interim cash flows are reinvested at 4% per year.

(4) at the investment horizon, interest rates for similar sequential-pay bonds decrease by 200 basis points to 5%.

(5) a drop in interest rates of 200 basis points increases the prepayment speed at the end of the investment horizon to 250 PSA from 165 PSA.

According to these assumptions, the cash flow generated from principal repayments, coupon interest, and reinvestment income would be $682,100. The price of the tranche at the end of the investment horizon would be 111-17. The sale price plus accrued interest for $9,650,000 of original par value is $10,819,100. The total future dollars would then be $11,501,200.

Since the bonds are assumed to be purchased at 100-09, the price paid for this tranche is $9,677,141 (100.2812 for $9,650,000 of original par value) plus accrued interest. The accrued interest is $56,292, so the total proceeds paid for this tranche would be $9,733,433. The monthly total return is then:

$$\left(\frac{\$11,501,200}{\$9,733,433} \right)^{\frac{1}{12}} - 1 = (1.181618)^{\frac{1}{12}} - 1 = 0.014004$$

The bond-equivalent yield is found as follows:

$$2\,[\,(1.014004)^{6} - 1] = 0.1740 = 17.4\%$$

The effective annual yield would be:

$$(1.014004)^{12} - 1 = 0.1816 = 18.16\%$$

Scenario Analysis

Note from the total return calculation that several assumptions are necessary. To test the sensitivity of total return to various alternative assumptions, a technique known as *scenario analysis* is helpful. Its limitation is that only a small number of potential scenarios can be considered, and it fails to take into consideration the dynamics of changes in the yield curve and the dynamics of the deal structure. A more powerful technique that addresses these considerations is Monte Carlo simulation, which we describe later.

Exhibit 1 shows the total return on a bond-equivalent basis for each regular interest class of FRR-03 for nine parallel interest rate shifts. For each interest rate shift, a different prepayment rate is assumed. In practice, the prepayment rate would be based on projections of a prepayment model.

Exhibit 1: Scenario Analysis for Four Regular Interest Classes of FRR-03

Assumptions:

One-year investment horizon
Horizon yield based on interest rate shift
Priced at: 165 PSA
Analysis at issuance; Settles: 8/31/92
Interest rates shift in one step of one month each
Cash flows reinvested to horizon date at 4%

Collateral prepayment assumptions:

Interest Rate Shift (bp)	PSA
+400	100
+300	130
+200	140
+100	150
+0	165

Interest rate shift (bp)	PSA
-100	200
-200	250
-300	300
-400	400

Scenario Analysis for Tranche A

Original par: $194,500,000; Coupon: 6.00% (fixed); Price: 99-25; Cash flow yield: 6%;
Par purchased: $19,450,000; Purchase price: $19,407,453; Accrued interest: $97,250;
Total proceeds paid: $19,504,703

Interest rate shift (bp)	Ending pre-payment (PSA)	Horizon Performance A/L (yrs)	Dur (yrs)	Yield (%)	Proceeds excl. sale ($100s)	Sale price ($100s)	Sale price (32nds)	Total dollars ($100s)	Total return (% BEY)
+400	100	4.17	3.37	10.01	22,836	161,333	87-08	184,168	-5.66
+300	130	3.35	2.87	9.01	25,019	167,286	91-20	192,305	-1.41
+200	140	3.15	2.75	8.01	25,673	171,788	94-16	197,461	1.23
+100	150	2.96	2.64	7.01	26,323	175,908	97-06	202,231	3.65
0	165	2.72	2.48	6.01	27,344	179,328	99-23	206,671	5.87
-100	200	2.29	2.14	5.01	29,857	180,361	101-26	210,218	7.63
-200	250	1.86	1.78	4.01	33,477	178,851	103-06	212,329	8.67
-300	300	1.56	1.52	3.01	37,076	176,652	104-07	213,728	9.36
-400	400	1.18	1.18	2.01	44,384	168,879	104-11	213,263	9.13

Scenario Analysis for Tranche B

Original par: $36,000,000; Coupon: 6.50% (fixed); Price: 100-01; Cash flow yield: 6.5%
Par purchased: $3,600,000; Purchase price: $3,601,125; Accrued interest: $19,500;
Total proceeds paid: $3,620,625

Interest rate shift (bp)	Ending pre-payment (PSA)	Horizon Performance			Proceeds excl. sale ($100s)	Sale price ($100s)	Sale price (32nds)	Total dollars ($100s)	Total return (% BEY)
		A/L (yrs)	Dur (yrs)	Yield (%)					
+400	100	9.96	6.89	10.51	2,428	27,566	76-01	29,994	-17.97
+300	130	8.06	6.08	9.50	2,417	30,289	83-19	32,706	-9.91
+200	140	7.56	5.87	8.50	2,406	32,291	89-05	34,697	-4.21
+100	150	7.12	5.66	7.51	2,395	34,260	94-20	36,655	1.24
0	165	6.53	5.33	6.51	2,384	36,184	99-31	38,568	6.42
-100	200	5.46	4.63	5.51	2,374	37,815	104-16	40,189	10.71
-200	250	4.39	3.85	4.51	2,363	38,940	107-20	41,303	13.61
-300	300	3.65	3.28	3.51	2,352	39,750	109-28	42,102	15.67
-400	400	2.71	2.50	2.51	2,341	39,795	110-00	42,136	15.76

Scenario Analysis for Tranche C

Original par: $96,500,000; Coupon: 7.00% (fixed); Price: 100-09; Cash flow yield: 7%
Par purchased: $9,650,000; Purchase price: $9,677,141; Accrued interest: $56,292; Total proceeds paid: $9,733,432

Interest rate shift (bp)	Ending pre-payment (PSA)	Horizon Performance			Proceeds excl. sale ($100s)	Sale price ($100s)	Sale price (32nds)	Total dollars ($100s)	Total return (% BEY)
		A/L (yrs)	Dur (yrs)	Yield (%)					
+400	100	14.92	8.11	11.00	7,008	69,922	71-28	76,930	-22.19
+300	130	12.44	7.68	10.00	6,977	77,371	79-19	84,347	-13.82
+200	140	11.75	7.63	9.00	6,945	83,764	86-07	90,709	-6.93
+100	150	11.11	7.54	8.00	6,914	90,429	93-04	97,343	0.01
0	165	10.26	7.30	7.00	6,883	97,274	100-07	104,157	6.89
-100	200	8.65	6.56	6.00	6,852	103,516	106-22	110,368	12.97
-200	250	7.0	5.63	5.00	6,821	108,191	111-17	115,011	17.40
-300	300	5.84	4.89	4.00	6,790	111,749	115-07	118,539	20.71
-400	400	4.32	3.79	3.00	6,759	112,232	115-23	118,990	21.13

Scenario Analysis for Tranche Z

Original par: $73,000,000; Coupon: 7.25% (fixed); Price: 100-20; Cash flow yield: 7.25%
Par purchased: $7,300,000; Purchase price: $7,345,625; Accrued interest: $44,104;
Total proceeds paid: $7,389,729

Interest rate shift (bp)	Ending pre-payment (PSA)	A/L (yrs)	Horizon Performance		Proceeds excl. sale ($100s)	Sale price ($100s)	Sale price (32nds)	Total dollars ($100s)
			Dur (yrs)	Yield (%)				
+400	100	23.69	9.01	11.25	5,491	50,127	68-02	55,617
+300	130	21.71	9.34	10.25	5,466	55,237	75-02	60,703
+200	140	21.04	9.75	9.25	5,442	60,666	82-16	66,108
+100	150	20.36	10.12	8.25	5,417	66,871	91-00	72,288
0	165	19.37	10.36	7.25	5,393	73,874	100-19	79,267
-100	200	17.19	10.12	6.25	5,368	81,243	110-22	86,611
-200	250	14.53	9.44	5.25	5,344	88,041	120-00	93,385
-300	300	12.41	8.71	4.25	5,320	94,041	128-07	99,360
-400	400	9.36	7.21	3.25	5,295	96,390	131-14	101,686

Note: This analysis was performed using the Multiscenario Analysis Feature of WallStreet Analytics, Inc.

Projection of Price at the Horizon Date

The most difficult part of estimating total return is projecting the price of the CMO tranche at the horizon date. The price depends on the characteristics of the tranche and the spread to Treasuries at the horizon date. The key determinants are the "quality" of the tranche, its average life (or duration), and its convexity.

Quality refers to the type of CMO bond. Consider, for example, that an investor can purchase a CMO tranche that is a PAC bond but as a result of projected prepayments, could become a sequential-pay tranche. As another example, suppose a PAC bond is the longest average life tranche in a reverse PAC structure. Projected prepayments in this case might occur in an amount to change the class from a long-term average life PAC tranche to effectively a support tranche. The converse is that the quality of a tranche may improve as well as deteriorate. For example, the effective collar for a PAC tranche could widen at the horizon date when prepayment circumstances increase the par amount of support tranches outstanding as a proportion of the deal.

Exhibit 1 demonstrates how the average life and Macaulay duration can change materially, depending on the scenario, although perhaps not in the desired direction. For example, consider once again tranche C of FRR-03. From Exhibit 1 we can see that if interest rates increase by 400 basis points, the Macaulay duration increases from 7.3 years to 8.11 years, and the average life increases from 10.26 years to 14.92 years. Thus, one year later this tranche will become a longer-term security, and in all likelihood it will be priced relative to a longer-benchmark Treasury security. Rather than rolling down the yield curve, this security would roll up the yield curve. For support bonds and other exotic bond classes, the drift of Macaulay duration and average life can be quite substantial.

While we have not focused on convexity in our discussion, the same is true for this parameter. It can drift to an undesirable value, thereby adversely affecting price.[2]

OAS-TOTAL RETURN

The total return and OAS frameworks can be combined to determine the projected price at the horizon date. This requires an OAS model and a

---

[2] For a further discussion, see David P. Jacob and Sean Gallop, "Duration and Convexity Drift of CMOs," Chapter 30 in Frank J. Fabozzi (ed.), *The Handbook of Mortgage-Backed Securities* (Chicago: Probus Publishing, 1992).

prepayment model. At the end of the investment horizon, it is necessary to specify how the OAS is expected to change. The horizon price can be "backed out" of the OAS model.

Assumptions about the OAS value at the investment horizon reflect the expectations of the money manager. It is common to assume that the OAS at the horizon date will be the same as the OAS at the time of purchase. A total return calculated using this assumption is sometimes referred to as a *constant-OAS total return*. Alternatively, active total return managers will make bets on how the OAS will change — either widening or tightening. The total return framework can be used to assess how sensitive the performance of a CMO tranche is to changes in the OAS.

SIMULATION

The performance of an MBS or MBS portfolio depends on the outcome of a number of random variables.[3] A portfolio's total return will depend on the magnitude of the change in Treasury rates, the spread between CMO tranches and Treasury securities, changes in the shape of the yield curve, and actual and expected prepayment speeds. Moreover, each random variable may have a substantial number of possible outcomes. Consequently, evaluation of all possible combinations of outcomes in order to assess the risks associated with an MBS portfolio may be impractical.

Suppose that a money manager wants to assess the performance of an MBS portfolio over a one-year investment horizon. Suppose further that the portfolio's performance will be determined by the actual outcome for each of nine random variables, and that each of the nine random variables has seven possible outcomes. There are thus 4,782,969 (9^7) possible outcomes representing all possible combinations of the nine random variables. Furthermore, each of the 4,782,969 outcomes has a different probability of occurrence.

One approach for a portfolio manager is to take the "best guess" for each random variable, and determine the impact on the performance measure. The best-guess value for each random variable is usually the expected value of the random variable.[4] There are serious problems with

---

[3] A random variable is one that can take on more than one possible outcome.

[4] The expected value of a random variable is the weighted average of the possible outcomes, where the weight is the probability of the outcome.

this shortcut approach. To understand its shortcomings, suppose the probability associated with the best guess for each random variable is 75%. If the probability distribution for each random variable is independently distributed, the probability of occurrence for the best-guess result would be only 7.5% (0.75⁹). At this level of probability, no portfolio manager would have a great deal of confidence in this best-guess result.

Between the extremes of enumerating and evaluating all possible combinations and the best-guess approach is the simulation approach. Simulation is less a model than a procedure or algorithm. The solutions obtained do not represent an optimal solution to a problem. Rather, simulation provides information about a problem so that a portfolio manager can assess the risks associated with an MBS or an MBS portfolio.

There are many types of simulation techniques. When probability distributions are assigned to the random variables, the simulation technique is known as a *Monte Carlo simulation*, named after the famous gambling spot on the French Riviera. Monte Carlo simulation enables portfolio managers to determine the statistical properties of various investment characteristics such as total return and average life of an MBS portfolio. Armed with this information, a portfolio manager can assess the likelihood of meeting an investment objective and determine whether the portfolio should be rebalanced.

Steps for Monte Carlo Simulation

There are 12 steps in a Monte Carlo simulation:[5]

Step 1: A performance measure must be specified. The performance measure could be total return over some investment horizon or net interest (spread) income.[6]

Step 2: The problem under investigation, including all important variables and their interactions, must be expressed mathematically. The variables in the mathematical model will be either deterministic or random. A *deterministic variable* can take on only one value; a *random variable* can take on more than one value.

---

[5] A more detailed explanation and illustration is provided in Chapter 23 of Frank J. Fabozzi, *Fixed Income Mathematics: Analytical and Statistical Techniques* (Chicago: Probus Publishing, 1993).

[6] Liabilities can also be simulated, particularly when liabilities exhibit interest-rate sensitivity.

The variables that are typically assumed to be deterministic in a Monte Carlo simulation to assess the total return performance of a CMO tranche include:

- the volatility of short-term Treasury rates
- the volatility of long-term Treasury rates
- the correlation between the movement in short-term and long-term Treasury rates
- a prepayment model

The random variables are typically:

- short-term rates
- long-term rates
- the shape of the yield curve
- the relationship between long-term Treasury rates and mortgage rates

The horizon price of a security can be calculated using the static cash flow yield methodology or the OAS methodology. The interest rate paths generated in the simulation can be used to determine the horizon price, but an OAS value at the horizon date must be assumed.[1]

Step 3: A probability distribution for the random variables must be specified.

Step 4: Probability distributions for random variables must be converted into cumulative probability distributions.

Step 5: For each random variable, representative numbers must be assigned on the basis of the cumulative probability distribution to each possible outcome specified.

Step 6: A random number must be obtained for each random variable.

---

[1] For an illustration of how this can be done to assess the six-month performance (as measured by total return) of an interest-only (IO) trust under various yield curve scenarios, see: Lakhbir Hayre, Charles Huang, and Vincent Pica, "Realistic Holding-Period Analysis: Technology and Its Impact on Valuation Metrics." *Study #14*, Financial Strategies Group, Prudential Securities, August 13,1992.

Step 7: For each random number, the corresponding value of the random variable must be determined.

Step 8: The corresponding value of each random variable found in the previous step must be used to determine the value of the performance measure mathematically expressed in step 2.

Step 9: The value of the performance measure found in step 8 must be recorded.

Step 10: Steps 6 through 9 must be repeated many times, say, 100 to 1,000 times. The repetition of steps 6 through 9 is known as a *trial*.

Step 11: The values for the performance measure for each trial recorded in step 9 become the basis for construction of a probability distribution and cumulative probability distribution.

Step 12: The cumulative probability distribution constructed in step 11 is analyzed in terms of summary statistics such as the mean, standard deviation, and the range.

Usually more than one simulation analysis is undertaken in order to test sensitivity to changes in the deterministic variables. A money manager may rerun the simulation using a different volatility assumption for short-term and long-term rates. To test sensitivity to prepayment rates, the simulation could be rerun assuming prepayment rates that are a specified percentage higher or lower than that projected from the model (e.g., 80% lower, or 120% higher).

Generating Random Numbers

In order to implement step 6, it is necessary to have a procedure to obtain random numbers. Any procedure used must provide that the probability of selection must be equal for each number that could be selected.

Several procedures can be used for generating random numbers. Random number tables provide random numbers. Add-in features in spreadsheets and other software also can be used to generate random numbers. LOTUS 123, for example, provides a function @RAND that will generate a random number between 0 and 1. To get a two digit number the value generated by @RAND can be multiplied by 100.

Exhibit 2: Total Return Distributions: FHLMC 151 C versus U.S. Treasury Benchmark

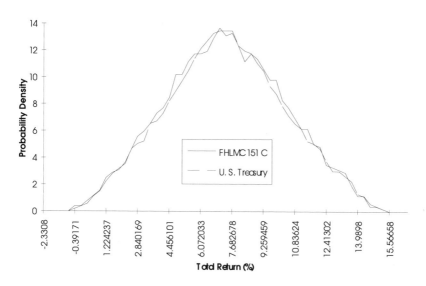

Illustrations

To illustrate the application of simulation, we use several total return simulations provided by David Canuel of Aeltus Investment Management, Inc.[2] In all illustrations, the investment horizon is two years. Interim cash flows are assumed to be reinvested in Treasury strips that mature at the horizon date. The total return for each trial is calculated assuming a constant OAS. There are 200 trials for each simulation.

In the first example, FHLMC 151 C tranche (a PAC tranche) is compared to a U.S. Treasury benchmark consisting of a combination of three-year and five-year on-the-run Treasuries. The coupon rate for the tranche and the passthrough coupon rate are both 9%. Exhibit 2 graphs the results of the simulation, a total return distribution for the tranche versus the U.S. Treasury benchmark. The PAC tranche has a total return distribution similar to that of the Treasury benchmark because of the high degree of prepayment protection at the time of issuance (an initial collar of 90 to 270 PSA).

---

[2] These illustrations were presented at the various Collateralized Mortgage Obligations Tutorials sponsored by Frank J. Fabozzi Associates.

Exhibit 3: Total Return Differences: FHLMC 151 C versus U.S. Treasury Benchmark

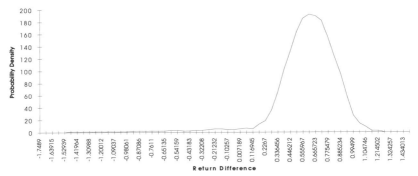

Exhibit 3 shows the distribution for the spread between the tranche and the Treasury benchmark for each trial. This exhibit provides further insight into the relative performance of the tranche and the Treasury benchmark that is not evident from Exhibit 2. The distribution has a tail to the left, due to the negative convexity of the PAC tranche, which reduces the mean of the distribution significantly. The mean of the PAC distribution is 59 basis points above that of the Treasury distribution, while the cash flow yield spread of the PAC was 75 basis points. The difference between (1) the cash flow spread and (2) the spread between the two distributions is attributable not only to the option cost (i.e., negative convexity of the distribution), but also to the fact that the Treasury benchmark rolls down the yield curve more rapidly than the PAC over a two-year horizon.

Besides comparing a CMO tranche to a Treasury benchmark, simulation can be used also to look at the relative performance of competing mortgage-backed securities. Exhibit 4 graphs the total return distributions for FHLMC 151 D tranche (a PAC tranche) and a newly originated FNMA 8.5% passthrough. Both mortgage-backed securities exhibit a slight negative convexity, but the passthrough exhibits more. This difference reflects differences in (1) option exercise during the horizon, (2) option cost embedded in the end-of-horizon price, and (3) rolling down the yield curve. Assumptions regarding reinvestment of cash flows also affect the difference between the distribution means. For example, if reinvestment were at 0% over the horizon, the difference would be large, and the security with more rapid prepayments would experience low realized returns. If reinvestment occurred at the Treasury rate plus a fixed spread, the difference between distribution means is a rough measure of the differences in option cost. The option cost is sensitive to other factors as well.

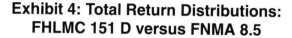

Exhibit 4: Total Return Distributions: FHLMC 151 D versus FNMA 8.5

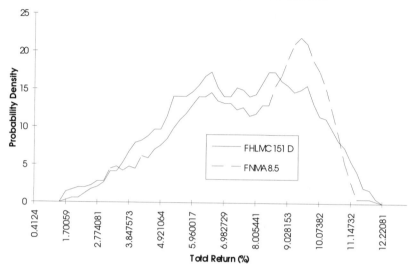

Simulation can also be used to assess the impact of differences in collateral on total returns. Exhibit 5 shows results of two simulations of an actual sequential-pay tranche returns, assuming collateral of 9% and 9.5%.[3] The exhibit indicates that in rising interest rate environments, the nature of the collateral makes little difference in performance. In declining interest rate environments, however, the tranche with the lower-coupon collateral will outperform the tranche with the higher-coupon collateral. The mean difference in total return is 20 basis points. The tranche at the time of issuance had 50% 9% collateral and 50% 9.5% collateral. With seasoning of mortgages and interest rate changes, the character of the collateral will change over time, so in the future simulation results may be quite different.

The same type of analysis for PAC IOs appears in Exhibit 6. The exhibit shows the total return distributions for FHLMC 194 F tranche. At issuance, the average life for this tranche was 16 years. The passthrough rate for the collateral is 8.5%. Shown in the exhibit are total return distributions assuming passthrough coupon rates of 8.5% and 9% (with the WAC 50 basis points higher). The mean difference in the total return distribution over the two years is 24 basis points.

---

[3] The deal is Kidder Peabody Mortgage Assets Trust Three issued in 1987. The tranche simulated is Class D.

Exhibit 5: Sequential-Pay Total Returns: Impact of Collateral Differences

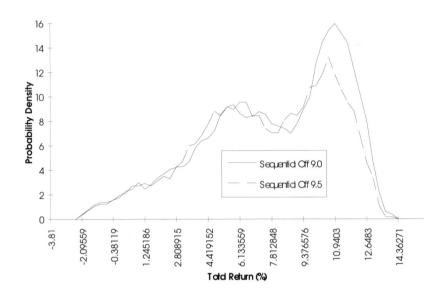

Exhibit 6: PAC-IO Total Returns: Impact of Collateral Differences

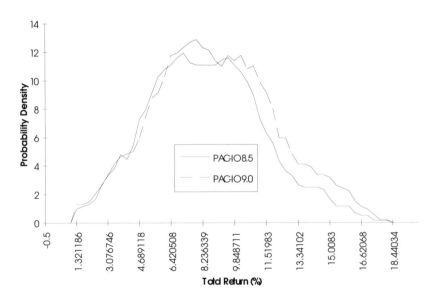

SUMMARY

Total return is the correct measure for assessing the performance of CMO tranches over a specified investment horizon. The static cash flow yield and option-adjusted spread methodologies can be incorporated into a total return framework to calculate the CMO price at the horizon date.

Scenario analysis is one way to evaluate the risk associated with investing in a CMO tranche, but the dynamics of interest rates cannot be captured by scenario analysis. Monte Carlo simulation provides a better assessment of the performance of a CMO tranche through generation of a total return distribution.

Chapter 12

ANALYSIS OF INVERSE FLOATERS

In Chapter 5, we explained what an inverse floater is and how it is created. An inverse floater can be created from a support tranche, a PAC tranche, or an IO tranche. Our purpose in this chapter is fourfold. First, we explain how the value of an inverse floater is determined. Second, we look at its performance as the yield curve changes. Then we discuss the effective position of the owner of an inverse floater. Finally, we explain how a synthetic security can be created either to enhance return relative to a benchmark Treasury or to control interest rate risk.

VALUING AN INVERSE FLOATER

As we stated in Chapter 9, the value of any financial asset is the present value of its expected cash flow. It is difficult to value an inverse floater in these terms because of uncertainty about future values for the reference rate. Fortunately, the valuation of an inverse floater is not complex as we shall see.

In our discussion of inverse floater valuation, we shall refer to the fixed-rate tranche out of which the floater and inverse floater were created as "the collateral." We can express the relationships among the collateral, the floater, and the corresponding inverse floater as follows:

Collateral = Floater + Inverse floater

This relationship applies in terms of cash flows as well as valuation.

That is, the sum of the value of the floater and the value of the inverse floater must be equal to the value of the collateral from which they are created. This value is sometimes referred to as the *creation value*. If this relationship is violated, arbitrage profits are possible.

An alternative way to express the relationship is:

Value of inverse floater = Value of collateral – Value of floater

This expression states that the value of an inverse floater can be found by valuing the collateral and valuing the floater, then calculating the difference between the two values. In this case, the value of an inverse floater is not found directly, but instead inferred from the value of the collateral and the floater.

Valuing the Collateral

The value of the collateral is found by determining the cash flow according to some prepayment assumption and then discounting at an appropriate interest rate. The appropriate discount rate depends on (1) the level of Treasury rates, and (2) the spread of the collateral to Treasuries. The spread depends on the value of the option granted to homeowners.

Valuing a Floater

The value of a floater depends on two factors: (1) the spread over the reference rate, and (2) the cap on the floater. As explained in Chapter 5, all floaters have a cap, which means we can view the security as a package of an uncapped floater (a floater without a cap) and a cap. That is:

Capped floater = Uncapped floater – Cap

The reason for subtracting the value of the cap from the value of an uncapped floater is that the holder of a capped floater has effectively sold a cap.

Assuming that the spread over the reference rate required by the market has not changed since issuance, the uncapped floater should sell at its par value. The value of a capped floater thus can be expressed as follows:

Value of a capped floater = Par value – Value of cap

If the reset coupon rate (reference rate plus spread) is far below the cap, the value of the cap will be close to zero, and the capped floater will trade at par value. However, if the reset coupon rate is close to the cap or above the cap, the value of the cap will be positive, and the value of a capped floater will be less than its par value.

The question therefore is how to determine the value of the cap. A cap is an agreement between two counterparties whereby one party, for an upfront premium, agrees to compensate the other if a designated benchmark interest rate (called the reference rate) is above a predetermined level (called the strike rate).[1]

In the over-the-counter market, caps are valued using an option pricing model, since a cap is nothing more than an option or series of options. Two key factors that affect the value of a cap are: (1) the relationship between the current reference rate and the strike rate, and (2) the expected volatility of the reference rate. The farther the reference rate is below the strike rate, the less the value of the cap. As the reference rate approaches the strike rate, the cap increases in value. With respect to expected volatility of the reference rate, a cap has more value the greater the expected volatility.

Factors that Affect the Value of an Inverse Floater

Given that the floater created from the collateral is a capped floater, the value of an inverse floater can be expressed as:

Value of inverse floater = Value of collateral – Value of capped floater

The factors that affect the value of inverse floaters are the factors that affect the value of the collateral and the value of a capped floater. The factors that affect the collateral are (1) prepayment rates, (2) Treasury rates, and (3) the spread of the collateral to Treasuries. The factors that affect the value of a capped floater are those that affect the value of the cap: (1) the relationship between the reset coupon rate and the cap, and (2) the expected volatility of the reference rate.

---

[1] The terms of an interest rate agreement include: (I) the reference rate; (2) the strike rate that sets the ceiling; (3) the length of the agreement; (4) the frequency of settlement; and (5) the notional principal amount.

Leverage and Valuation

It is informative to recast the valuation of inverse floaters by looking at the importance of the leverage that is selected. Suppose that the creator of the floater and inverse floaters divides the collateral into 100 bonds, 20 inverse floater bonds and 80 floater bonds.[2] This means that the leverage in this structure is 4:1 of floater bonds to inverse floater bonds. Then, the following relationship must hold:

$$100\,(\text{Collateral price}) \ = \ 20\,(\text{Inverse price}) + 80\,(\text{Floater price})$$

This can also be expressed as:

$$20\,(1+4)\,(\text{Collateral price}) \ = \ 20\,(\text{Inverse price}) + 20\,(4)\,(\text{Floater price})$$

Dividing both sides by 20, we get:

$$(1+4)\,(\text{Collateral price}) \ = \ (\text{Inverse price}) + (4)\,(\text{Floater price})$$

This can be generalized for any leverage L as follows

$$(1+L)\,(\text{Collateral price}) \ = \ (\text{Inverse price}) + (L)\,(\text{Floater price})$$

Solving for the inverse price we have:

$$(\text{Inverse price}) \ = \ (1+L)\,(\text{Collateral price}) - (L)\,(\text{Floater price})$$

There are two important implications of this price relationship. First, typically it is not difficult to price the floater. The greater difficulty is often in determining the collateral's price. Notice the implication of mispricing the collateral. The greater the leverage, the greater the impact of mispricing of the inverse floater resulting from mispricing the collateral. Specifically, every one point mispricing of the collateral results in a 1 + L point mispricing of the inverse floater. So with a leverage of 3, a 4 point mispricing of the inverse results for each one point mispricing of the collateral.

---

[2] William R. Leach, "A Portfolio Manager's Perspective of Inverses and Inverse IOs," Chapter 10 in Frank J. Fabozzi (ed.), *CMO Portfolio Management* (Summit, NJ: Frank J. Fabozzi Associates, 1993).

The second implication is that the price of the inverse floater is not related to the level of the reference index as long as the floater cap is not affected. What in fact affects the price performance of an inverse floater is explored next.

PERFORMANCE OF AN INVERSE FLOATER

A common misconception is that the value of an inverse floater should change in a direction opposite from the change in the reference rate. Thus, if the reference rate falls (holding collateral value constant), the value of an inverse floater should rise. This view is incorrect because the value of an inverse floater is not solely dependent on the reference rate. The reference rate affects the value of the inverse floater only through its effect on the value of the cap of the capped floater, and does not take account of the other factors that we have noted will affect the value of an inverse floater.

To see the importance of these relationships for the value of an inverse floater, assume that:

- the reference rate for an inverse floater is one-month LIBOR, and currently one-month LIBOR is 6.5%
- the capped floater created from the same collateral has a spread of 100 basis points and a cap of 7%
- the collateral would trade at a spread of 120 basis points to a comparable Treasury and that the comparable Treasury (one with an intermediate-term maturity) has a yield of 9.5%

Now consider three scenarios six months from now. For each scenario we make an assumption about (1) one-month LIBOR six months from now, (2) the expected volatility of one-month LIBOR six months from now, and (3) the yield on a comparable Treasury and the spread to that Treasury security. We will look at the effect on the value of the collateral and the value of the capped floater. The difference between these two values is the value of the inverse floater.

Scenario 1: Six months from now (1) one-month LIBOR declines to 4.5%, (2) expected volatility of one-month LIBOR declines, and (3) the spread widens to 140 basis points and the yield on a comparable Treasury (an intermediate-term maturity) rises to 11%. Thus, short-term rates are assumed to have declined, and intermediate-term rates to have increased. This means that the yield curve is assumed to steepen.

Given this scenario, the value of the capped floater will increase for two reasons. First, today the coupon rate on the capped floater is 7.0% since one-month LIBOR is 6.5% and the spread is 100 basis points but the cap is 7%. Six months later the capped floater's value increases because the coupon rate falls below the cap (the new coupon rate is 5.5%), thereby reducing the value of the cap. Second, expected volatility for one-month LIBOR decreases. The value of the collateral declines because both the relevant intermediate-term Treasury rate has increased and the spread to the Treasury has widened. Since the value of an inverse floater is the difference between the value of the collateral (which has decreased) and the value of the capped floater (which has increased), the value of the inverse floater has declined. Notice that this effect occurs in this scenario despite the fact that one-month LIBOR has declined.

Scenario 2: Now assume that six months from now (1) one-month LIBOR rises to 7%, (2) expected volatility of one-month LIBOR increases, and (3) the spread narrows to 100 basis points and the yield on a comparable Treasury (an intermediate-term maturity) falls to 8%. Thus, short-term rates are assumed to rise and intermediate-term rates to fall. This means that the yield curve has flattened. Since one-month LIBOR has risen further above the cap and expected volatility has increased, the value of the capped floater six months from now will fall. The value of the collateral will rise. Thus, the value of the inverse floater will increase. This occurs even though the reference rate has increased.

Scenario 3: Finally, assume that six months from now that (1) one-month LIBOR declines to 4.5% (as in scenario 1), (2) expected volatility of one-month LIBOR decreases (as in scenario 1), and (3) the spread narrows to 100 basis points and the yield on a comparable Treasury (an intermediate-term maturity) falls to 8% (as in scenario 2). Under this scenario, the value of the collateral will rise. The value of the inverse floater can either rise or fall, as the collateral has risen in value and the capped floater has risen in value. The net effect depends on the relative increases of the collateral and the capped floater.

These three scenarios do not consider another key factor: how changes in interest rates affect prepayments, and therefore the collateral from which the floater and inverse floater are created. The overall effect will depend on how the collateral used to create the CMO structure is affected by prepayments. Thus, a change in interest rates affects not only the discount rate used to determine the present value of the cash flow from the collateral (i.e., tranche) from which the floater and inverse floater are created, but also the cash flow from the underlying collateral for the CMO structure.

Typically, dealers analyze inverse floaters for a potential buyer by modeling the performance under various scenarios. Usually, performance assumptions cover a rise or decline in interest rates of up to 400 basis points. Such analysis can be misleading for several reasons. First, there is no such thing as an "interest rate." Rather there is a structure of interest rates as depicted by the Treasury yield curve, and we demonstrated above that changes in the shape of the Treasury yield curve can affect the value of a floater. Simply assuming that "interest rates" rise or fall by a particular number of basis points means that all interest rates along the Treasury yield curve change by the same amount (i.e., that there is a parallel shift in the Treasury yield curve). Our discussion should make it clear that the value of an inverse floater requires more in-depth analysis than one simple assumption of parallel shifts in the yield curve.

Duration of an Inverse Floater

The duration of an asset is a measure of its price sensitivity to a change in interest rates. Because valuations are additive (that is, the sum of the floater and the inverse floater equals the value of the collateral), durations are additive as well. Thus, the duration of the inverse floater is related to the duration of the collateral and the duration of the floater. Assuming that the duration of the floater is close to zero, it can be shown that the duration of an inverse floater is:[3]

$$\text{Duration of inverse floater} = (1 + L)\,\text{Duration of collateral} \times \frac{\text{Collateral price}}{\text{Inverse price}}$$

For an inverse IO, the duration is:

$$\text{Duration of inverse IO} = \text{Duration of collateral} \times \frac{\text{Collateral price}}{\text{Inverse price}}$$

---

[3] Leach, "A Portfolio Manager's Perspective of Inverses and Inverse IOs," p. 159.

INTERPRETATION OF AN INVERSE FLOATER POSITION

Since the capped floater and inverse floater are created from fixed-rate collateral, the following relationship is true:

Long fixed-rate collateral = Long a capped floater + Long an inverse floater

Recasting this relationship in terms of an inverse floater, we can write

Long an inverse floater = Long fixed-rate collateral – Long a capped floater

Or, equivalently,

Long an inverse floater = Long fixed-rate collateral – Short a capped floater

Thus, the owner of an inverse floater has effectively purchased fixed-rate collateral and shorted a capped floater. But shorting a floater is equivalent to borrowing funds, where the interest cost of the funds is a floating rate where the interest rate is the reference rate plus the spread. Consequently, the owner of an inverse floater has effectively purchased a fixed-rate asset with borrowed funds.

APPLICATION OF INVERSE FLOATERS

Inverse floaters have been used in three ways: (1) to bet on the movement of the reference rate; (2) to create synthetic fixed-rate securities with a better total return performance; and (3) to reduce interest rate risk.

Betting on the Reference Rate

As we explain in Chapter 5, the formula for the coupon rate on an inverse floater is

$$K - L \text{ (Reference rate)}$$

The L or multiple in the formula to determine the coupon rate is the coupon leverage and K is the cap on the inverse floater.

For example, for the inverse floater tranche S of FNMA 90-138, the coupon rate is:

$$42.56 - 3.8 \text{ (1 month LIBOR)}$$

.   If LIBOR is 4%, the coupon rate is 27.36%, a fairly hefty coupon in an environment of low rates for the reference rate.

It is important to note that while the coupon rate on the inverse floater is indeed attractive in our example, the total return depends also on its price performance, which is affected by the additional factors discussed in the previous section.

Let's consider the appropriateness of using inverse floaters to bet on the movement of the reference rate. All financial intermediaries such as depository institutions, insurance companies, and investment companies take on intermediary risks. That is their role. The question is which types of intermediary risks are acceptable. For depository institutions and insurance companies, the acceptable risks and the amount of exposure to such risks are set forth by regulators. As we explain in Chapter 13, all mortgage derivatives classified as high-risk mortgage securities are closely regulated by the appropriate supervisory agency. In general, regulators do not want depository institutions to use inverse floaters that may be classified as high-risk mortgage securities to speculate on rates. The exception is that financially strong depository institutions with a knowledgeable management may actively trade inverse floaters; there must be a board-approved investment policy specifying the maximum exposure, and that exposure must be monitored periodically.

Regulations with respect to mortgage derivatives are discussed in Chapter 13. Investment companies must set forth their investment objectives in the prospectus. Speculating on the reference rate may be perfectly acceptable if specified in the prospectus.

Creating Synthetic Fixed-Rate Securities

The market for CMOs can be described as fragmented. There is no centralized reporting system for trades as there is for stocks, and each CMO structure is unique. Such fragmented markets present opportunities for enhancing returns. By enhancing returns we mean earning a total return greater than a comparable Treasury (or Treasury combination) after adjusting for risk.

One strategy using inverse floaters is to combine them with floaters from similar collateral to create a synthetic fixed-rate security that will outperform a comparable Treasury. Institutions authorized to use the interest rate swap market can create a synthetic fixed-rate security by using this market. The governing issue is that the actual performance of a synthetic security will depend on many assumptions about the factors that affect the value of the inverse floater and the floater used in the synthetic.

Unfortunately, typical analysis of a synthetic calls for looking at the cash flow yield over a range of parallel shifts in the Treasury yield curves. There are two pitfalls to this approach. First, as we explain in Chapter 9, cash flow yield is not a measure of the potential performance of a security. The same is obviously true for a synthetic. Instead, the total return approach should be used. Second, the parallel shift assumption is not adequate in testing the sensitivity of the performance of a synthetic.

Thus, there are no "free lunches" in the CMO market. It is unlikely that one can create a fixed-rate synthetic using an inverse floater and either a floater or a swap position that will outperform a comparable Treasury in all scenarios. Rather, total return analysis that takes into account the relevant risks will indicate the relative risks associated with the two positions. While there are no free lunches, however, there are some that are much more tasty and less expensive than others.

Reducing Interest Rate Risk

All financial institutions are subject to interest rate risk. A drop in interest rates may increase the value of portfolio holdings of fixed-rate securities, but it will also reduce interest income generated from some assets. For example, a decline in short-term rates reduces interest income from floating-rate instruments. A decline in mortgage refinancing rates will accelerate prepayments for both mortgages and passthroughs with a higher coupon rate, forcing an institution to reinvest at a lower rate. For institutions that service mortgages, a drop in mortgage refinancing rates will also reduce the value of their portfolio of servicing rights.

An inverse floater provides a leveraged means for reducing the risks should a key interest rate that will affect an institution fall. The danger is that the analysis undertaken to assure realization of that objective is all too often done not on a cash flow basis, but on some type of cash flow yield basis without carefully assessing the relevant risks.

As we explain in Chapter 13, regulators of depository institutions recognize the use of high-risk mortgage securities to reduce interest rate risk. Now, however, they demand more adequate analysis and documentation to support the purchase of any CMO tranche for the purpose of reducing interest rate risk.

SUMMARY

The value of an inverse floater is determined by the value of the collateral from which the inverse floater and the floater are created. The factors that affect the value and performance of an inverse floater are those that affect the value of the collateral from which it is created — the yield on a comparable

Treasury, the spread off a comparable Treasury, and prepayment rates — and the value of the floater — the value of the cap. The owner of an inverse floater has effectively purchased a fixed-rate asset and borrowed on a floating-rate basis.

Inverse floaters have been used to speculate on the reference rate, create synthetic fixed-rate securities, and reduce interest rate risk. Analysis of the potential outcome of any of these applications should be based on a total return framework, not on a cash flow yield. It should also reflect the wide range of possible outcomes for the factors that affect the values of the inverse floater and the other securities in the strategy.

SECTION IV: ACCOUNTING AND REGULATORY CONSIDERATIONS

Chapter 13

ACCOUNTING FOR CMO INVESTMENTS

This chapter provides an overview of the generally accepted accounting practices (GAAP) for reporting investment in CMO tranches and mortgage passthroughs. Guidelines for classification of mortgage-backed securities and CMO's, as well as rules for accounting for the cash flows of MBS's and CMO's, are established by the Financial Accounting Standards Board, otherwise known as FASB. The FASB has released several statements and bulletins that address these topics. The primary documents are the Financial Accounting Standards Board Statement No. 91, "Accounting for Nonrefundable Fees and Costs Associated with Originating or Acquiring Loans and Initial Costs of Leases," released in 1986; the Emerging Issues Task Force Issue 89-4, "Accounting for a Purchased Investment in a Collateralized Mortgage Obligation Instrument or in a Mortgage-Backed Interest-Only Certificate," released in 1989; and Financial Accounting Standards Board Statement No. 115, "Accounting for Certain Investments in Debt and Equity Securities," released in 1993. FASB 115 supersedes FASB Statement No.12, "Accounting for Certain Marketable Securities" and alters other previously issued FASB pronouncements.

---

* This chapter is coauthored with Cathy Hansen of Frank J. Fabozzi Associates.

VALUATION AND CLASSIFICATION: FASB 115

According to FASB 115 there are two methods to value any security, including a CMO tranche: (1) amortized cost (i.e., historical cost with adjustment for amortization of a premium or discount), or (2) mark to market. Despite the fact that the real cash flow is the same regardless of the accounting treatment, there can be substantial differences in the income reported using these two methods. The lower of cost or market method is no longer used.

Illustration of Valuation Methods

To illustrate the two methods, we use a hypothetical security that has a principal (or par value) of $100,000 and an 8% coupon rate. Exhibit 1 shows the balance sheet value and the income reported for three years assuming the end-of-year prices shown. We assume that the security is purchased at the beginning of the year so that the coupon interest for the year is $8,000.

In the amortized cost method, the value reported in the balance sheet reflects an adjustment to the acquisition cost only for the amortization of a discount or premium. For a security acquired at a premium, the adjustment decreases the reported value; the amortization of a discount increases the reported value. If the security is held to maturity date, the amortized cost method would report a balance sheet value equal to the par value at that date. In our case, since the security is assumed to be purchased at par there is no balance sheet adjustment.

The income statement in this method reflects the coupon interest adjusted for the amortization. The amortization of a premium reduces income for the year while amortization of a discount increases income for the year. Since there is no amortization in our illustration, the income reported is just the $8,000 coupon interest.

In the mark-to-market method, the balance sheet reported value is the market value. The gain or loss for the year is reflected in the income statement or in shareholder's equity, depending upon security classification discussed later in this chapter. For example in the first year, the market value declined to $96,000 resulting in a loss of $4,000. This loss is reflected in the income statement or shareholder's equity. At the end of the second year, the market value rebounds to $103,000 and an unrealized gain of $7,000 is reflected. As Exhibit 1 clearly indicates, there is considerable variation in the reported balance sheet value under the two methods.

Exhibit 1: Comparison of Accounting Methods for Securities

		Accounting Method		
	Market Value	Amortized Cost	Trading Mark-to-Market	Available for sale Mark-to-Market
Balance sheet effects: Assets				
At acquisition date	$100,000	$100,000	$100,000	$100,000
End of year 1	96,000	100,000	96,000	96,000
End of year 2	103,000	100,000	103,000	103,000
End of year 3	98,000	100,000	98,000	98,000
Balance sheet effects: Shareholder's Equity				
End of year 1		0	0	-4,000
End of year 2		0	0	7,000
End of year 3		0	0	-5,000
Income Statement Effect				
End of year 1		8,000	4,000	8,000
End of year 2		8,000	15,000	8,000
End of year 3		8,000	3,000	8,000

Classification of Securities

Accounting treatment required for a security depends on how the security is classified. There are three categories of investment accounts: (1) held for trading, (2) available for sale, and (3) held to maturity.

In general, a security is classified as held to maturity if the investor has the ability and the intent to hold it to maturity. If a security is classified as held to maturity the amortized cost valuation method is used.

A security that is acquired for the purpose of earning a short-term trading profit from market movements is classified as held for trading. These securities are valued based on current market value, or the mark-to-market method. Unrealized profits and losses from market changes on held for trading securities are to be included in earnings.

A security that is classified as available-for-sale is also to be valued based on current market value. A security is classified as available for sale if it is not purchased for short-term trading and the investor does not have the ability or the intent to hold the security to maturity. Unrealized gains and losses for available-for-sale securities are to be excluded from earnings and reported in a separate component of shareholders equity until gains or losses become realized. Realized gains or losses in any category are to be reported in earnings.

Original classification of securities are to be consistent. Transfers between accounts may call into question the investor's intent and ability to hold securities to maturity and subject the entire portfolio holdings to mark-to-market accounting. However, there are circumstances under which transfers are allowed without calling intent and ability into question. These circumstances are:[1]

1. Significant deterioration is the issuer's creditworthiness.

2. Changes in tax law that reduces or eliminates tax-exempt status of interest on the security (but not a change in tax law that revises the marginal tax rates applicable to interest income.)

3. Major business combination or major disposition (such as sale of a segment) that necessitates the sale or transfer of held-to maturity securities to maintain the enterprise's existing interest rate risk position or credit risk policy.

---

[1] FASB 115, p. 3.

4. Change in statutory or regulatory requirements significantly modifying either what constitutes a permissible investment or the maximum level of investments in certain kinds of securities, thereby causing an enterprise to dispose of a held-to-maturity security.

5. Significant increase by the regulator in the industry's capital requirements.

6. Significant increase in the risk weights of debt securities used for regulatory risk-based capital purposes.

Two conditions exist under which securities may be sold from the held-to-maturity account which consider the security as matured. They are: (1) maturity date is so near that interest rate risk is no longer a pricing factor[2] and (2) a substantial portion of the principal outstanding (at least 85%) at acquisition date has been returned prior to the sale of the security. This means 85% of par value purchased, not 85% of original par value.

Interest income, including amortization of premiums and discounts at purchase, is to be included in earnings for all categories of classification. No changes for calculation of premium/discount amortization and interest income were made by FASB 115.

ACCOUNTING FOR MORTGAGE-BACKED SECURITIES AND THEIR DERIVATIVES

Accounting for the cash flows (monthly principal and interest payments) of mortgage-backed securities, by applying actual income earned to the income statement and returning capital to the asset accounts, has been a topic for discussion since the MBS was created. The creation of CMOs and IO/PO strips further complicated the issue. FASB issued its Statement No. 91 in December 1986 to establish standards of financial accounting and reporting for the cash flows, discounts, and premiums associated with the purchase of loans and other debt securities, in addition to nonrefundable fees and costs associated with lending activities.

---

[2] The example used in FASB 115 is three months.

FASB 91

FASB 91 states that a constant effective yield (or internal rate of return) is to be calculated according to some reasonable assumption of projected prepayments. The calculated yield will determine the amount of income to be booked on the basis of the outstanding dollars invested. The balance of the cash flow will be the return of capital. FASB 91, paragraph 19, further states that should actual prepayments differ from projections, the yield (or IRR) is to be recalculated, and net investment amounts, as well as income, are to be adjusted to the amount that would have existed had the new yield been applied since acquisition.

The mechanics are as follows. A reasonable prepayment speed is determined to project cash flows. Once the cash flows have been determined, the IRR, referred to as the "mortgage yield," is calculated using the purchase price of the bond. The yield is calculated in the same way as the cash flow yield discussed in Chapter 9, although annualization of the monthly or quarterly yield to calculate a bond-equivalent yield is not performed. The periodic yield is annualized instead by compounding.

The initial beginning book value of the security is the cost of the purchase. The income from the investment is calculated monthly by multiplying the yield (IRR) by the beginning book value (dollars invested). The difference between the monthly cash flow payment and the calculated income is the return of capital. Each month the book value (dollars invested) is reduced by the amount of capital returned (a credit to the asset account) until the original cash investment is totally returned to the investor over the life of the bond.

Another way to arrive at the same results is to calculate the NPV (net present value) of the projected cash flows using the IRR as the discount rate. The NPV becomes the new beginning book value. The amount necessary to reduce current dollars invested to the NPV is the return of capital; the remaining cash flows are interest income. Under these two methods of calculation, assuming the same prepayment speed and discount rate, income and return of capital amounts will be the same as will newly calculated book values.

Therefore, all cash flows in excess of the original cost are the security holder's earnings or income. Exhibits 2 and 3 show the initial accounting schedules for a discount and a premium bond.

Exhibit 2: Accounting for a Discount Passthrough Using the Initial Schedule
FASB 91 – Interest Method

Face value:	15,000,000	Coupon:	9.5%	Factor: 1.00
Purchase price:	95.00	WAM:	348	CPR: 6.00
Effective yield:	10.396%			

Income 1 Year:	1,436,551
Ret of cap 1 Year:	932,087
Cash flow 1 Year:	2,368,638

Payment Month	Beginning Balance (A)	Principal (B)	Interest (C)	Total Cash flow (D)	Beginning Book Value (E)	Income (F)	Return of Capital (G)	Ending Book Value (H)	Book Price (I)
1	15,000,000	84,479	118,750	203,229	14,250,000	123,453	79,776	14,170,224	95.003
2	14,915,521	84,067	118,081	202,149	14,170,224	122,762	79,387	14,090,837	95.006
3	14,831,454	83,658	117,416	201,074	14,090,837	122,074	79,000	14,011,837	95.010
4	14,747,795	83,251	116,753	200,005	14,011,837	121,389	78,615	13,933,222	95.013
5	14,664,544	82,846	116,094	198,941	13,933,222	120,708	78,232	13,854,989	95.016
6	14,581,698	82,444	115,438	197,882	13,854,989	120,031	77,851	13,777,138	95.020
7	14,499,254	82,043	114,786	196,829	13,777,138	119,356	77,473	13,699,665	95.023
8	14,417,211	81,645	114,136	195,781	13,699,665	118,685	77,096	13,622,569	95.026
9	14,335,567	81,248	113,490	194,738	13,622,569	118,017	76,721	13,545,848	95.030
10	14,254,318	80,854	112,847	193,701	13,545,848	117,352	76,348	13,469,500	95.033
11	14,173,464	80,462	112,207	192,669	13,469,500	116,691	75,978	13,393,522	95.037
12	14,093,002	80,072	111,570	191,642	13,393,522	116,033	75,609	13,317,913	95.040

A: Par value of bond
B: Principal payments-monthly
C: Monthly interest payments
D: Monthly total (B + C)
E: First month = Bond cost
Subsequent months = Bal fwd: I – previous month

F: Book value x IRR/12
G: Total CF (D) less Income (F)
H: Beg. book value (E) less Ret. of cap (G)
I: Ending book value (H)/ Par value (A) after payment

Exhibit 3: Accounting for a Premium Passthrough Using the Initial Schedule
FASB 91 – Interest Method

Face value:	15,000,000	Coupon:	9.5%	Factor:	1.00	Income 1 Year:	1,308,728
Purchase price:	106.50	WAM:	348	CPR:	6.00	Ret of cap 1 Year:	1,059,910
Effective yield:	8.452%					Cash flow 1 Year:	2,368,638

Payment Month	Beginning Balance (A)	Principal (B)	Interest (C)	Total Cash flow (D)	Beginning Book Value (E)	Income (F)	Return of Capital (G)	Ending Book Value (H)	Book Price (I)
1	15,000,000	84,479	118,750	203,229	15,975,000	112,518	90,710	15,884,290	106.495
2	14,915,521	84,067	118,081	202,149	15,884,290	111,879	90,269	15,794,020	106.490
3	14,831,454	83,658	117,416	201,074	15,794,020	111,244	89,830	15,704,190	106.485
4	14,747,795	83,251	116,753	200,005	15,704,190	110,611	89,394	15,614,796	106.480
5	14,664,544	82,846	116,094	198,941	15,614,796	109,981	88,959	15,525,837	106.475
6	14,581,698	82,444	115,438	197,882	15,525,837	109,355	88,527	15,437,310	106.470
7	14,499,254	82,043	114,786	196,829	15,437,310	108,731	88,098	15,349,212	106.465
8	14,417,211	81,645	114,136	195,781	15,349,212	108,111	87,670	15,261,542	106.459
9	14,335,567	81,248	113,490	194,738	15,261,542	107,493	87,245	15,174,297	106.454
10	14,254,318	80,854	112,847	193,701	15,174,297	106,879	86,822	15,087,474	106.449
11	14,173,464	80,462	112,207	192,669	15,087,474	106,267	86,402	15,001,073	106.443

A: Par value of bond
B: Principal payments-monthly
C: Monthly interest payments
D: Monthly total (B + C)
E: First month = Bond cost
Subsequent months = Bal fwd: I – previous month

F: Book value x IRR/12
G: Total CF (D) less Income (F)
H: Beg. book value (E) less Ret. of cap (G)
I: Ending book value (H)/ Par value (A) after payment

The book price of a bond is the relationship between the security holder's book value and the outstanding current face of the bond. All book prices will move from the original price of the investment toward par, except in the case of an interest-only strip, whose unit cost will move from purchase price to zero.

As FASB 91 states, should actual prepayments differ from projections (and they will), a new yield is to be calculated using actual payments received. Adjustment must then be made as if the new yield had been used from inception. The carrying value is to be adjusted with a corresponding reduction or increase in interest income. FASB does not define how often these adjustments are to be made. The nature of the investor's business is an integral factor in determining how often to adjust earnings, as well as the severity of the discrepancy of projected prepayment from actual prepayment. Exhibits 4 and 5 provide the actual payment schedules assumed in our illustration. Exhibits 6 and 7 show adjustments for the new prepayments.

For certain CMO tranches, there may be no cash flow, or it may be interest only, for a number of months or years. Z (or accrual) bonds and inverse floaters are examples. In this case, there is either no cash or insufficient cash to cover the calculated income. In this case, income is calculated and booked. The shortfall of cash creates a negative book value reduction, which means an increase to the book value. Additional debit entries necessary to cover income applied to the income statement then come from the asset itself. Income earned, but not received in the form of cash, is considered phantom income, and is taxable. Once the investment begins to pay principal, the entries to the asset account become positive again, resulting in a reduction of book value (dollars invested) until complete retirement.

EITF 89-4

The Financial Accounting Standards Board's EITF 89-4 further clarifies methods of application of income and capital returned to the income statement and balance sheet for debt securities. The consensus reached by the task force is that accounting for investment in a CMO needs to be consistent with the type of the investment. Some CMO tranches (namely, the residuals) are issued in equity form. But some of the "equity" tranches consist only of future cash flows that will be collected under conditions existing at issue. A set of six criteria govern. An asset meeting all six criteria is accounted for according to the accounting method prescribed for nonequity investments. The criteria for nonequity classification of a CMO issued in equity form are as follows:

Exhibit 4: Accounting for a Discount Passthrough Using the Actual Payments
FASB 91 – Interest Method

Face value:	15,000,000	Coupon:	9.5%	Income 1 Year:	1,446,584
Purchase price:	95.00	WAM:	348	Ret of cap 1 Year:	2,596,303
Effective Yield:	11.076%	Factor:	1.00	Cash flow 1 Year:	4,042,887

Actual CPR: Month 1: 12%; Month 2: 15%; Month 3: 17.5%; Month 4: 20%; Month 5: 22%; Month 6 thru maturity: 18%

Payment Month	Beginning Balance (A)	Principal (B)	Interest (C)	Total Cash flow (D)	Beginning Book Value (E)	Income (F)	Return of Capital (G)	Ending Book Value (H)	Book Price (I)
1	15,000,000	166,237	118,750	284,987	14,250,000	131,528	153,459	14,096,541	95.030
2	14,833,763	206,798	117,434	324,232	14,096,541	130,112	194,120	13,902,421	95.047
3	14,626,965	239,815	115,797	355,611	13,902,421	128,320	227,291	13,675,129	95.051
4	14,387,150	272,187	113,898	386,085	13,675,129	126,222	259,863	13,415,266	95.043
5	14,114,963	296,285	111,743	408,028	13,415,266	123,824	284,205	13,131,061	95.024
6	13,818,678	233,628	109,398	343,026	13,131,061	121,200	221,826	12,909,236	95.025
7	13,585,050	229,739	107,548	337,287	12,909,236	119,153	218,135	12,691,101	95.027
8	13,355,311	225,914	105,730	331,644	12,691,101	117,139	214,504	12,476,597	95.028
9	13,129,397	222,153	103,941	326,094	12,476,597	115,160	210,934	12,265,663	95.029
10	12,907,244	218,453	102,182	320,635	12,265,663	113,213	207,423	12,058,240	95.031
11	12,688,791	214,815	100,453	315,268	12,058,240	111,298	203,969	11,854,271	95.032
12	12,473,976	211,236	98,752	309,989	11,854,271	109,416	200,573	11,653,697	95.033

A: Par value of bond
B: Principal payments-monthly
C: Monthly interest payments
D: Monthly total (B + C)
E: First month = Bond cost
Subsequent months = Bal fwd: I – previous month

F: Book value x IRR/12
G: Total CF (D) less Income (F)
H: Beg. book value (E) less Ret. of cap (G)
I: Ending book value (H)/ Par value (A) after payment

Exhibit 5: Accounting for a Premium Passthrough Using the Actual Payments
FASB 91 – Interest Method

Face value:	15,000,000	Coupon:	9.5%	Income 1 Year:	1,121,938
Purchase price:	106.50	WAM:	348	Ret of cap 1 Year:	2,920,949
Effective Yield:	7.668%			Cash flow 1 Year:	4,042,887

Actual CPR: Month 1: 12%; Month 2: 15%; Month 3: 17.5%; Month 4: 20%; Month 5: 22%; Month 6 thru maturity: 18%

Payment Month	Beginning Balance (A)	Principal (B)	Interest (C)	Total Cash flow (D)	Beginning Book Value (E)	Income (F)	Return of Capital (G)	Ending Book Value (H)	Book Price (I)
1	15,000,000	166,237	118,750	284,987	15,975,000	102,082	182,905	15,792,095	106.460
2	14,833,763	206,798	117,434	324,232	15,792,095	100,914	223,319	15,568,777	106.439
3	14,626,965	239,815	115,797	355,611	15,568,777	99,487	256,125	15,312,652	106.433
4	14,387,150	272,187	113,898	386,085	15,312,652	97,850	288,235	15,024,417	106.443
5	14,114,963	296,285	111,743	408,028	15,024,417	96,008	312,020	14,712,397	106.467
6	13,818,678	233,628	109,398	343,026	14,712,397	94,014	249,012	14,463,385	106.465
7	13,585,050	229,739	107,548	337,287	14,463,385	92,423	244,864	14,218,520	106.463
8	13,355,311	225,914	105,730	331,644	14,218,520	90,858	240,785	13,977,735	106.461
9	13,129,397	222,153	103,941	326,094	13,977,735	89,320	236,774	13,740,961	106.459
10	12,907,244	218,453	102,182	320,635	13,740,961	87,807	232,829	13,508,132	106.457
11	12,688,791	214,815	100,453	315,268	13,508,132	86,319	228,949	13,279,184	106.455
12	12,473,976	211,236	98,752	309,989	13,279,184	84,856	225,133	13,054,051	106.453

A: Par value of bond
B: Principal payments-monthly
C: Monthly interest payments
D: Monthly total (B + C)
E: First month = Bond cost
Subsequent months = Bal fwd: I – previous month

F: Book value x IRR/12
G: Total CF (D) less Income (F)
H: Beg. book value (E) less Ret. of cap (G)
I: Ending book value (H)/ Par value (A) after payment

Exhibit 6: Accounting for a Discount Passthrough Using the Initial Schedule and Using the Actual Payments: FASB 91 – Interest Method

Using the Initial Schedule

Payment Month	Beginning Balance	Principal	Interest	Total Cash flow	Beginning Book Value	Income	Return of Capital	Ending Book Value	Price
1	15,000,000	84,479	118,750	203,229	14,250,000	123,453	79,776	14,170,224	95.003
2	14,915,521	84,067	118,081	202,149	14,170,224	122,762	79,387	14,090,837	95.006
3	14,831,454	83,658	117,416	201,074	14,090,837	122,074	79,000	14,011,837	95.010
4	14,747,795	83,251	116,753	200,005	14,011,837	121,389	78,615	13,933,222	95.013
5	14,664,544	82,846	116,094	198,941	13,933,222	120,708	78,232	13,854,989	95.016
6	14,581,698	82,444	115,438	197,882	13,854,989	120,031	77,851	13,777,138	95.020
Totals:		500,746	702,533	1,203,279		730,417	472,862	13,777,138	

Using the Actual Payments

Payment Month	Beginning Balance	Principal	Interest	Total Cash flow	Beginning Book Value	Income	Return of Capital	Ending Book Value	Price
1	15,000,000	166,237	118,750	284,987	14,250,000	131,528	153,459	14,096,541	95.030
2	14,833,763	206,798	117,434	324,232	14,096,541	130,112	194,120	13,902,421	95.047
3	14,626,965	239,815	115,797	355,611	13,902,421	128,320	227,291	13,675,129	95.051
4	14,387,150	272,187	113,898	386,085	13,675,129	126,222	259,863	13,415,266	95.043
5	14,114,963	296,285	111,743	408,028	13,415,266	123,824	284,205	13,131,061	95.024
6	13,818,678	233,628	109,398	343,026	13,131,061	121,200	221,826	12,909,236	95.025
Totals:		1,414,950	687,020	2,101,970		761,206	1,340,764	12,909,236	

Projected cash flows (6 mos): 1,203,279   Income booked from schedule: 730,417   Return of capital from schedule: 472,862   Proj. carrying value (6 mos): 13,777,138   Income adjustment: 30,789

Actual cash flows (6 mos): 2,101,970   Actual income: 761,206   Actual return of capital: 1,340,764   Actual carrying value (6 mos): 12,909,236   Capital returned adjusted: 867,902

Difference: 898,692   Difference: 30,789   Difference: 867,902   Difference: 867,902   898,692

Income understated

"1. The assets in the special-purpose entity were not transferred to the special-purpose entity by the purchaser of the CMO instrument.

2. The assets of the special-purpose entity consist solely of a large number of similar high-credit monetary assets (or one or more high-credit-quality mortgage-backed securities that provide an undivided interest in a large number of similar loans) for which prepayments are probable and the timing and amounts of prepayments can be reasonably estimated.

3. The special-purpose entity is self-liquidating; that is, it will terminate when the existing assets are fully collected and the existing obligations of the special-purpose entity are fully paid.

4. Assets collateralizing the obligations of the special-purpose entity may not be exchanged, sold, or otherwise managed as a portfolio, and the purchaser has neither the right nor the obligation to substitute assets that collateralize the entity's obligations.

5. There is no more than a remote possibility that the purchaser would be required to contribute funds to the special-purpose entity to pay administrative expenses or other costs.

6. No other obligee of the special-purpose entity has recourse to the purchaser of the investment.

The ability of a purchaser of a CMO instrument to call other CMO tranches of the special-purpose entity generally will not preclude treatment of the purchaser's investment as a nonequity instrument provided all the above are met."

The Task Force further concluded that the level of risk of nonequity CMO instruments is required to be determined before accounting methods are determined. If a significant portion of the original investment is at risk because of (1) interest rate changes, (2) prepayment of underlying collateral, or (3) reinvestment earnings of collected but not distributed cash flows, the instrument is declared high-risk. Interest-only certificates and/or tranches (including PAC IOs, TAC IOs, Inverse IOs, etc.) also fit the high-risk description, in that their purchase price consists of only premium, and is subject to substantial loss of original investment due to prepayment risk. Hence, IOs are to be accounted for in the same method as set forth for high-risk CMOs (the 89-4 method).

Exhibit 7: Accounting for a Discount Passthrough Using the Initial Schedule and Using the Actual Payments: Interest Method – FASB 91

Using the Initial Schedule

Payment Month	Beginning Balance	Principal	Interest	Total Cash flow	Beginning Book Value	Income	Return of Capital	Ending Book Value	Price
1	15,000,000	84,479	118,750	203,229	15,975,000	112,518	90,710	15,884,290	106.495
2	14,915,521	84,067	118,081	202,149	15,884,290	111,879	90,269	15,794,020	106.490
3	14,831,454	83,658	117,416	201,074	15,794,020	111,244	89,830	15,704,190	106.485
4	14,747,795	83,251	116,753	200,005	15,704,190	110,611	89,394	15,614,796	106.480
5	14,664,544	82,846	116,094	198,941	15,614,796	109,981	88,959	15,525,837	106.475
6	14,581,698	82,444	115,438	197,882	15,525,837	109,355	88,527	15,437,310	106.470
Totals:		500,746	702,533	1,203,279	15,525,837	665,588	537,690	15,437,310	

Using the Actual Payments

Payment Month	Beginning Balance	Principal	Interest	Total Cash flow	Beginning Book Value	Income	Return of Capital	Ending Book Value	Price
1	15,000,000	166,237	118,750	284,987	15,975,000	102,082	182,905	15,792,095	106.460
2	14,833,763	206,798	117,434	324,232	15,792,095	100,914	223,319	15,568,777	106.439
3	14,626,965	239,815	115,797	355,611	15,568,777	99,487	256,125	15,312,652	106.433
4	14,387,150	272,187	113,898	386,085	15,312,652	97,850	288,235	15,024,417	106.443
5	14,114,963	296,285	111,743	408,028	15,024,417	96,008	312,020	14,712,397	106.467
6	13,818,678	233,628	109,398	343,026	14,712,397	94,014	249,012	14,463,385	106.465
Totals:		1,414,950	687,020	2,101,970	14,712,397	590,355	1,511,615	14,463,385	

Projected cash flows (6 mos): 1,203,279
Actual cash flows (6 mos): 2,101,970
Difference: 898,692

Income booked from schedule: 665,588
Actual income: 590,355
Difference: -75,233
Income understated

Return of capital from schedule: 537,690
Actual return of capital: 1,511,615
Difference: 867,902

Proj. carrying value (6 mos): 13,777,138
Actual carrying value (6 mos): 12,909,236
Difference: 973,925

Income adjustment: -75,233
Capital returned adjusted: 973,925
898,692

Accounting methods for high-risk CMOs are similar to FASB 91's interest method, in that upon purchase an effective yield is calculated on the basis of purchase price and projected cash flows. These are to be based on prepayment assumptions consistent with those set by marketplace participants for comparable investments. The resulting effective yield is then used to calculate income on the initial investment balance for the first accounting period. The cash flow received is first applied to the amount of income accrued, with any excess applied to the carrying value of the investment.

The major difference between the 89-4 method and the FASB 91 method is that, for each subsequent period, the yield must be recalculated on the basis of the amortized cost of the instrument and the new projected cash flows. The new yield at each reporting period is used to determine income on the outstanding dollars invested. These steps are repeated until the investment is retired. An illustration is provided in Exhibit 8.

No "catch-up" is necessary, as with FASB 91's interest method. At each reporting period, the carrying value of the investment will equal the net present value of the projected cash flows at the current effective yield. The effective yield cannot be negative. In the event that the newly generated present value is less than the present value of the same projected undiscounted cash flows, the loss is to be taken in the current period, and income for that period will be zero.

Premiums and discounts for nonequity CMO instruments are to be accounted for as described in FASB 91 and illustrated in Exhibits 2 through 7.

Exhibit 8: Accounting for an IO Using the Actual Payments
EITF 89-4 Method

Face value:	15,000,000	Coupon: 9.5%
Purchase price:	35.00	WAM: 348
Effective Yield:	5.792%	Factor: 1.00

Income: 434,382
Ret of cap(-loss): 379,702
Cash flow: 814,085

Actual CPR: Month 1: 6%; Month 2: 10%; Month 3: 4%; Month 5: 8% Month 6: 20%; Month 7: 25% for loss adjustment

Payment Month	Beginning Balance	Principal	Interest	Total Cash flow	Beginning Book Value	Income	Return of Capital	Ending Book Value	Price	Yield (%)
1	15,000,000	0	118,750	118,750	5,250,000	87,495	31,255	5,218,745	34.989	19.999%
2	14,915,521	0	118,081	118,081	5,218,745	68,219	49,862	5,168,883	34.977	15.686
3	14,777,805	0	116,991	116,991	5,168,883	95,161	21,830	5,147,053	34.966	22.092
4	14,720,253	0	116,535	116,535	5,147,053	76,623	39,912	5,107,141	34.954	17.864
5	14,610,948	0	115,670	115,670	5,107,141	89,590	26,080	5,081,061	34.942	21.051
6	14,541,222	0	115,118	115,118	5,081,061	17,294	97,824	4,983,237	34.931	4.084
7	14,265,992	0	112,939	112,939	4,983,237	0.00	369,876	4,613,360	33.140	-2.225

Cash flow for this period: 112,939   Net loss: 256,937   New adjusted carrying value: 4,613,360

FASB 91 Accounting (for comparison purposes only)

Beginning Book Value	5.572% Income	Return of Capital	Ending Book Value	Price	Yield (%)
5,250,000	25,340	93,410	5,156,590	34.377	5.792
5,156,590	25,889	92,192	5,063,398	33.947	5.792
5,063,398	24,439	92,552	4,970,846	33.637	5.792
4,970,846	23,993	92,542	4,878,304	33.140	5.792
4,878,304	23,546	92,124	4,786,180	32.757	5.792
4,786,180	23,101	90,017	4,694,163	32.282	5.792
4,694,163	22,657	90,282	4,603,882	32.272	5.792
Total FASB 91:	167,966	646,118			
Total 89-4:	434,370	636,642	256,937		
Net:	266,414	-9,477			

Chapter 14

REGULATORY CONSIDERATIONS

In this chapter we review regulations covering CMO investments for depository institutions and insurance companies. Regulations for depository institutions are in place and are undergoing fine-tuning, although at the time of this writing the National Association of Insurance Commissioners had not adopted regulations. We discuss the regulatory changes that are likely to be forthcoming.

DEPOSITORY INSTITUTIONS

The Federal Financial Institutions Examination Council (FFIEC) is a government advisory organization consisting of five member agencies: the Board of Governors of the Federal Reserve System, the Federal Deposit Insurance Corporation, the National Credit Union Administration, the Office of the Comptroller of the Currency, and the Office of Thrift Supervision. In December 1991, the FFIEC approved a policy statement entitled "Supervisory Statement on Securities Activities," which subsequently became effective for depository institutions regulated by these agencies.[1]

The supervisory policy statement addresses:

1. how depository institutions should select securities dealers.

2. requirements for establishing prudent strategies for securities transactions.

3. the identification of sales or trading practices viewed by the agencies as unsuitable.

4. the characteristics of loans held for sale or trading.

5. tests for identifying when certain mortgage derivative products are to be classified as high-risk mortgage securities and thereby held either in a trading account or available-for-sale account.

Our focus here is to discuss the last issue and its application to CMO tranches. While the tests apply only to depository institutions, all market participants should be aware of them because they will affect the number of potential buyers of a mortgage derivative security.

General Principle

The general principle underlying the tests is that a CMO tranche that exhibits an average life or price volatility that is greater than a benchmark fixed-rate 30-year passthrough security is to be classified as a "high-risk mortgage security" and is not a suitable investment for depository institutions. (The tests for classifying a CMO tranche as a high-risk security are discussed later.)

Accounting Treatment

Under the newly implemented FASB 115, a CMO tranche can be classified in of three accounts of a depository institution: (1) a held-to-maturity

---

[1] In April 1988 the FFIEC issued a supervisory policy statement entitled "Selection of Securities Dealers and Unsuitable Investment Practices." In January 1991 it issued a proposed supervisory policy statement entitled "Concerning Selection of Securities Dealers, Security Portfolio Policies and Strategies and Unsuitable Investment Practices, and Stripped Mortgage-Backed Securities, Certain CMO Tranches, Residuals, and Zero-Coupon Bonds." This supervisory policy statement was revised following evaluation of 110 comment letters. The supervisory policy statement discussed in this chapter reflects the revised statement.

account; (2) an available-for-sale account; or (3) a trading account. In the held-to-maturity account, the CMO is tranche is reported at amortized cost; in both the available-for-sale and the trading accounts, it is reported at market value.

The financial accounting treatment of CMO tranches is as follows. If a CMO tranche is classified as a high-risk mortgage security, and acquired after the agency adopted the supervisory policy statement, it must be carried in the institution's trading account or as an asset in the available-for-sale account.

As of this writing, there is an outstanding controversy regarding accountants' interpretation of the FFIEC high-risk test in terms of FASB 115. Under the FFIEC supervisory policy statement, if a CMO is classified as high-risk subsequent to acquisition, the regulators may require that the institution dispose of the CMO in an orderly fashion. In this event, the accountants argue that the institution effectively losses it s ability to hold the CMO to maturity. Therefore, accountants maintain that the chances of such a reclassification must be considered "remote" for an institution to categorize a CMO-tranche as held-to-maturity. The FFIEC has stated that the accountants strict interpretation of the high-risk test exceeds the original intent of their guidelines. The FFIEC has formed a task force which is in the process of redefining the high-risk test to allow depository institutions more leeway in classifying CMOs as held-to-maturity.

Rationale for and Capacity to Invest in High-Risk Mortgage Securities

The supervisory policy statement does not specify that a depository institution cannot acquire a CMO tranche that is classified as a high-yield mortgage security. Rather, it (1) states how a CMO tranche must be treated for accounting purposes, (2) discusses what the motivation should be for acquiring such a security, and (3) addresses the capacity of a depository institution to accept the risks and understand those risks.

In general, a CMO tranche classified as a high-risk mortgage security must reduce the institution's interest rate risk in accordance with safe and sound practices. The management of a depository institution must be able to demonstrate that it understands the risks associated with the CMO tranche and can effectively manage those risks. We suppose a good rule in this regard is that if the examiner knows more than the institution's management about the risks, the institution should not be holding the security because under some circumstances an examiner may require an orderly disposal of high-risk mortgage securities. (In such instances, the CMO tranche or tranches would be reported in the held-for-sale account.)

The degree of trading activity in high-risk mortgage securities should be reasonably related to the depository institution's (1) capital, (2) ability to sustain losses, and (3) in-house expertise. The supervisory policy statement does not foreclose a depository institution that has strong capital, earnings, and liquidity from obtaining CMO tranches for the sole purpose of trading. In such instances, the depository institution must specify detailed investment policies and internal controls.

Classification of a CMO Tranche as a "High-Risk Mortgage Security"

The rule for classifying a CMO tranche as a high-risk mortgage security has been quantified by the supervisory policy statement. A high risk mortgage security is defined as any CMO tranche that at the time of purchase, or at a subsequent testing date, meets any one of three tests. Any CMO tranche that fails all three tests is classified as a "non-risk mortgage security."

The three tests are referred to as the average life test, the average life sensitivity test, and the price sensitivity test.

1. *Average life test*: The average life of the CMO tranche is greater than 10 years.

2. *Average life sensitivity test*: The average life of the CMO tranche either (a) extends by more than four years assuming an immediate and sustained parallel shift in the yield of plus 300 basis points, or (b) shortens by more than six years, assuming an immediate and sustained parallel shift in the yield curve of minus 300 basis points.

3. *Price sensitivity test*: The estimated change in the price of the CMO tranche due to an immediate and sustained parallel shift in the yield curve of plus or minus 300 basis points is more than 17%.

There are two critical assumptions in the price sensitivity test: (1) the prepayment assumption, and (2) the appropriate rate to discount the cash flow when yields are changed. With respect to the prepayment assumption, the same assumption used in the average life test must also be used in the price sensitivity test. The appropriate rate to discount the cash flow is specified in the supervisory policy statement.

The procedure for determining the discount rate is as follows. First, calculate the yield spread over a comparable average life Treasury. The yield on the Treasury is based on the bid side of the market. "Yield" for the CMO tranche while not specified in the policy statement, means the cash flow yield that we discussed in Chapter 9. Then the calculated yield spread is added to the Treasury rate when the yield curve is assumed to shift plus and minus 300 basis points. The initial price to be used in the price sensitivity test is determined by the offer side of the market and used as the base price.

Applicability of Tests to Certain CMO Classes: Not all CMO bond classes are subject to the three tests. A CMO tranche such as a CMO IO cannot be tested with respect to an average life test or an average life sensitivity test, since there is no principal received. In such cases, the CMO tranche is still subject to the price sensitivity test.

A floating-rate CMO debt class is not subject to the average life and average life sensitivity tests if the following three conditions are satisfied at the time of purchase or a subsequent testing date:

1. the rate is below the cap.[2]

2. the rate adjusts at least annually on a one-for-one basis with the index.

3. the index is a conventional, widely used market interest rate index.

This exemption does not apply to inverse floaters or floating-rate non-debt classes such as residuals.

Frequency of Testing and Reclassification: The three tests must be conducted prior to executing a trade and at subsequent dates depending on the current classification of the CMO tranche. If a CMO tranche is classified as a non-high-risk mortgage security, it must be retested no less

---

[2] The cap can be removed by purchasing an interest rate cap.

than annually to determine if it requires reclassification as a high-risk mortgage security. Thus, it is important for not only depository institutions but also all potential investors to be aware of the economic conditions that will result in a reclassification, as a reclassification will affect their ability to dispose of the CMO tranche.

A CMO tranche currently classified as a high-risk mortgage security can be reclassified as a non-high-risk mortgage security. The supervisory policy statement specifies that this can occur if at the end of two consecutive quarters it does not meet the definition of a high-risk mortgage security.

Other Important Considerations

Managers of depository institutions should be aware of several key aspects of the supervisory policy statement when they are contemplating the acquisition of a CMO tranche.

1. All the assumptions in analysis of the CMO must be reasonable and available to the examiner. The supervisory policy statement gives the examiner the authority to challenge the prepayment assumption to reduce the likelihood that an institution will use a prepayment rate that will make a CMO tranche fail all three tests. Specifically, if the prepayment assumption differs significantly from the median prepayment assumption of several major dealers selected by the examiner, the examiner may use the median prepayment assumption in the tests.

2. If a depository institution plans to purchase a CMO tranche that would be classified as a high-risk mortgage security, a monitoring and reporting system must be in place to evaluate the security's expected performance with respect to reducing overall interest rate risk, and then to monitor actual performance at least quarterly to determine if the interest rate risk reduction is actually being achieved.

3. An analysis of whether a CMO tranche is a high-risk mortgage security must be undertaken prior to acquisition. The supporting documentation must be retained and made available to the examiner. Any analysis and supporting documentation performed after an acquisition in order to justify the acquisition is subject to

examiner criticism. Reliance on analysis by a dealer firm or other outside party without supporting internal analysis is also subject to examiner criticism.

4. In undertaking the analysis, the depository institution can rely on industry "calculators" used in the mortgage-backed securities marketplace, and considered independent. For newly issued CMO deals whose cash flows are not modeled yet by independent services, the deal must be reverse engineered so that analysis can be performed. Seasoned CMO deals have typically been modeled by independent services. For some services, prepayment assumptions must be input, while for others prepayment assumptions of major dealer firms are built into the system. If a depository institution relies on an independent service, it must make sure that the assumptions and analysis are reasonable.

5. Documentation must be maintained to demonstrate that reasonable steps were taken to assure that the price paid for a CMO tranche classified as a high-risk mortgage derivative was fair market value. This can be accomplished by obtaining quotes from at least two dealers prior to executing a trade. When a CMO tranche is unique, particularly either when a structure is a new innovation and just being introduced, or when a depository institution requests a tranche be created for its particular needs, the requirement of at least two quotes is not possible. In such cases, the reasons for not obtaining a quote from more than one dealer must be documented.

6. There must be a board-approved policy for high-risk mortgage securities setting forth the goals and objectives expected to be achieved by using these securities. Limits on the amount or portion of the portfolio that may be allocated to these securities must be specified.

7. The board of directors must meet at least quarterly to review all high-risk mortgage securities to assess whether they are performing as expected, and the board must be made aware of the risks associated with prepayments.

INSURANCE COMPANIES

The National Association of Insurance Commissioners (NAIC) is increasingly concerned with a lack of understanding of CMOs among the companies it regulates. Two examples are the $14 million loss on certain CMOs held by State Fund Mutual Insurance Co., which wiped out the net worth of this Minneapolis insurer with $104 million in assets,[3] and the $43.8 million write-down of certain CMOs by ICH Corp., a Kentucky holding company for insurance companies, in the first quarter of 1991 on its $1.1 billion holding.[4]

As we noted at the outset, the regulations for insurance companies had not been finalized by the NAIC at the time of this writing. The key provisions that are likely to be adopted are reviewed here.

There are three main working groups of the NAIC that are responsible for establishing the investment policy for insurance companies with respect to investing in mortgage-backed securities: the Invested Asset Working Group, the Invested and Admitted Asset Model Law Working Group, and the Valuation Office Support Working Group. The key committee dealing with mortgage-backed securities is the Invested Asset Working Group. In Spring 1992, the advisory committee to this group recommended that the regulations adopted by the FFIEC for classifying a mortgage-backed security as high-risk not be adopted by the NAIC.

What the group did recommend and what is likely to be adopted are three changes in the statutory reporting requirements. First, to make it easier to identify an insurance company's holdings of CMOs, a separate section for CMO reporting will be provided in Schedule D, Part 1 of the Statutory Blanks.[5] CMOs have generally been listed in either the U.S. Government section or the Industrial and Miscellaneous bond section. Second, the types of CMO bonds must be disclosed.

Finally, there is the possibility that beginning with the 1994 Statutory Blanks, cash flow volatility ratings will be assigned to the CMO securities held. There are two proposals for determining the volatility rating: (1) a formula or guidelines will be specified so that an insurance company can determine the

---

[3] This insurer was seized by Minnesota regulators.

[4] Susan Pulliam, "Insurance Regulators Express Concern Over Safety of Certain Types of CMOs," *The Wall Street Journal* (Monday, June 15,1992), p. A5.

[5] More specifically, the category for fixed-income securities will be expanded to the following four subcategories: bonds, loan-backed bonds (for example, passthrough securities and asset-backed securities), structured securities, and CMOs.

rating, or (2) a rating assigned by a rating agency. In the former case, steps have already been taken by the actuary profession, which in July 1991 adopted professional standards for actuaries performing cash flow testing.[6]

A concern with reporting volatility ratings and types of CMO bonds is that financial analysts and regulators will fail to recognize that it is the overall volatility of the portfolio, not that of individual CMO tranches, that affects the economic well-being of an insurance company. The classic example is the holding of an IO and PO security from the same collateral. On an individual security basis, it would seem that the portfolio has considerable risk, while instead the portfolio has only the risk of the underlying collateral.

It should be noted that regulators are making no attempt to limit investments in CMOs. In New York State, for example, Section 1409: Limitation of Investments, exempts mortgage-backed securities from the restriction that no more than 10% of admitted assets may be invested in the securities of any one institution. Section 1409(c) states that the restriction is not applicable to mortgage-related securities, or to securities issued or guaranteed by Freddie Mac or Fannie Mae. It does specify, however, that "if the aggregate amount of such securities exceeds 70% of admitted assets, the balance of such securities over 70% thereon shall be limited by and apportioned according to a ratio of 1:2 respectively, between mortgage-related securities and government obligations."

SUMMARY

This chapter has reviewed the regulations for depository institutions adopted by regulatory agencies and the likely regulatory changes for insurance companies. The FFIEC statutory policy statement sets forth tests for classifying a CMO tranche as a high-risk mortgage security. The tests involve average life, average life sensitivity, and price sensitivity. Management is required to analyze a CMO tranche prior to executing a trade and to monitor high-risk mortgage securities.

New insurance regulations are likely to involve three statutory reporting changes: (1) disclosure of the amount of holdings of CMOs, (2) the types of CMOs, and (3) provision of cash flow volatility ratings for individual holdings.

---

[6] Actuarial Standard of Practice No. 7, "Performing Cash Flow Testing for Insurers."

INDEX

Credit Rating

Investors need to understand credit considerations affecting residential housing and mortgage markets in order to make informed investment decisions. Duff & Phelps Credit Rating Co. provides in-depth research on significant developments in the credit analysis of mortgage-backed transactions.

The following topical reports and publications are available to you free of charge. Please call for more information.

- Rating Policy for Residential Mortgage-Backed Securities

- Innovative Deals Rated Under New Residential Policy

- Securitization of B & C Quality Loans

- Los Angeles Area Housing Prices

- The Impact of U.S. Military Base Closings on Private-Label Residential Mortgage-Backed Securities

- Rating of Prepayment Sensitive Cash Flow Securities

- Credit Enhancement for Mortgagor Bankruptcy Risk in Residential Mortgage-Backed Securities

- Credit Enhancement for Special Hazard Risk in Residential Mortgage-Backed Securities

The Rating Guide alphabetically lists all companies and transactions with their ratings. This monthly handbook is supplemented by a weekly newsletter, *Credit Decisions*, updating readers to any interim rating activity.

Structured Finance Review provides a bi-monthly review of newly rated structured securities and includes timely articles on industry trends.

Press releases on recently rated transactions are mailed weekly to investors and are also available through real time electronic delivery.

Franklin Institutional Services Corporation

One Source

Institutional investors can look to *one source* for professional investment management and comprehensive service.

Franklin Institutional Services Corporation is part of Franklin/ Templeton Group, an industry leader with over $85 billion in assets under management.

Defined Contribution Plans

401(k) Investments

- ◆ GIC Alternative
- ◆ Balanced
- ◆ International
- ◆ Capital Growth
- ◆ Income
- ◆ Money Market

Defined Benefit Plans

Investment Management Styles

- ◆ Short Duration Fixed Income
- ◆ Value Equity
- ◆ International Fixed Income
- ◆ Mortgage-Backed Securities

If you are responsible for corporate treasury, pension or 401(k) investments, Franklin can help. Call John Murray, Vice President at: **415-312-3939 or 1-800-632-2000.**

Default Risk is the
PRIMARY RISK
in NonAgency Securities
and Whole Loans

MORTGAGE RISK
ASSESSMENT CORPORATION
HAS THE BEST AND MOST
COMPREHENSIVE DATA
TO ANALYZE DEFAULT RISK

Housing Price Indices
Second Mortgages
Credit Scores

AT CRITICAL TIMES...
DOES YOUR DATA VENDOR
LEAVE YOU HANGING?

In today's highly competitive market, the on-time delivery of accurate information is crucial to your operations. Wondering if your information will be delivered on-time can be like wondering if your chute will open before you hit the ground.

You need a data vendor you can rely on.

ABSG provides the most comprehensive prepayment date delivery of factor information for MBS, ABS, and CMO/REMIC securities. As an independent pricing source, we ensure impartiality on our extensive valuations of CMO/REMIC, ABS, MBS, and ARM securities.

As for meeting those critical deadlines, you can be assured of fast, reliable delivery through any one of our innovative delivery methods, ranging from 9-track tape, thru interactive on-line, to High Speed Transmissions.

To find out more about additional ABSG products and services and how we can help streamline your operations, call ABSG marketing at (212) 754-1011 today.

ABSG

TREPP ▾ BOND BUYER ▾ ALMONT

ASSET BACKED SECURITIES GROUP
477 MADISON AVENUE, NEW YORK, NY 10022

A THOMSON FINANCIAL SERVICES COMPANY

CAMRA Makes Managing Your Investment Picture *This Easy.*

Now, CAMRA™ makes it even easier to manage and account for complex investment vehicles and portfolios.

CAMRA puts Complete Asset Management, Reporting and Accounting at your fingertips. With a click of the mouse or a press of a key, you can get accurate and timely investment information in a flash.

For a full picture of the CAMRA system, contact SS&C for this detailed information package. Or for a quicker response, call us today at (800) 234-0556. It's that easy.

SS&C
SECURITIES
SOFTWARE &
CONSULTING

We speak your language.

Corporate Place
705 Bloomfield Avenue
Bloomfield, CT 06002
(203) 242-7887
FAX (203) 242-8897

Regional Offices:
Atlanta
Los Angeles
St. Louis

Windows is a registered trademark of Microsoft Corporation

PROVIDING INVESTMENT
MANAGEMENT SERVICES
TO INDIVIDUALS, FAMILIES,
FOUNDATIONS, ENDOWMENTS,
AND PENSION PLANS SINCE 1968

Thomas A. Wimberly, CFA
Marvin H. McMurrey, Jr.
Nicholas N. Wentworth, CFA
Elinor G. Ashworth, CFA
Vance M. Arnold, CFA
Steven C. Gammage, CFA

INVESTMENT ADVISORS, INC.

For additional information,
call Thomas A. Wimberly
at (713) 659-2611.

BARRA's U.S. Bond Analysis Service will give you a better understanding of what happens when you mix complex fixed-income assets. It can help ensure that your portfolios don't blow up in your face.

There might be another way to blend a domestic bond portfolio, but the mixture could be volatile.

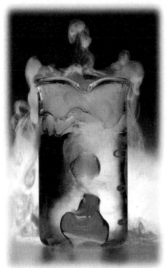

Creating software as sophisticated as the U.S. Bond Analysis Service (B2) required thousands of hours of research and development. The resulting analytical rigor – combined with our state-of-the-art OAS model and our path-dependent mortgage prepayment model – means you can focus on managing your portfolio with greater confidence than ever before.

Not just another slice-and-dice spreadsheet, B2 offers a powerful, cogent framework that facilitates and sharpens your insights. And we apply this framework consistently to all asset classes: Treasuries, Agencies, Corporates, MBS, CMOs, ABS, futures, options on futures, and private placements.

As you might expect, the U.S. Bond Analysis Service displays your interest rate, sector and quality bets. But it goes beyond that.

It applies our understanding of the riskiness of those bets to precisely quantify your portfolio's volatility, both on an absolute basis and relative to your benchmark. In addition, B2's sophisticated performance attribution identifies the returns to your interest rate, sector and quality bets.

What's more, B2 offers scenario analyses so you can explore the impact of changing market conditions on your portfolio's return. And an optimizer that lets you rebalance your portfolio to optimally trade off risk and return.

B2. It can be the difference between a profitable solution and blowing up the lab. For more information or a demonstration, call BARRA at (510) 548-5442. For an instant fax packet, call 1-800-75-BARRA, ext. 482 and request document number 2300.

BERKELEY   MONTREAL   NEW YORK   ∞   LONDON   PARIS   FRANKFURT   ∞   TOKYO   HONG KONG   SYDNEY

You can get asset-backed securities pricing from one source, factors from another, descriptive data from a third...

Or you can get it all from Interactive Data.

Managing asset-backed securities can be a juggling act. If you're automated and getting your data from multiple feeds, you know about the hassles. Multiple applications. Delayed or incomplete transmissions. Working late to catch up.

When you don't have the data you need, you don't get your income projections and statements done on time. Your customers are not happy and they let you know it.

Get all the data you need... when you need it.

We can provide you with daily updated pricing, factors, and descriptive data on GNMAs, FNMAs, FHLMCs and CMOs. We also have coverage on other asset-backed securities including CARS and CARDS. You choose the format, frequency and data items from our full universe of securities, or create custom files based on your specific needs. If you run into a problem, we have the best service group in the business. And our reputation for accuracy and information quality is known throughout the financial world.

You have enough operational and system delays in-house without importing more. Get all your asset-backed securities data via one single feed from Interactive Data and eliminate multiple sources, multiple applications, and multiple hassles.

So, you can learn to juggle. Or you can call Interactive Data at 212-306-6999 and let us take the act out of managing your asset-backed securities.

Interactive Data

a company of
The Dun & Bradstreet Corporation

Boston   Chicago   Hong Kong   London   Los Angeles   New York

Wall Street Analytics, Inc. has been producing financial software since 1988, and is the premier vendor of structured financing systems. WSA's client list includes nineteen major investment banks, Freddie Mac, The Office of Thrift Supervision, a "Big 6" accounting firm, the GNMA Remic program, and dozens of thrifts and insurance companies.

The premier commercially available tool for asset securitization is WSA's Structured Financing Workstation (SFW). This has been designed for the structuring and analysis of CMO/REMICs and has been used to create over $60 billion of new issuance. It fully supports whole loans, senior-subordinated, and asset-backed securities, as well as collateralized bond obligations (CBOs), collateralized loan obligations (CLOs), and remic-on-remic structures. The SFW is widely used not only by issuers, but also by fund managers involved in the purchase of Remic securities. In a matter of minutes it enables a new deal to be completely reverse-engineered from a faxed term sheet, and then provides the capability to produce numerous graphs, reports and analyses for any prepayment or default scenario. The types of analysis supported include multiscenario, bivariate, stochastic, option-adjusted spread (OAS), FFIEC suitability, total horizon return, and many others.

WSA also supplies the leading commercially available tool for portfolio management — The Portfolio Management Workstation (PMW) provides a comprehensive framework for analyzing the complete fixed income asset/liability balance sheet of a financial institution. It can handle investments ranging from the most basic Treasury security to the most arcane mortgage derivative and is currently being used by many of the nation's largest investment and commercial banks to manage over $100 billion of assets. Like the SFW, it provides a wide variety of analyses, including portfolio sub-aggregation, OAS analysis, Monte Carlo simulations, asset/liability hedging, interest rate sensitivity scenarios, and holding period total return. The user can fully specify his own prepayment/foreclosure model as well as nonparallel shifts of the yield curve.

The full compatibility of all WSA products permits direct interchange of data files between the SFW and PMW systems, allowing for example CMO/REMICs designed by the SFW to be immediately analyzed in a full portfolio context or hedged by the PMW. Alternatively, CMO tranches may be imported into the PMW from WSA's extensive CMO/REMIC database, which contains 99% of Agency deals and numerous whole loan and private placement deals, all ready-modeled. The systems also provide full facilities for the import and export of data to other programs or files. All features of WSA software are accessed by simple popup windows, and an extensive online help library and comprehensive technical support make the systems extremely simple to learn and use. For more information, Wall Street Analytics, Inc. can be contacted directly at (415) 853-0360.

Wall Street Analytics, Inc.